The
Relationship
Garden

The Relationship Garden

Jock McKeen, M.D. and
Bennet Wong, M.D.

PD Publishing
Haven By-the-Sea
RR#1, 240 Davis Road
Gabriola Island, British Columbia, Canada V0R 1X0
Internet: jockben@mail.island.net

Canadian Cataloguing in Publication Data
McKeen, Jock, 1946-
    The relationship garden

    Includes bibliographical references.
    ISBN 0-9696755-3-4

    1. Interpersonal relations. 2. Intimacy (Psychology) 3. Self-
actualization (Psychology) I. Wong, Bennet, 1930- II. Title
BF575.I5M34 1996   158'.2   C96-910331-X

Printed and bound in Canada by Hignell Printing Ltd.

∞ This book is printed on acid-free paper.

Dedication

We dedicate this book to one another,
and our Relationship Garden which
we have been privileged to tend.

Contents

Foreword

I am a Roman Catholic priest working in the area of spirituality and religion. Religion for me must be about real life, about deepest convictions and ideals. Religion must always be grounded in my own experience. I believe all religious traditions can be traced back to one common experience of belonging that is expressed in diverse ways. This is what it means to be fully human and united to others.

Over the years some very special people have managed to touch my life. They are people who possess the uniqueness of this present age, but in their own lives are able to penetrate and personalize more deeply and freely than others. They are artists of human being-ness. Ben and Jock are such people.

Much of this book has been worked out in the unique relationship of these two men. They are not the kind of people who are cautious about every comma. They want us to recognize what they have seen, because it has brought them a life of love and joy, a range of wholeness not commonly experienced.

> *Each moment from all sides rushes to us the call to love.*
> *We are running to contemplate its vast green field.*
> *Do you want to come with us?*
> *This is not the time to stay at home,*
> *But to go out and give yourself to the garden.*
> *The dawn of joy has arisen,*
> *And this is the moment of union, of vision.* —Andrew Harvey[1]

For me, Ben and Jock's relationship (which grounds this book) does not fit ordinary categories. Their relationship allows a multifaced wholeness to emerge in response to personal and archetypal experiences. It suggests that countless configurations are inherent in each individual soul. My own insights, and the insights of others to whom I minister, are illuminated by delving into the wealth that Ben and Jock have found in their own relationship. I myself am just beginning to discover the boundlessness of human spirituality that can occur in the kaleidoscope of patterns in human relationships.

Several years ago Ben and Jock invited me to rethink, to revision, and to re-imagine my religious belief system. This enterprise invited me into new life.

With them I discovered a spiritual vitality that has lifted me up, taken me out of myself, and made me present to myself and others on a level of being I did not know before. My relationship with them became a vehicle for a life, which continues to unfold. We learned from one another what we already knew in our hearts.

The Relationship Garden is not a religious book. Instead, it is a practical, all-encompassing, culturally neutral, spiritually profound work, for people of all sorts, who are willing to challenge abusive understandings, of life in general and the spiritual in specific. In contemplating a new vision, people can move from limited concepts (of perfectionism, guilt, fear, violence, sin, sex, threats of hell, superiority, exclusivity, black/white values, power, submission) and take a journey into humanness, wholeness, the right to choose, the strength to bend, personal responsibility, and especially the Divinity within.

The Relationship Garden is a book of faith, not beliefs. Religion and beliefs are what people hold to be true because someone else experienced it. To me, faith comes not from indoctrination (words I pour into myself), but from the Spirit of God bursting from inside me. Faith is experiencing myself actively on a journey; it is a way of life, of confidence and curiosity. Beliefs are what are seen or imagined along the way, gleanings from the fields passed by on the journey. The heart of becoming fully human is faith, not beliefs. The "Garden" that Ben and Jock write about continues to be explored by them as they walk the journey with faith.

In this book Ben and Jock awaken me to the common territory of this garden —an experience that differs in depth for each of us. Their real function is not to provide maps, but to sharpen our own sense of direction so that when we really get going we can travel without maps.

Religious traditions can point beyond themselves and their churches toward this larger territory. Each uses its own imagery for description. Christianity for instance, names it and explores it as the "Kingdom of God," a place of becoming fully human, a way of life that is soul making, a place of renewal; similarly, Buddhism points to enhanced dimensions of awareness, rooms where consciousness is enhanced.

When Ben and Jock speak of strength and grace in relationships I hear them speak of God. For myself, because I work in the field of personal and institutional transformation, this book is a wonderful tool. Dualisms, as traps, as alienating language, are laid to rest as I listen to these men speak passionately of the human/divine strength that brings humanity to life. In their writing I see, touch and taste this strength—this God as me.

In this book my senses come alive; relationships become vehicles of grace calling me into strength and the "seat of God" within me. There I discover the clues, the inspiration, the grace of God grounded in me. This is pure experience,not doctrine, not something laid under a tree, but the tree itself. Each religious tradition finds imagery to express this. In Christianity this experience is called "conversion" or "metanoia," a deep glimpse at a new awareness, a turning around, a shift, a constant confirming of one's own self as a personal life reality, not just an idea. The authority for this is placed in the hearts of those who choose the journey. Thus people already know about it as they stand on their own two feet. I believe Jesus touched people to awaken them to their self-respect and deepest possibilities for relationship, precisely by reminding them this was never lost.

At one time I became very involved in social justice issues. Gradually I realized that the very cultural lifestyle that kept me from knowing myself as a "gardener" also perpetuated injustice in the world. I've learned we are all linked, and to whatever extent I realize and express what wants to manifest through me, the world will unfold. This book invites us to take seriously what many would call "simply personal," as a base for anything later labelled as social or political. Joseph Campbell suggests that if you really want to help this world, what you really will have to teach is how to live in it.[2]

Laughter, for me, is holy and important to the spiritual life. Its gift is a therapy of the heart. When we can laugh around man-made institutions, claims and moralisms, we can realize that the facts of the world within and without are never the end of the matter, never the last word. The laughter present in this book and in the authors' seminars is an experience of faith, a way "back to the garden."

My religious training has taught me very little about sexuality; basically it has ignored sexuality, or treated it negatively. In the seminary I heard it as suffocating and alienating. In this writing of Ben and Jock I experience a great rediscovery of the body, of embodiment, of a manifestation of the life power that enters into everything one does, especially in relationships.

Jesus said, "I have come that they may have life and have life in fullness" (John 10:10). This tells me all areas of life are to be cultivated and savored—poetry, music, painting, sculpture, imagination, relationship, passion, fantasy, sexuality—

all contributing to new fire leading me beyond to see a new world. There is the dark as well as the light to befriend.

Ben and Jock are mystics who enjoy their connection to the divine and so love the sound of human life as much as the silence of God.

> *Welcome, O life! I go to encounter for the millionth time the reality of experience and to forge in the smithy of my soul the uncreated conscience of my race.* —James Joyce[3]

Jack Sproule
Victoria, B.C.
December 1995

NOTES

1. A. Harvey, *The Way of Passion: A Celebration of Rumi* (Berkeley, CA: Frog Ltd., 1994), p. 314.

2. Joseph Campbell with Bill Moyers, *The Power of Myth* (New York: Doubleday, 1988), p. 149.

3. J. Joyce, *A Portrait of the Artist As a Young Man* (Middlesex: Penguin Books, 1960), p. 253.

The day will come when, after harnessing the winds, the tides, and gravitation, we shall harness for God the energies of love. And on that day, for the second time in the history of the world, man will have discovered fire.

—Pierre Teilhard de Chardin[1]

Introduction

BEN: *The year was 1970. After a decade of private psychiatric practice, specializing in problems of adolescence during the heady days of the "Hippie Revolution," I was filled with the excitement over what seemed to be a possible dream. My teachers were the youth themselves; my colleagues were too baffled by the rebellious energy to offer much information or support in my struggle to understand the phenomenon that was sweeping society. Much of the time, I felt isolated in my professional community; some of the time, I was obviously rejected by them. The situation reawakened my inner childhood angst, which found some relief in the emotional sharing of the endless numbers of teenagers that flowed through my office.*

JOCK: *After a childhood of loneliness and rejection by my peers, my academic and social successes at university were welcome relief. Now, newly married and heading to the west coast for my medical internship, I was filled with excitement over the prospects of being able to make a difference in people's lives. During the senior years of my medical training, I had discovered a meaningful existence while working with the street gangs of youth, helping them with their problems of drugs and dropout behaviours. My intention was to complete my medical internship, then study psychiatry so that I could be more effective. Wishing me well as I left our street clinic, many of the youth advised me to look up the psychiatrist Ben Wong in Vancouver. After settling into the responsibilities of my internship at the Royal Columbian hospital in New Westminster, B.C., I arranged to visit this Dr. Wong to discuss the possibility of an elective time studying with him in his office. I was confident that he would accept me as had all of my mentors throughout my training. I knew how to impress. With my fashionable clothes, long wavy hair and de rigueur moustache, he would immediately know that I was "with it" in the youth culture that he knew so well!*

BEN: *I wondered, "Just what does this young doctor hope to learn from me? I guess that I will soon learn as he is due to arrive here at my office any minute now." My receptionist announced the arrival of Dr. McKeen, and I asked her to send him down the corridor to my office. In response to his knock, I invited him to "come on in!" As the door swung open, I rose to offer my handshake. But I was struck dead in my tracks! To my astonishment, this young Dr. McKeen was a dead-ringer copy of singer Tony Orlando, moustache, sideburns and*

1

all! Completely losing all control, I broke into a hilarious laugh, exploding with the words, "You gotta be kidding!" After settling down, I was able to carry on a decent discussion with Jock, whom I soon discovered to be a paragon of narcissism. However, he also quickly revealed a most nimble mind, full of curiosity and adventure, willing to experiment and expand, while yearning to be in touch through his self-involvement. He was an old soul in a youthful, agile body! Within fifteen minutes of our initial contact, I knew that we were destined to create something together. In language that he might understand without freaking, I told him that I believed that we could work together sometime in the future. That seemed to please him.

After that momentous meeting, we planned our subsequent learning situations. Knowing that the field of psychiatry had little to offer in the areas in which Jock was particularly interested, Ben discouraged him from pursuing postgraduate training in that discipline. Eventually, Jock went to England to study acupuncture and traditional Chinese medicine in Oxford. Since then, we have devoted our attention to combining our understanding of western and eastern philosophies and healing traditions.

You might well ask, "Why are two men writing a book about loving and the stages of development of intimacy? What could they possibly know about such matters, which usually involve a man and a woman, or members of a family?" For the past twenty-six years, we have been in a most unique relationship, where we have made the study of loving and intimacy our central concern. Both of us were trained as scientists: Ben studied psychiatry and psychoanalysis following his medical degree; Jock trained in traditional Chinese medicine and acupuncture, after he graduated from medical school. Both of us had been fascinated with religions and spirituality, and were very involved in working closely with people as they delved into the concerns of their lives. It seemed that relationship and loving were central concerns of most people we met. And yet, we could not find any authorities who could answer "What is love?", "What is intimacy?", and "How can I deepen in relationship without losing myself?"

The Project

Over the years, we have been embarked upon a project of self-exploration together. In the spirit of the investigative seventies, we made an agreement with each other to explore intimacy together. By "intimacy" we mean knowing one another deeply, being revealed to one another; the Latin root of the word is *intimus*, meaning "inside." From the beginning, we approached the whole endeavour as two scientists, interested in discovering as much as we could. Our ground rules were simple, but rigorous. We each agreed to grant access to the other; this meant that upon request, one person could ask "What are you thinking?" and the other would agree to tell as much as he knew at that time. We did leave a provision for censoring; it was an appropriate response to say, "I choose not to tell you." This was humorously important when Ben was carefully holding back telling what he had bought for Jock as a birthday gift; the fun of a surprise could be dampened by the scientific rigour of being forced to tell. So honest revelation included being able to openly censor.

As well, we agreed to share our feelings, perceptions and judgments with each other, spontaneously, as soon as we could. Thus, there was no requirement for questioning; each person's responsibility was to willingly offer the information, so that the other could be included in his world. At the beginning, Jock was not too good at this. He was ready to offer the bare facts; however, he did not realize that Ben wanted *details*! So, we began to distinguish between factual, cool reporting of editorialized summaries, and embodied revelations. What we wanted to share to go deeper was the *experience*—the thoughts, feelings, sensations and impressions of moment by moment. As trained scientists, this was a struggle for us, to move deeper, into the layers where we *personally* lived. We were moving from the *objective* world of reporting, into a realm where we needed to develop our language and communication to share the *felt experience* of our lives.

It was in this project that we developed and honed the Communication Model, we outlined this model in our previous book, *A Manual For Life*.[2] The ground rules are simple, but rigorous and stringent. Deception is the enemy of intimacy. Jock discovered that he was a liar—not by conscious intent, but certainly through a lifetime of trying to put on the most appropriate presentation to win the affection and approval of others. We were not practised at *revelation*; we were programmed to deceive, to withhold, to minimize, to deflect. In other words, we found that we had adopted many socially established programs that interfered with open communication. The Communication Model helped us to patiently work through this.

A significant attitude we took from the beginning was that there was no truth, no objective reality. We each had our own experiences, coloured by our past, and our built-up prejudices, and there was no "truth" outside of this. So we could share our perspectives without one having to be right or wrong. This helped to lay a structure to develop a relationship without blame, and with full *responsibility* by each party. As well, we assumed that in any instance, neither person would be *right or wrong*. We would only be sharing viewpoints, perspectives; we did not have to decide who was "correct" in any circumstance. Hence, we avoided the legalistic structures in which most people become mired.

In this project, we found that most of what we had previously believed about loving, and relationships, and sex and intimacy simply were not so for us. We gradually built up a language to describe our experience together. We investigated further by comparing our results with the findings of many people who were around us. We talked openly with friends, colleagues and clients, with the intention of finding out what was so, rather than what was supposed to be so, or what other people said was so. We discovered many unexpected elements of relationships; these principles that we found continue to hold up to scrutiny over the years.

> JOCK: *What we were discovering about ourselves specifically, and about relationships in general, was breathtakingly beautiful! At the same time, I felt an uncomfortable gnawing somewhere deep in my gut, some unspeakable and unrecognizable fear for which I could find no explanation. My unconscious needs for survival would often overpower me. I began to recognize that whenever I would feel especially close to Ben, I would discover many reasons why I had to curtail my visits to him—I would become too busy or have conflicting appointments. Then I would not phone him for weeks. In past relationships, the other person would ultimately contact me to renew contact. Ben never would. How puzzling!*

At the beginning, each of us was living in our respective marriages, and only had a social relationship with each other, as well as a collegial interest in matters psychological. We found our times together to be stimulating and provocative. When Jock returned from his acupuncture studies in England, he set up an office next door to Ben's, sharing a common waiting room. We would meet each day to discuss our approaches with our patients (yes, they were "patients" in those days—we had not moved from the medical model of the therapist and patient yet). And we would talk about what we were doing with people, and what approaches seemed to bring the most benefit. Certainly, our approach with our patients was psychological; each of us had adopted a belief that peoples' lives could only change when their attitudes and approaches changed. So, even when the patients' complaints were physical in nature, we were most interested in how these people related to their world. Our medium of investigation was often the relationship that we established with them. It was apparent that people were openly sharing many of the intimate, painful details of their lives, and were thus opening themselves to us, in the therapeutic relationship.

As we met in our clinical conferences to discuss our patients, we were interested in how we could deepen our contact with them; it was apparent that the more significant the contact we had with them, the more ground they could gain in working with their concerns about their lives. In other words, if we could know them more, they could know themselves more, and they could see their lives in a different perspective; thus their healing would be facilitated. Consequently, we wanted to learn what stood in the way of our getting to know them more deeply.

We could see that one of the barriers was the professional distance into which we had been indoctrinated. It was acceptable for the patients to share their lives and concerns with us; we were supposed to keep an objective distance from them. And this was obviously (to us) an obstruction to the therapeutic endeavour. In the spirit of the times, we decided to try to open up ourselves, and become people with our clients (when we opened up and shared, the "patient" became a "person" instead of an object—hence the word "client" now applied). But we found that we had our own defences, and limited the relationship with each client with our own prejudices, and fixed attitudes about how things "should" be, rather than to simply appreciate how they were.

In our morning meetings together, where we were now discussing our "clients," we began to be more interested in how our own limitations as people restricted the relationship with our clients. We wanted to find out about our walls and defences, to overcome our habitual ways of keeping distant, so that the healing process could deepen. We decided in this spirit to investigate how we kept ourselves barricaded and distant from each other. In short, we decided to see how close we could get with each other, and to work through each defence that prevented such a closeness.

We began to talk about our feelings with and about each other. We found we were shy and inexperienced in giving words to them. We were comfortable at picking up a tab in a restaurant, or praising each other, as expressions of interest and affection. But to directly say "I like this about you" was very difficult. And even more difficult were the negatives that inevitably came up: we were too polite to say, "I don't like this about you." We realized that in order for our intimacy to deepen, we had to give voice to these feelings, positive and negative. And as we did, we would find breakthroughs in our morning meetings. Soon, we were not talking much about our clients; increasingly, we were involved in talking about our feelings for each other, and for ourselves. This process took more time, and we began to come to the office an hour ahead to "process." This grew into an hour and a half, and then into two hours pre-client time. We would also meet at the end of the day to talk about what we had thought and felt during the day, to keep in touch with each other. As well, we spent an hour on the phone each night.

As we became more familiar with each other, we also began to know ourselves and our own processes more. As we would discover something new in the morning meeting, we would be surprised to find that we saw this same issue in many of the clients during the day. It was as if the issue could not be seen until we faced it in ourselves, and in our own primary relationship. We began to theorize that professionals could only go with their clients where the professionals were prepared to go themselves.

The clients were fascinated, if somewhat taken aback. They began to practise the interpersonal skills that we introduced in the clinical hour with their families and friends. We found that they were coming early to their appointments, to talk with the secretary, who also was involved in interpersonal communication. And the clients were talking with each other, developing friendships in the waiting room! Because our client populations were quite different, this made for some interesting dynamics. Ben's clients were mostly adolescents dealing with life directions and parental and school issues; Jock's clients were elderly folk with chronic pain and idiosyncratic complaints that western medicine did not seem to touch. These two groups met in the melting pot of the waiting room, and really came to appreciate each other, and to learn from the relationships that they developed. The little old ladies brought cookies for the young hoodlums; we were never quite sure what substances the youngsters brought to initiate the older folk!

To our surprise, we found that people were becoming more interested in each other, and less interested in the "doctor." They even invited each other to their appointments, and took increasing charge of their hour. By the end of the day, we often had stacked up several people in our offices, who had simply stayed after their appointment was over, and flowed into the next client's hour. We were having group communication process, and in the midst of it, people's complaints were getting better!

Then we began to leave our practices for brief periods to lead residential experiential learning programs in a rural setting; all our work there was done in group process. From our experiences with our waiting room and office, we had already seen the benefit of people working together in groups. We were thrilled with the gains that people could make in the group setting—so much more extensive, and hopefully more substantial than the limited work in private counselling. Group process helped to avoid what Carl Whitaker used to refer to as the "emotional incest" of individual psychotherapy.[3] We began to dream about having a farm or rural facility that would serve as a large version of our waiting room, where people could come together, to meet, to get to know one another, to help one another to heal.

Then we faced living together, and sharing personal time, as well as the professional hours of the day. We had each separated from our wives by this time, and our sons were living with their respective mothers. So we were unattached, and decided to live together as two bachelors. As we worked out our domestic situation, we made everything grist for the mill. Nothing was too small to investigate. In Zen tradition, every minute is eternity, and every small action contains the entire universe. We would talk, examine, argue about the smallest details. We learned to observe grace or heavy-handedness in how we washed the dishes together. When we would have our meals together, there was an aesthetic as to how we would share the tasks involved in selecting and preparing the food. If Jock brought Ben a spoon he did not need, this would be cause for a long discussion and investigation into the lack of presence.

In short, we were learning to be *present* with one another, and to acknowledge when we fell out of presence. We were becoming sensitive to each other, acknowledging when we departed from this sensitivity.

> BEN: *Our project was enjoying a large measure of success! Often, I could tangibly feel the contact that was growing between Jock and myself! I suddenly flashed back to my senior high school days when, for an assignment, I had written an essay titled "My Best Friend." In it I had described in detail the kinds of things that would be felt between myself and an imagined true friend. My teacher was apparently uncomfortable with the revealing of my inner wishes; although she gave me an "A" for my writing, she appended a brief note cautioning me never to reveal the contents of the essay to anybody else! Jock and I were now living out in detail all that I had described some twenty-two years before.*

So, although we happen to be two men who have lived through this experiment, we see ourselves as two persons trying to determine the parameters of loving, *to discover intimacy.* In our living and exploring together, we have discovered many elements in relationship. Also, we have learned that these principles apply to any relationship. In our seminars, we now teach that there are common processes and issues that occur in relationships of any length; hence, people can come together for a weekend, never having met each other, and work on the patterns of relating that they bring to this short-term relationship.

In a similar fashion, people who have been together for many years have the same issues to contend with as those who are simply newer in their interactions.

Neither does the nature of the relationship particularly matter. As long as any two people are willing to commit themselves to being honest and curious with each other, they can work on a deepening intimacy. Thus, although the principles are very important to married couples, they also apply to parents in relation with children (and vice versa), siblings, business partners, same-sex friends, and opposite-sex friends of a Platonic sort.

Overcoming Control

Early in our relationship, we recognized the urgent desire to *control* one another: the greater the control, the higher the level of safety experienced. Yet we could also see that all such control leads to the ultimate destruction of any relationship; so we became determined to always unearth any underlying motives or means of control that might arise. How would we know when we were controlling and not just desiring? If we did not get what we wanted, we felt fine if all we were doing was desiring something to happen; if we had been controlling, we would feel resentful and angry.

JOCK: *Now I understand that my pattern of withdrawing from intimacy is a symptom of fear. All of my life, I have been afraid of being captured. I believed that all of my human contacts had always wanted something from me, something for their own pleasure and not mine. To beat them all to the punch, I developed extraordinary means of capturing them before they captured me, using seduction, pleasing, succeeding and acting—all to get my own way. Ben was totally different—he appeared to want nothing from me, and never would pursue me, no matter how hard I tried! I didn't know what to make of this.*

BEN: *My friends were concerned about me in relationship to Jock. They believed that he was out to use me, to get what learning he could from me and ultimately dump me, leaving me heartbroken and hurt. I could only reassure them that I knew that certainly he was trying to do just that, but that I understood myself well enough to know that I would never give away anything that I did not want to give, and that I could only be manipulated in areas in which I wanted to be manipulated. I knew that we only have to fear that which we want to do, and that if we participate, we are responsible for the consequences. With Jock I was finding a sense of fulfilment that I had hitherto only fantasized about in my youth.*

Relationships built on *need* are always controlling relationships. Controlling people tend to locate their centre in others. At separation, the controlling person becomes a victim, full of resentment and anger. On the other hand, a whole person experiences sadness over the loss, devoid of resentment. Needy people become enmeshed with one another, without effective boundaries; they do not grow. Whole persons in relationship become *more of themselves*. The relationship serves as a garden that provides the nurture for everyone (children as well as parents) to flourish and grow into the full potential of themselves. Even if they separate, they continue to appreciate one another for what they have learned together.

JOCK: *Ben has been a shepherd to my process, for the transformation and revelation of my soul. I went through several stages in discovering what it was that I was seeking. When I was a child, my statement would have been, "My soul wants to be seen." Later, after I was less afraid of close contact, I would have said instead, "My soul wants to be touched." Once I had moved through much of my dependency needs, and realized that I didn't need to be loved, but rather I need to love, I would then say, "My soul needs to be born."*

The Relationship Garden

Since the beginning of our relationship, we set as our goal the care and maintenance of a relationship garden in which each of us could best grow. Even though this task has necessitated an incredible investment of time and energy, with our rarely being outside of one another's vision for more than a few days a year over a span of over twenty-five years, we believe that what we have discovered will help others to manage the same with a more realistic time frame. Our friends have been concerned that we may have become enmeshed in this project, and that we may be deceiving ourselves in our assessment of our individual autonomous growth. Perhaps that may be so; the real test will occur if and when we are ever separated. We feel a sense of confidence that we will successfully pass such a test. However, as we have grown older and wiser, we have come to believe in the eternal aspects of loving; hence, we are beginning to believe that we will *never* be separated. We know of no earthly test of that!

What thou lovest well remains,
   the rest is dross. —Ezra Pound[4]

Notes

1. Pierre Teilhard de Chardin, quoted in E.H. Sell, *The Spirit of Loving* (Boston: Shambhala, 1995), preface.

2. B.R. Wong & J. McKeen, *A Manual for Life* (Gabriola Island, BC: PD Publishing, 1992), pp. 6–10.

3. Carl Whitaker, personal communication.

4. Ezra Pound, "Cantos LXXXI," in *Selected Poems of Ezra Pound* (New York: New Directions Publishing, 1957), p. 174.

Resonance

Original Energy

We are born into a sea of energy that has a wave action of expansion and contraction ("x" on the figure, "The Self and Connections," page 12). At conception, each being is unique, yet also connected to this pulsating energy; this participating connection is what we will refer to as "universal" or "cosmic" loving. This is the basic, true nature of loving to which we aspire throughout our lives, but rarely feel. Some compelling imperative appears to ordain that we experience separation in order to *individuate*—to become our individual selves before we are able to achieve a greater sense of that universal love in a larger and more highly evolved form. Such is the task set before us. Like the search for the Holy Grail, this journey is beset with danger and tests that will either strengthen the self or destroy it in the process. Nevertheless, there is no greater, more enjoyable goal. It is a challenge of equal magnitude for paupers and kings, lepers and athletes, victims and perpetrators, atheists as well as priests.

Separation

The human being's estrangement from the universal wholeness goes far beyond the physical separation that occurs at birth. Although we do not know the experience of other creatures, it is possible that animals other than humans feel very little separation even after birth. Some animal experiments with subtle energy suggest that even when a mother is artificially separated from her offspring, there remains an energy connection within both.[1]

For humans, who have a capacity for consciousness, the more remarkable consequence of separation is psychological in nature. The foetus is not only physically close to the mother, but also seems to be psychologically linked with her; the inner emotional climate of the pregnant mother probably has effects on the developing embryo. Many clinicians and researchers believe that unwanted children can feel in the womb their mothers' strong feelings of rejection toward them. If this is so, the pulsating life force energy in such children would likely expand less and contract more; in this tendency toward closure, they would

The Self and Connections

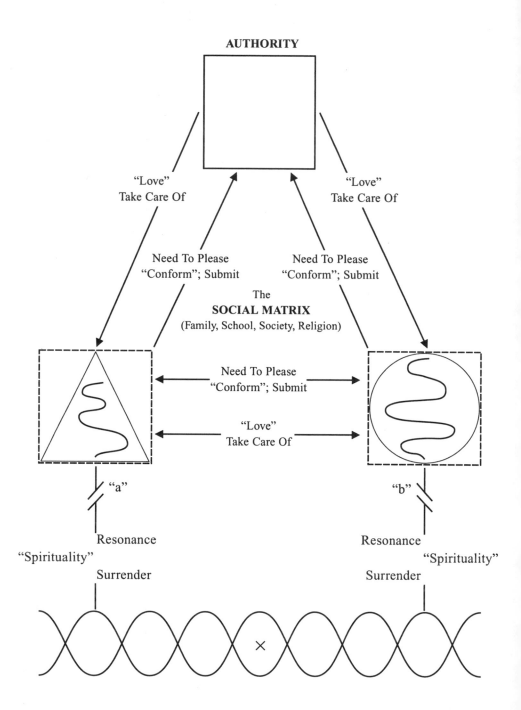

continue to feel unwanted after birth, with accompanying fears of rejection and problems with separation that would likely continue throughout their lives.

At conception, the universal energy flows without interruption within the developing human being. Each person has a core pattern similar to all other humans; at the same time, each person has an individual, unique pattern. In the diagram ("The Self and Connections," page 12), the unique patterns of two individuals are represented by a circle and a triangle within which the universal energy (represented by "x") freely flows. The square represents the authority figures that will be caretakers of these particular individuals. For the sake of simplicity, we have diagrammed two separate offsprings and one square caretaker. The square caretaker, representing the demands of culture, unconsciously motivates both offspring to surrender much of their individual differences, to conform to becoming square, to fit in.

Becoming Appropriate

The process of teaching appropriate cultural behaviour is both desirable and necessary—toilet training, healthy eating patterns, and appropriate interpersonal social behaviour are all necessary in any society. However, in order to conform, developing children must abandon or repress much of their own true nature. In order to be more square, the energy within each individual must be curtailed and controlled; the net result of such a process is that the pulsating energy within them diminishes in amplitude. With this freezing of core energy, the connection between the individual and the sea of universal energy is broken ("a" and "b" in the figure, "The Self and Connections"). This is the separation that is unique for human beings; it is what determines much of our goals and behaviour in life. This accounts for the basic inner feeling of isolation, which sets into motion all of our strategies to prevent us from being abandoned.

By the time children have become "good" children, they have effectively frozen most of their core energy and no longer experience their connection with the universal energy ("love"). In place of feeling connected to the universal love, people learn to "take care of" or "look after" one another, which is society's paradigm of what "love" is. As we described in *A Manual for Life*, in striving to be ideal, people lose connection with the Authentic Self (which is the original universal love vibration).[2]

Such "love" fulfills the needs of the developing (square) child as well as the caretaking (square) parent. Whereas the universal energy of love flows freely, this socially acceptable form of love is conditional (even though on a superficial level it would appear to be most selfless). This is the kind of love that builds societies and cultures. It is necessary, convenient and practical for the survival of the citizens; at the same time, it is the source of most of an individual's emotional problems. In conforming to the expectations of the square culture, people are cut off from the source of the universal love force. It is this very dilemma that motivates people to seek love and to develop relationships.

The Dilemma

Throughout people's lives, they are trapped between the choice of using better strategies to ensure that someone will take better care of them, or developing some means of reconnecting with their universal energy. Most relationships are based on the former; most spiritual practices and religions are based on the latter. In actuality, these circumstances occur on a spectrum. What we have experienced ourselves, and propose to others, is a combination of both; a relationship can serve as a nurturing and protective garden within which each person is able to grow in self-reliance, while remaining a responsible citizen. Human growth is a process of moving from the dependent condition of being cared for to the more autonomous state of being connected on the level of universal love.

Later, we will describe the movement in relationships beyond the early states of dependency and caretaking, which are known as the stages of Romance and Power Struggle (see "Developmental Stages of Relationships" p. 50). In such relationships, people experience feelings related to each other; however, they are mostly out of connection with the universe (and their deeper nature). Ownership of each other, and the bonds of social obligations, are substitutes for true connection.

Although most people lose their root connection with universal (love) energy, their inner vibrations do not entirely shut down. Usually, their energy just diminishes in amplitude; this occurs with individuals who do not have ready access to their feelings.

When feelings run high, the amplitude of vibration is large; this is evident in those who experience a high level of compassion and empathy. Such persons tend to remain in touch with the universal (love) energy and experience less fear over the possibility of being alone or rejected. These *individuated* people have little need to be taken care of by others; nor do they need to caretake others.

Thawing

In the workshops at PD Seminars, many people begin the sessions in a state of defensiveness, and are reluctant to share themselves. Their energy is a low intensity vibration, and they commonly report feeling tired or depressed. As some participants begin to reveal their inner hurts and fears, the other people begin to feel their own pain and anxiety *in resonance*. As the amplitude of these inner stirrings is increased, even the most frozen of them will begin to thaw. In that release, the inner energy is often reconnected with the universal (love) energy.

People tend to think that they are able to feel the pain of the others; they cannot. What they feel is their own pain that has begun to thaw in resonance with the pain of another. All that is required for that to happen is for the (observing) person to be fully present and more open. As the resonance increases in amplitude in a group, feelings will tend to spontaneously erupt among the participants, and an increasing feeling of unity and intimacy develops. We believe that this phenomenon of resonance is what happens in true *intimacy* in relationships. It can occur between friends and co-workers as well as between spouses and lovers.

Although this resonance often occurs in the process of sharing hidden pains, people do not connect only through pain. Indeed, when people are open with each other, they can resonate with any experience of others. The thawing can occur through sharing of all kinds of feelings, including anger, sadness, fear, grief, and joy.

Note that *feelings of resonance are empathetic, not sympathetic.* Sympathy involves objectification and a power-based condescension, accompanied by a desire to take care of the other. Empathy is personal, and involves an intimate participation through openness and vulnerability. Resonance connects people to their deepest nature.[3]

Sliding Toward Intimacy

Many believe that intimacy is an acquired skill; by this notion, humans are seen to be naturally separate, and have to learn to become close. In contrast to this common notion, we maintain that if people spend much time together, they will slide inexorably into a state of intimacy. Strangely, most of their time will be taken up with defending against this, to find ways to prevent that slide!

Interfering With Resonance

When intense resonance occurs between partners, one person sometimes tries to preserve that wonderful feeling of connection by attempting to control and possess the other. When this happens, their energy soon becomes blocked again, and they regress to a state of taking care of one another, hence losing the universal (love) connection. Unfortunately, this seems often to be the default position; people tend to become enmeshed with one another in this way, blocking the possibility for further growth. Resonance is frequently lost through blaming, denying, controlling, expecting, withholding, pleasing, taking care of one another, advising, intimidating, threatening, manipulating, misleading and lying, deceiving and judging. These are all some of the means of *defending* against the threat of intimacy.

Faith

When the parties involved in a healthier relationship reach this state of high resonance and harmony, they will resist the urge to freeze the experience by ownership or control. Instead, they will develop a sense of *faith*, assured that similar opportunities can always occur between them, so long as they remain open and compassionate with one another.

Love is the drive towards the unity of the separated. —Paul Tillich[4]

Notes

1. S. Ostrander & L. Schroeder, *Psychic Discoveries Behind the Iron Curtain* (New York: Bantam Books, 1971), pp. 141–42.

2. B.R. Wong & J. McKeen, *A Manual for Life* (Gabriola Island, BC: PD Publishing, 1992), pp. 15–19.

3. Ibid., p. 63.

4. P. Tillich, *Love, Power and Justice* (Oxford: Oxford University Press, 1954), p. 25.

Intimacy

A Confusion in Terms

Much confusion exists over the meaning and use of the word "intimacy." Commonly, it is used as a euphemism for sexual relations—which are frequently anything but intimate!

Here, we use the word in its original meaning of "closeness" and "being known." The word is derived from the Latin *intimus* meaning "innermost, deepest, most profound, most secret."[1] Intimacy is a state of being wherein the most inner parts of the self are revealed to another, and to oneself, without pretense or defence. Hence, intimacy involves a state of vulnerability and knowing that is achieved through revelation, quite apart from the roles and obligations that frequently exist in interpersonal relationships. With this definition, one person may be intimate—that is, revealed and vulnerable—with someone who might not be intimate in return. In an *intimate relationship*, such revelation and vulnerability are mutual.

The use of the word "intimate" to apply to sexual relations is based in part on a confusion with the verb "to intimate" meaning "to put, drive or press into, to announce," which is derived from a different Latin root (*intimare*). [2] This meaning associates to the penetrating quality of sexual contact, giving rise to the use of "being intimate" to mean having sexual relations.

Further confusion arises from the meaning implied in the verb "to intimate," which means "to suggest obscurely or indirectly, to hint";[3] this can be associated with the secrecy, privacy and innuendos associated with sexual interactions.

In this book, we will reserve the use of "intimate" to mean closeness and knowing. Hence, intimacy often—indeed, usually—occurs without sexuality.

The Loss of the Feeling of Connection

In the original state at conception, human beings are at one with universal (love) energy. Because they *are* one, they have no need to be known by another. However, from infancy, people become separated through the expectations for them to conform and play roles (see "Resonance," p. 11); by so doing, children learn to make *objects* of one another as well as of themselves. This is a necessary function of socialization. The process of learning for the developing child involves objectification, and language supports this by facilitating the naming of things. The price to be paid for this socialization is the loss of the deepest connection with the universal (love) energy; this connection is replaced by the act of taking care of one another, which becomes the more familiar meaning of the word "love." As well as losing contact with the universal vibration, the socialized person loses the ability to know the self. This process of objectifying continues throughout life, and people increasingly lose touch with their deeper nature.

The Developing Child

At the beginning, children are not aware of much outside of themselves. The parents or guardians provide for their wants and needs. The infant is dependent, and focused on developing of the sensorimotor systems. In this primary narcissism, children experience everything as extensions of themselves. As they achieve some degree of competence with the body and its functions, they gradually become more aware of the world around, and develop a curiosity in relating to it. In this way, children begin to distinguish self and other, and learn to see themselves in relationship with the rest of the world. They become increasingly social, and interested in others; initially, this seems to be quite self-serving, looking to others to provide sustenance, care and stimulation. As they learn to relate more sensitively to parents, siblings and other people, the early movements of the development of loving are taking place. Having learned to objectify others, they then are challenged to move beyond the objectification into having genuine empathy for the humanness of others.

The development of children involves a movement from dependency and field relatedness into self-reliance and individuation. In the early phases of psychological development, a child's perspective is relatively fixed, based on a black-and-white morality. As children grow, the possibility increases for seeing that other people have concerns, feelings and interests that are different from themselves. As they learn to conceptualize the separateness of others, there is a movement from the isolated narcissism into the beginnings of real relationships with other persons. As they progressively learn to recognize the world of others, the possibility opens for the freedom and creativity of being truly autonomous, caring individuals. Such people can accept the differences of others, thus being in harmony with them. Sensitive and responsible, they can learn to utilize their personal will to act in concert with the desires of the self, other people and the community at large, without being in conflict.

Alone and Separate

The existential condition of the human being is to be alone and separate. People live inside their own skins, and one person can never fully know another. Individuals can only know *their experience* of one another. People cope with the separation by social conveniences, and by living in an objectified world; but there is always separation. Intimacy involves acknowledging and accepting this existential separation, and standing in the strength of knowing one's *relatedness* with others. Togetherness comes with sharing aloneness. We have written at length on this subject elsewhere.[4]

At the core of human experience is a root anxiety, called "existential anxiety" or dread. Most of human activity involves attempts to cope with this basic feeling. Most people try to bury or deny this feeling, and occupy themselves with diversions to provide the illusion that they can be joined with another.

Indeed, most people seek relationships in order to overcome this root anxiety. Often, they are trying to fulfill a neurotic need to have someone else take care of them; they wish for someone else to fill their internal emptiness. Commonly, they want to own their partner as a possession, to have the illusory security of controlling another—in the same way that an infant wants to own the parent, and wants the security of having enough control to assure that the parent will always return.

The illusions of security and control work against intimacy. As long as people are invested in controlling their image of their objectified partners, their capacity for intimacy and loving will be limited.

Object Constancy

Throughout their lifetimes, all persons face the enormous task of moving from the infantile state in which all others are "objects" to recognizing them as persons. It is natural to see "mother" as provider and nurturer because of her caretaking functions; it is almost impossible to recognize her as a person in her own right, with her own desires and fears, her own history of life experiences, her own fallible virtues and vices. Too often, children remain mired in the early stage of assessing their parents as "good" or "bad" without taking the important step in accepting that in their parenting, they have been "good enough."

From the beginning, the child's sense of security is directly related to the quality of caring provided by the parent figures who at this stage are completely seen as providing *objects*—and not as real people. An infant's basic fear of annihilation is assuaged by the loving *presence* of a caretaker, which is primarily assessed by the quality of touch and sight, along with the certainty of being fed and provided with the means for safety and comfort. At the time the child learns to crawl and walk, making voluntary physical separation a real possibility, more importance is attributed to the *visual* presence of the parent. This is evident in the tendency for the newly crawling child to look over the shoulder at mother (making sure that she is still there).

After practicing separation and testing the certainty of the parent's presence over a sufficient period (which varies with each individual), the child will usually reach a stage of comfort over the parent's physical absence. This is accomplished by the child having sufficient memories of the constant presence of the parent; it is as though the image of the (object) mother has been taken into the child's inner self where it can provide uninterrupted caring. This process is referred to as *object constancy*.

When a state of object constancy is being established, the child has an increasing tolerance of the parent's absence. During that time, the child may make use of "transitional objects" such as dolls, teddy bears or some favorite blanket that provide some substitute comfort and reassurance along the way to becoming separate. This important process can be interrupted by any events that the child finds threatening—anxious and undependable parents, family breakup for whatever reasons, violence on television, abusive experiences, *unpredictable* or frequent absence of the caretaker. In such cases, the child is unable to develop an inner stable image of a caring authority figure whose presence is reliable. Over the ensuing years, such persons remain *field dependent*, constantly seeking reassurance and security from "objects" (people and things) outside of themselves. They crave attention and tend to control, possess and cling to their partners, feeling insecure when left alone; or they fill their world with transitional objects that they can purchase and collect.

Placed in a Relationship Garden in which they are encouraged to discover, express and acknowledge such insecure infantile longings, without their partners being controlled by them, these people who lack internal stable objects can slowly continue to proceed through the necessary stages of development in which they had been arrested. For that purpose, it is important to use the "Communication Model" of relating, in which intentions, imaginings, and reality checks are fully revealed.[5] Use can also be made of such tools as the "five-minute cling" that will be described later (see "Working Through the Power Struggle," p. 119). With increasing autonomy, such people can develop stable internal objects.

The Fear of Intimacy

Becoming intimate and revealed to another would help people to rediscover themselves, by overcoming the objectification. Instead, people tend to do everything they can to prevent such intimacy from flourishing, believing at some level that to do so would be to *lose* the self! At the beginning, there is no self—there is only an energy centre with a potential to develop a self. The earliest separation experiences give roles to play, and people learn how to objectify one another. "Mother" becomes a provider and protector; siblings tend to become rivals; fathers become authority figures. These are all *objectified versions* of real people, who may never be known for themselves beyond the objectifications. Children never think to ask their parents who they really are, what their hopes and fears are, where their passions lie. Even if they did, what parents would give them some straight answers? Probably most parents would not know the real answers for themselves. In this way walls are built, roles are established, and lifetime patterns of behaviour are created. Most persons become identified with their walls as they lose touch with what is real in their centres!

Unfortunately, because of a lifetime habit of self-preservation, people tend to believe that the revelation of the true self would result in judgment, rejection and abandonment by others. It is difficult to believe that anyone could ever accept the demons of our inner natures—our hurts, angers, pettiness, jealousies, spitefulness, evil desires, and shameful lusts. Our own parents would never accept these things in us—why would our partners or friends, who thought we were wonderful and all good! How could we now reveal to them that we have been deceiving them all along? Becoming intimate and revealed would be tantamount to signing our own banishment or death warrant! No! No! Better we should become more perfect partners, try harder to please, repress our own horrible natures all the more. So what if it means that we become more depressed, or more addicted to drugs and alcohol, or develop more serious physical illnesses—at least we will not be abandoned, and being a chronic patient is better than becoming abandoned and nothing at all!

Lost and Found

In later adulthood, after years of identifying with protecting walls, people often begin to feel the stirrings of a desire to know who they *truly* are—to find the Authentic Self. They begin to understand that they are more than their defences, that all such identifications are illusions. This may be the stimulus for a spiritual search for the self, using a wide spectrum of meditative and self-denying methods to do so. Unfortunately, many times such attempts result in self-delusions of a new sort, or despair of a deeper level, as the capacity for self-deception is so subtle and far-reaching.

In a relationship of an intimate nature, people have a greater capability to discover their own walls, identify them, acknowledge them and lower them—thus opening the pathway to the revelation of the Authentic Self. If people do not protect either themselves or their friends and partners, and are committed to share with someone else what they are discovering, then they have a unique and effective way to find themselves. An intimate relationship is the garden in which people can grow!

Roles and Images

From birth, people are expected to become appropriate citizens. Families teach their children how to be socialized through a myriad of expectations and subtle demands, wherein they are rewarded for their performance and achievement, and where little notice is given to internal feelings and personal wishes. Thus, from an early age, people learn to play roles, and fulfill duties and objectified images. Although these roles and images bring some measure of comfort and security, later on they often stand in the way of developing intimacy.

Sartre's view about the human condition was that human beings are not what they are, and are what they are not.[6] By this, he suggested that people live the images of themselves, but they don't know their deeper nature, which is hidden beneath the masks of roles and cultural expectations.

Generally, children adopt an attitude of pursuing achievement, and develop an image of an "Ideal Self"[7] that serves to please others (at first parents, and later others in the world). They learn to be "good" and "appropriate," but they don't know their inner being. Indeed, by the time they reach adulthood, they generally have suppressed so much of their own personal feeling and opinion that they scarcely know their own authentic natures at all. When these individuals come into relationship, they generally offer their roles and achievements, and what they can *do for* each other, without coming to know themselves or their partners more deeply. Because intimacy involves sharing of the self, these people are limited in their capacity for closeness by their limited awareness of themselves.

Image Projection

People usually don't know one another; they relate instead to the images they project upon each other. This phenomenon, known clinically as "projection" and "transference," and in popular language as "ghosting," is a normal condition. Children learn to relate to parent objects, much in the way that they learn to relate to the stuffed toy object. That there is a person present beneath the projections of roles and expectations is a fact that slowly dawns, and is part of the developmental process of intimacy.

So, in relationship, people tend to relate to their partners as if they were parents or teachers or other authority figures; they also might relate as if the partner had characteristics of a child, a family pet, or teddy bear. Only by acknowledging and relating these projections can people move closer to their own feelings and discover a more personal perspective where they entertain thoughts about the uniqueness of their partners.

Many people are afraid to look beyond their roles and projections because they fear that who they really are will be unacceptable to others; they are afraid that if they are revealed, they face the danger of rejection and abandonment. Indeed, this is the risk of intimacy. Fearing to take this risk, many people opt for remaining hidden—playing roles, controlling, projecting and withdrawing. The Relationship Garden then becomes a playground in which fantasies are enacted but no growth is possible.

Taking Care or Caring About

Taking care of others is different from *caring about* (caring for) them. Caring for others often involves leaving them with their feelings, and not trying to help them or fix them. Generally, people are motivated to *caretake* others (take care of them), to infantilize them, in order to try to relieve pain or anxiety. At the root, the caretaker is trying to be important to the recipient of the caring;

this pseudo-parenting of another is often a way of coping with the caretaker's root anxiety.

Genuine caring about others doesn't mean trying to take away their feelings or their experience, even if these involve pain or suffering. Caring involves sharing in another's feelings, without trying to take them away. When people take care of others, they minimize their experience, and devalue the feelings by trying to get rid of them. When people take care of others, they are actually not caring about the others; they are defending against their own existential anxiety. Caring about someone involves acceptance of the self and the other. To take care of someone involves trying to control the other and the other's experience.

Most people have unresolved childhood issues that are commonly attributed to the "child within." Much passion in life is directly related to satisfying this child part—spontaneous play, being taken care of, being seen as special, being able to feel irresponsible, and even being allowed to throw a temper tantrum. Any intimate relationship should provide for the possibility of expressing these passions. However, from the outset, they should be acknowledged as immature and irresponsible behaviours that will be shared *for a limited time*, thus diminishing the danger of using them for control.

Presence

Presence is a prerequisite for intimacy. In order to relate in an intimate way, it is important that both parties come *present* for the interaction. In the earliest years, people discover that presence has some gratifying results in the ability to control others—parents at first, then the entire world. By becoming present, it is possible to bridge the gap between oneself and others, providing a means of reciprocal give and take. However, some have found through life experience that the external world is unsafe; this can occur through physical violence or sexual abuse at one end of the scale, or some parental inconsistency or thoughtlessness on the milder end. Whatever the circumstances, most have learned to withdraw and to become non-present. Originally this was for protection and sometimes even survival; for a helpless child, going non-present may be a self-preservative mechanism to avoid pain. Having learned to become non-present, people can later use this for purposes other than the original ones. For example, when going non-present has some desirable effect upon one's partner (such as arousing concern), it can become a manipulative, controlling device. When one person is fully present, a retreat from presence by the partner often results in hurt and disappointment within the one who remains present.

In its extreme form, going non-present is a prelude to splitting off, wherein the self separates from the body. Although such mechanisms might have been useful to a helpless child under assault, they become a handicap to any responsible adult attempting to establish an intimate relationship. "Flashbacks" (spontaneous regressions to past traumatic experiences) are stimulated by events in the present that the person is emotionally unprepared (or stubbornly refuses) to deal with in a responsible, mature way; they remain victims to their past. Withdrawal and splitting off, once useful behaviours, now have become defensive mechanisms to interrupt the development of intimacy. Of course, as with all established bad habits, merely knowing this does not make it easy to quit doing it. But the first step is to begin acknowledging the process to an intimate partner whenever it is happening, thus reducing the possibility of using these mechanisms for the purpose of control.

In the extreme form of splitting off, a person may leave too quickly to have time for such acknowledgement. In these instances, people might have to call their partners back into presence by holding or touching hands while identifying themselves. Sometimes, loud shouting is necessary to reach the split-off person. Ultimately, every person is responsible for remaining present, and for returning from splitting off; all parties should be held able and accountable for playing their part in the developing relationship. While being accountable, remember that splitting off is not a symptom of being "bad"; although everyone is responsible, no one is at fault. Becoming non-present, or splitting off, are weeds in the Relationship Garden that can be dealt with *together*.

Many people confuse intensity with presence. They believe that they are present when they are only being highly charged or deeply involved with a person or an activity. Obsessions involve intense involvement without presence. Obsessed people are intensely bound to their ideas about the other person, and are not present to be truly engaged. Obsessive lovers are more tied to their ideas of love, rather than intimate with the one they believe they love; their consciousness has been captured by their own concept of romance, thus interfering with their ability to be truly present with the other. In this way, they lose the possibility for an intimate relationship, while suffering from intense desires that they might misidentify as love or presence.

Presence is not necessarily conscious awareness; it is possible even in sleep. Throughout the night, sleeping mothers frequently remain present with their babies; even a slight agitation in a child is often sufficient to arouse its mother. People in relationship are able to be fully occupied with other activities, and still remain present with one another. Distances do not matter; even with physical separation and death, people who are intimate with one another continue to feel the partner's presence. Some would argue that this is merely a sign of good "object constancy" in which the image of the other has been internalized and carried within the self as a constant memory. We believe that the development of object constancy is quite dependent upon a high level of presence of both parties. In intimate relationships, partners resonate through their continuing presence with each other.

Vacancy and Non-Presence

Presence means to have one's attention and involvement in a situation; when one is present, one is revealed. Vacancy involves giving up the self; when people are vacant, they are not being true to their own real nature. One can be present and not vacant, or present and vacant. Or one can be non-present and not vacant, or non-present and vacant. The following chart illustrates.

	Vacant (Unreal)	Inhabited (Real)
Present	Geisha (Caretaker)/Warrior Line Worker (no person, role)*	Real Person+ (available for intimacy)
Non-Present	Hysteria, Obsessions, Addictions* (no person, no role)	Achievers, CEOs* (real, but unavailable)

* = involved in control, power; invulnerable
+ = intimate; vulnerability, strength

Geishas/Caretakers are present, but vacant. They wish to please others and do not take account for themselves. This is also seen in the "mother syndrome," where a woman gives up her own interests to be pleasing and to take care of the family. The emphasis is on giving up the self in pleasing the field. Beneath the compliant stance of Geishas is often a fear of abandonment.

Warriors, like the Geishas/Caretakers, are present, and vacant; they give up themselves in battling the foe. The stance of the Warrior is to refuse to accept a situation as it is; often Warriors give themselves away toward a "higher" political purpose. They are fighters; often beneath their aggressive stance is a fear of anger or destructive impulses.

Hysterics will become non-present, and vacant. They will give themselves away. They commonly have an underlying fear of the passion that they are unwilling to experience. They abandon themselves by becoming vacant; they are often afraid to experience the erotic impulses of the body. *Obsessions* and *addictions* represent other means to abandon the sensations in the body, and to become numb; these are variations of the non-present/vacant stance.

Achievers and people who are very caught up in being in charge (*CEOs*) are often real but unavailable; although they are often non-present, they will not abandon themselves. They are not truly present, although they have not given up their value systems or ethics; nevertheless, they are not personally available to be intimate. Their driven activity often expresses an underlying fear of failure and low self-acceptance. These people can be found as directors of many business enterprises, where the real person is hidden but is not relinquished.

Real Persons are present, and hence available for intimacy. Because they do not abandon themselves or their principles, the dialogue with these people is authentic.

In relationships, people tend to look for a specific type of person, their "microdot."[8] For example, a non-present, non-vacant person might be looking to establish a relationship with an hysteric. All combinations are possible, with different relationships emerging from the positions that are interacting. Note that *an intimate relationship is only possible when both persons are present and non-vacant.* All other combinations are managed with control and withholding; hence, intimacy is restricted.

Responsible Communication

Responsible, respectful communication is critical in developing intimacy. The Communication Model that we outlined in *A Manual for Life* has been the cornerstone of our relationship project.[9] As well, it has been the centre of our teaching in workshops over almost three decades. In this process, the thrust is toward becoming more present and less vacant. People return many years after attending one of our residential programs to report, "The Communication Model is the single most important thing I learned." We believe that people could overcome virtually any standoff in relationship by remaining curious, while using this model of relating in a caring manner.

One important point is that *no one can make another feel anything.* One person does not turn another on or off; nor does that person excite or bore another; one does not make another angry or happy. Individuals turn themselves on and off, excite themselves and bore themselves; people generate their own anger and happiness. Indeed, as a responsive being, each individual is responsible for all of his or her feelings, thoughts, attitudes, and experiences. Although this is usually unconscious, people nevertheless are responsible at some level for their own experiences. Yet, people generally have been indoctrinated to think that their feelings and thoughts are the result of others' behaviours and input. Indeed, feelings are the expression of the internal physiology of the individual human organism; they are generated from within the individual. Although thoughts can be copied from someone else, the individual internally chooses to copy the thoughts. Ultimately, each individual is responsible for his or her own thoughts, prejudices, attitudes, feelings, responses and desires. It is a malignant social convention that places the responsibility for such things on another person, inviting people to make others responsible for their feelings. In order to arrive at this position of responsibility (and freedom), people have to work through their fixed indoctrinated attitude. Strangely, as people begin to take responsibility for themselves, they begin to appear unusual. Language and culture serve to inculcate the belief that other people pull our marionette strings, and the "normal" position is one of being a victim of others.

For many, a most difficult aspect of this responsibility model is the realization that it is impossible to hurt anybody else's feelings. Certainly, people often *intend* to hurt one another with what they say; but in actual fact, they cannot. The physiological mechanisms of hurt feelings are within the person who hurts, controlled within his or her own brain by what *perceptions* and *interpretations* are made of what the other is saying. People are in charge of their own perceptions and interpretations; to hurt, they can use these perceptions and interpretations as weapons to stab themselves, to hurt their own feelings. So it is illegitimate to blame another for hurt feelings. But it is possible to share the hurt feelings so that the partner can know what kinds of things one will tend to hurt over. By sharing their hurt feelings, people can stop using them to control their partners. In this vulnerability, they are more revealed; this is how intimacy grows.

No Blame

Although all are responsible for their own feelings, this does not give licence to be insensitive. Neither person is to blame for the feelings of the other; neither person is responsible for the other; neither is obligated to the other. There is tremendous freedom in this: if people do come together in relationship, it is because they both choose to, by their own free wills and desires. When people are genuinely *curious* about themselves, and about each other, their relationship can flower without either having to feel guilty or blamed for what does or does not transpire. If they don't try to control each other, they can instead have a genuine interest in each other, in which loving and feeling for life can be revealed. When people become caught up in power, control and domination, the possibilities for intimacy and loving are eclipsed.

Both partners do not have to agree, or have the same perceptions and interpretations. When one partner shares feelings related to different interpretations, the other does not have to abandon his or her position. But it is important that they respect each other's position, and especially refrain from diminishing or belittling one another. Sometimes that leaves people in an uncomfortable state of disagreement that they need to learn to accept and live with. Any relationship benefits from this increasing capacity to accept differences while living with some tension between the parties.

Prejudices (*pre*-judgments) and interpretations are ways of organizing the world, but they prevent people from knowing one another. Indeed, people only know *their version* of anyone else. By sharing fixed attitudes and preconceptions, people become revealed. In this *revelation*, the window opens, and intimacy can flourish. The "Communications Model" presupposes there to be no right or wrong—all that is possible is to agree or disagree. When people are angry because they believe that they have been treated unfairly, that indeed is their reality; *but it never is right!* Indeed, others might even agree with this perspective; but that still does not make it right—it only means that they are in agreement. At the same time, people can disagree, and neither of them would be wrong. Because all feelings are generated by interpretations of the perceptual signals being received, it is important that people check their interpretations with each other. It is remarkable how many people suffer in silence over some imagined slight, becoming emotionally distant or angry from someone they love—all because they did not check out their interpretation of an event!

Many relationships head for the rocks because the parties become involved in legalistic battles of who is right or wrong; usually, it is obvious that they are merely disagreeing, and that neither is right or wrong. When people step beyond this child-like behaviour, they can learn to respect and accept one another's opposing views without giving up their own, and thus can live together in harmony. Instead of becoming defensive, partners can always become curious about themselves and each other, to discover more about how they have arrived at whatever opinions they have. Such an approach provides each person with more information about themselves and each other, hence strengthening their intimacy.

Guilt, Shame and Forgiveness

Much confusion exists concerning guilt and shame. Generally, they are both seen as negative states. We ourselves make a very clear distinction between the two.[10] Guilt operates against personal development and intimacy; shame can be very useful in personal growth and can enhance intimacy.

Guilt is the painful internal tension generated by the conscience of a person, who has *interpreted* that thoughts or deeds have broken some law or rule imposed from the external environment. Guilt sees the self as a transgressor, an object that deserves punishment. Guilty people seek forgiveness for having done something that they believe they would not ordinarily do; thus, guilt denies the true nature of the self, by attempting to divorce the self from actions. To be guilty is to be in a position of irresponsibility. A statement of guilt could include: "I'm not the kind of person who does this kind of thing."

On the other hand, shame is a flooding of feelings generated by a *recognition* of the self; no amount of forgiveness can erase the knowledge that the person is indeed the kind of person revealed by his or her words or deeds. A statement of shame could include an acknowledgement that "I am the kind of person who does this kind of thing." In Buddhist philosophy, shame is seen to be a highly nutritive state of consciousness, in the same degree of importance as faith and empathy.[11] With shame comes revelation and recognition—both key factors in returning to one's authentic nature.

Shame should not be confused with guilt, or what is often referred to as "toxic shame" (which we see as another form of guilt, with all its negative consequences). Parents produce confusion when they angrily point an accusing finger with an accompanying "Shame on you!" when what they mean is "Guilt on you!"

Physiologically, guilt closes the person down to feel small and worthless; the energy body is tightened and compressed. Shame opens up the energy body, flooding the self with warmth and expansiveness; the person experiences that there is no place to hide. Because guilt results in a shutting down and denial of the self, it works against intimacy. Shame involves a recognition of the self, which allows for true revelation of one to the other—which is the very basis of intimacy.

If while dancing with you, I step on your foot, I automatically say "I'm sorry," to beg your forgiveness so that I will not have to feel guilty. In effect, I am proposing that I am not normally the kind of person that steps on feet, so this time was perhaps an accident. However, when I view this event in a responsible way, I cannot deny that, indeed, I am the kind of person that steps on people's feet, because I just did so! Recognizing this, I am flooded with shame (and embarrassment, which is a particular form of shame), knowing that you cannot forgive me for being who I really am; I am caught, revealed as the klutz I am. To dance with me is to take the risk of being stepped on! Knowing this, I cannot any longer ask for your forgiveness; I can only ask for your recognition and acceptance. This attitude of acceptance of shame brings me closer to you (and myself), while the guilt approach further separates us through power dynamics.

People generally think of *forgiveness* in *moral* terms. In this way of seeing, I judge you for having done something *wrong*, and I banish you, moving you away from me. When I forgive you, I permit you to come near again. This involves a hierarchical, one-up/one-down view, where one person is in the right and is a *victim* of the transgressor's behaviour.

A more responsible way to view forgiveness is to recognize that *neither person is wrong*. When I do not like what you have done, I may feel hurt, become angry, and withdraw from you. My act of forgiveness is my letting go of my anger to return to be present with you. In forgiving, I do not permit you to come back to me (you might not have gone anywhere); as *I have moved away*, it is I who returns.

Familiarity Is Not Intimacy

Familiarity arises from having much information about one another. For example, a spy knows his adversary, and a boxer knows his opponent well; in war, generals know how enemies are likely to act, and the soldier in the trenches is hypervigilant to the activities of his counterpart across the battlefield. People who live together for a long time know one another's predictable habits. In all of these examples, the people have much information about one another, establishing a high level of *familiarity*, but not necessarily very much intimacy. To become more intimate would require the addition of more *vulnerability* and a greater access to one another's feelings.

This movement from familiarity to intimacy is movingly illustrated in the play *Shadowlands*, in which C.S. Lewis is depicted as discovering about intimacy and loving in his later years. In the following scene, Lewis' wife already knows that she is dying of cancer:

JOY: We'll have journeys.

LEWIS: And little by little I shall dwindle into a husband.

JOY: And I shall fatten into a wife. I know your footsteps. I can tell it's you long before you reach the house. I know it's you coming up the road.

LEWIS: I never thought I could be so happy, so late in life. Every day when I come home, there you are.

JOY: The first words you speak, I know what kind of a mood you're in. Just from the sound of your voice. Even if you don't speak, I still know, from the lines on your face. I watch you when you're working at your desk. I study you. I learn you.

LEWIS: Every day when I come home, there you are. I can't get used to that. Every day it surprises me. There you are. It's the sheer availability of the happiness that takes my breath away. I reach out and there you are. I hold you in my arms. I kiss you. All I have to do is reach out, and there you are. You've made the world kind to me. You've made me so grateful. Grateful for all the ordinary domestic pleasures.[12]

Hierarchy in Intimacy

It is not possible to be equally intimate with large numbers of people. Because time is limited, there is little possibility of sharing a great deal of personal information with more than just a few others. People have a different location and perspective in each of their relationships. Some relationships are more important than others, while others are only different. In families, all persons have a particular place in each other's lives; some relationships are more intimate than others, while some are merely different in nature. For example, the kind of intimacy that exists between parents is likely different from the closeness shared with children. What is shared with each child may be different, even if the intimacy is of the same degree.

The levels of intimacy for each person form concentric circles of increasing distance. Closest to the centre is the person with whom you are establishing a *primary relationship*, the person with whom you are willing to share the most about yourself, and from whom you can expect the greatest amount of feedback. Such a relationship is developed and maintained by a commitment to openness and honesty. Here you will feel the most vulnerable, discover your deepest feelings, and stimulate the greatest growth of your Authentic Self.

In the next closest concentric ring of intimacy will be a variable number of different people—perhaps your children, your friends, your family. Each individual locates these people in different places; there is no right way to do this. When children are involved, we recommend that parents locate their primary relationship solidly with one another. Parents who depend upon their children for their primary relationship will contribute towards the children developing feelings of obligation for the parents' health and happiness, along with increasing amounts of guilt and resentment. Furthermore, such children tend to develop unrealistic feelings of entitlement, which may hobble their future initiatives in emotional and vocational endeavours.

Even though each person has concentric rings of decreasing intimacy, the nurture generated within the garden of the primary relationship can be used at all the other levels. The co-creating style established by the process of mutual revelation will be inspirational to people at all the other levels within the sphere of influence of that relationship. What benefits one will benefit all.

Notes

1. J. Traupman, *The New College Latin and English Dictionary* (New York: Bantam Books, 1966), p. 156.

2. N. Webster, *Webster's Collegiate Dictionary* (Springfield, MA: G. & C. Merriam Co., 1947), p. 528.

3. Ibid., p. 528.

4. B.R. Wong & J. McKeen, *A Manual for Life* (Gabriola Island, BC: PD Publishing, 1992).

5. Ibid., pp. 6–10.

6. J.P. Sartre, *Being and Nothingness* (New York: Washington Square Press, 1972), p. 36.

7. B.R. Wong & J. McKeen, *A Manual for Life* (Gabriola Island, BC: PD Publishing, 1992), pp. 15–19.

8. Ibid., pp. 89, 90.

9. Ibid., pp. 6–10.

10. Ibid., pp. 45–50.

11. Lama Anagarika Govinda, *The Psychological Attitude of Early Buddhist Philosophy* (New York: Samuel Weiser, 1974), p. 121.

12. William Nicholson, *Shadowlands*, from Plays International, Vol. 5, No. 5, December 1989, p. 49.

Feelings and Closeness

Emotions and Feelings

Contrary to common opinion, everybody has feelings. Feelings are some of the parameters of the internal environment, just as temperature is one of the measures of the external environment. Some heat fluctuation is necessary in order to experience the temperature for what it is; the change allows for comparison. The same applies to feelings. Just as a person living in a constant temperature will lose heat sense, so it is with one whose internal feelings are invariable. The feelings are there; the problem is that when the feelings do not change, one does not notice feelings at all. A person who is experienced by others as "cool and controlled" likely has feelings and does not register them. Another possible cause of lack of sense of feelings might be that the person has a dysfunctional measuring instrument (as in a chronic brain syndrome or hysteria).

Emotions are not feelings; they are the vehicle through which feelings can be expressed. Emotions are feelings that move out from the internal environment to find expression on the surface in the external world. Thus, a person might feel sad inside, revealing that as emotion through weeping or withdrawing from social contact. Many people who claim to be afraid of feelings are actually afraid of the external manifestations, the emotions. When this is clarified, they can devote more attention to becoming familiar with their internal environment rather than spending so much energy at controlling what might be revealed. Being afraid of having emotions generally means being afraid of losing control or becoming too vulnerable. Such people develop a pattern of "moving into their heads," becoming rational and distant for the sake of security. Proposing that they allow some emotion is like suggesting a safari into a deep jungle without either provisions or weapons—a terrifying proposition!

Unemotional people need much understanding and encouragement to help them engage in emotional relationships. *Remember—everyone has feelings!* The unemotional person should not be viewed as wrong or bad—such an attitude tends to stimulate more defensiveness. Embarking upon a project of sharing feelings can be a mutually beneficial adventure in which all of the concerned parties can learn. The intention of sharing feelings should be discussed and clarified; when it is for the deepening of the relationship, perhaps even a frightened person might be willing to try. Any issues of control, intimacy and trust must first be addressed; the unemotional person must know that the environment is safe and accepting. Many find it valuable to review the past from the vantage point of discovering the situations that fostered the lack of safety for emotional expression. The imagined catastrophic possibilities that could happen in the present should be unearthed.

Responsibility for Feelings

Feelings are the inner subjective climates related to outer objective experience that help to direct our choices in life. Basically, there are two broad kinds of feelings—the positive that attract and the negative that repel. Painful feelings such as hurt and anxiety tend to motivate us to withdraw and protect ourselves from others, while the more positive feelings of attraction, closeness, warmth, pleasure and joy tend to drive us to move closer to others.

Close inspection shows that the generation of these feelings, and the responsibility for them, always originates within the self, never in the object or other. As my own perceptions and interpretations produce those feelings, they can become whatever serves me best. For example, as a parent, I could feel a sense of warmth and pleasure over my sons being engaged in a game of cops and robbers; but if I suddenly began to think that they were becoming too serious and real about the game, then my feelings might change to concern and worry. The difference need not be how they are playing; the difference lies in my capability to interpret their behaviour in a variety of ways!

In relationship, one person might begin to feel anxious when the partner begins to show signs of being secretive. After doing some sleuthing, she discovers that he is busy planning a surprise birthday party for her; as the interpretation changes, her concern fades and she feels a sense of loving warmth for him, even though he continues to be secretive and furtive. Some people would say that his secretive behaviour caused her to be anxious, thus making her a helpless victim to his activities. To take a more responsible position, one sees that all our feelings are all entirely our own, generated by ourselves through our interpretations of what we perceive. Before becoming distraught over any particular feeling, it is important to check out the interpretations that underlie the feeling with one's partner to see if the anxiety is warranted!

After coming to realize that all feelings are self-generated over our interpretations, we have a further choice. We can decide to share our feelings with the other person, or keep them to ourselves. If we share them, our own energy is released, we establish a greater sense of intimacy because we are better known and we feel closer to the other. If we choose to withhold feelings, our energy body must close down; then we feel more distant and unknown to the other— there is less intimacy. This happens frequently with negative feelings; if we do not acknowledge our feelings of repulsion, anger, jealousy or sadness, we become more distant from our partners in the withholding.

If I am uncomfortable with someone because of something that I find unlikable, I am probably afraid to tell her about the discomfort, for fear of hurting her feelings. But I cannot hurt her feelings; she can only hurt her own. Often I am more concerned that she will not like me for feeling the way I do and that she might reject me. If I withhold my feelings, I am less known by her and we are less intimate. Once I am confident that I can accept full responsibility for my feelings, then I can share them with her in a non-blaming way that does not demand that she change. The negative judgments then can be received as information that can be either useful or discardable. I can have no investment in the response being one way or the other. If I find that I am disappointed or resentful over the outcome, then I know that my sharing had been controlling rather than a true sharing; I would be endangering our intimacy.

Classification of Feelings

Viewed from an energetic perspective, feelings motivate us to either open and move toward experience ("positive" feelings) or to close and move away from experience ("negative" feelings). With positive feelings such as loving, we open up with expansive energy, becoming vulnerable and desiring contact and closeness. With negative feelings such as repulsion, we contract, close down our energy, and become walled, protective and isolated.

In his book *Feelings, Our Vital Signs*, Willard Gaylin sees feelings as "internal directives" or signals for survival, caution and success.[1] Borrowing from some of his classification, feelings can readily be qualified as being either negative (even though they indeed may serve a positive purpose) or positive. Although many would not agree, the reader is reminded that we believe all feelings are generated from within the self, and depend upon how that individual interprets the perceptions being received from the external world. Thus, our composite chart of feelings would look like this:

Positive Feelings	Negative Feelings
Feeling Excited	Feeling Anxious
Feeling Moved	Feeling Bored & Unmoved
Feeling Relaxed & Comfortable	Feeling Upset & Uncomfortable
Feeling Good, Joyful & Open	Feeling Closed
Feeling Energetic & Engaged	Feeling Tired & Withdrawn
Feeling Ashamed	Feeling Guilty
Feeling Appreciation	Feeling Jealous, Envious or Proud

Experiencing Feelings and Expressing Emotions

It is worthy of note that because feelings are always interior, they are always difficult to see from the outside. Even people experiencing feelings frequently have difficulty in articulating what they are. Because they are unable to name the feelings, or explain the causes for the feeling, they may believe that they are not having any at all. Actually, they should learn how to express whatever interior climate they are experiencing—a tightness inside the gut, a tension in the chest, an increased pulse rate, a choking sensation in the throat, a desire to move away, and so on. As the interpretation of these sensations is discussed and further examined, often the person will come to identify the feelings at some later time.

When feelings move to the surface, they are expressed in a limited number of ways as emotions. For example, crying may be either a manipulative strategy or an expression of a genuine emotion. If crying is related to an authentic emotion, it can be expressing a wide variety of feelings, ranging from sadness to anger, joy, guilt, or nervousness. In intimate relationships, it is important to keep one another informed about the meaning of the feelings, so that they don't become misinterpreted. More important, sharing the reasons for the feelings makes for deeper intimacy and knowing of one another; expressing the emotions deepens the way in which energy is shared, providing for a greater sense of connection.

Sharing Anger

Most people are afraid of anger. As children, most of our experience has been with anger that is accompanied by violence (our definition of "violence" is any act that crosses a known boundary). It is important to understand that *anger and violence are not the same!* Most anger is not primary—it usually is a reaction to some hurt, whether imagined or real. When people learn to share anger, it can enhance the intimacy and closeness. Too often, anger erupts with the intention of being intimidating, controlling and vindictive, all of which will serve to destroy a relationship. When the elements of safety and respect for one another are included, the expression of that same anger can create a greater knowing, understanding and closeness between partners and within families.

The usefulness of anger as an emotion is that it motivates toward action. This is of special importance in situations in which the person has withdrawn or regressed to a chronic state of helplessness in the face of a threatening or unmanageable power or authority, or after the loss of a loved one through rejection, death or any form of separation. Frequently, such withdrawal is accompanied by a denial or repression of feelings. The anger provides the energy to move out of this static, blocked state.

The sharing of anger can be accomplished through the use of such techniques as "fair fighting" that were first proposed by Dr. George Bach in his book *The Intimate Enemy.*[2] In the "Vesuvius technique" described by Bach, the angry person receives the consent of the rest of the family to blow out his feelings in front of them, after carefully setting the limits of safety and time. It is worth noting that in the expression of anger, some unfair blame and name-calling can creep in; this should be allowed with the provision that at the end of the Vesuvius, it will be cleaned up by the designated angry person, taking full ownership for his or her feelings. Other safe ways of expressing anger include using punching bags, pounding pillows or mattresses, tearing up old telephone books or catalogues, kneading bread, or chopping wood. With children, safe situations for expressing anger can be created through play, throwing rocks into the ocean, punching air bags, kicking mattresses, and hollering loudly. Keep in mind that the expression of anger should be boundaried and safe, always emphasizing the difference between sharing anger (which is encouraged) and sharing violence (which is prohibited).

Many times, people are afraid to express anger to or about people they love or depend upon, for fear of hurting those people's feelings. To deepen in intimacy, it is important to reassure them that nobody can hurt another's feelings, that each of us is responsible for our own feelings, and that it is safe to share them. Sometimes, at first, such people need to learn to express anger with the object of the anger being physically absent from the situation. Hopefully, they later can find the courage to share the anger in person; generally, it is advisable to explain the purpose first to the persons who are objects of the anger, to help them to understand the necessity of this process.

Sharing Jealousy

Jealousy is another feeling that people in relationship have difficulty in handling. This is because in the past, such feelings have mostly been used to control one another's behaviour—because I am hurting over what you are doing, you should stop doing it! Actually, as with all feelings, jealousy is self-generated. It stems from early childhood feelings of insecurity, fears of being not good enough, and fears of abandonment. In jealousy, one has made the other person more important than oneself, moving one's centre from within, and placing it in the other person. On the positive side, this kind of projection is a symptom of greatly valuing the other; on the negative side, the hurt and jealousy could be used to control and own the other. If jealousy is used for control, it can destroy any relationship. If jealousy is shared, rather than used for control, it can be viewed from a positive light; both members of the partnership can rejoice in how important they are to one another *so long as they agree not to allow those feelings to govern what they do!* People can hurt with their jealousies and share them, without any demands that their partners change their behaviour. When the partner responds to these fearful hurt feelings with sensitivity, understanding and acceptance, the result can be a high level of intimacy and caring. In a close relationship with an atmosphere of acceptance, people can feel safe enough to address past issues and to heal old wounds of unresolved hurt and rejection from childhood.

Sharing Sadness and Hurt

Most people believe that when they are sad or hurt in any way, others tend to see them in a negative light. Another common belief is that sadness should not be shared, as those who love us deserve to have enjoyable, rather than depressing, experiences. People who think that suffering should be felt in silence or isolation tend to repress all such hurts. This contraction of feelings results in a restriction of life energy, and the feelings tend to leak out in a minimal fashion over a prolonged time. This attitude has generally been learned in childhood from parents who say such things as "Stop your crying before I give you something to *really* cry about!" or "Go to your room! Nobody likes to see your long face!"

In this environment, children soon learn that their sad feelings are not respected; still, they frequently work to produce guilt in their parents so that they can get their own way. This is seen in the common mechanism of "feeling sorry for yourself." With hurt feelings, there is no better salve than self-pity; yet, too often this self-soothing has been abused and overused as a control mechanism to get one's own way. The pout, the extended lower lip, the whine and groan are all part of that process. As with jealousy, when self-pity is expressed freely without controlling the other, the experience can be truly healing. Because self-pity is too often linked to controlling, a productive solution is to remove yourself from the company of the other when you feel a good self-pity attack coming on, and give full vent to those delicious feelings in private. If you have an intimate partner, this event could be shared; but because it is always difficult for the other to stop being either judgmental or controlled by such feelings, it is sometimes best to describe the feelings *after* the self-pity party!

Intimacy and Familiarity

Intimacy involves sharing one with another; hence, with intimacy comes closeness. Because intimacy involves really knowing one another, people often assume that knowing will automatically bring closeness; but, this is not necessarily so. People can be familiar, and know one another, without any closeness. Enemies often know one another well without being close. In the same way, good athletes will have a good understanding of their opponent's moves and quirks, as will soldiers on the battlefield, without being close.

Thus, it is possible for two people in relationship to have lived with one another for a long time, knowing one another well, but never feeling close to one another. Because they do not share their inner feelings with each other, they are not intimate, and hence do not feel close. Whether they stay together for security, convenience or any number of other reasons, such people can live a satisfactory life together. However, their relationship will likely lack passion, caring or personal growth. For those experiences to occur requires the addition of the sharing of feelings, especially those of caring and loving. For a full relationship, the darker and more negative feelings must also be surfaced and shared.

Boredom and Apathy

Most people confuse these two feelings; yet they are distinctly different and require different solutions. The apathetic person has disengaged from real contact with the world and has settled into a low energy state with little interest or caring. In his book *Love and Will*, Rollo May describes apathy as "the withdrawal of love and will,"[3] and, as such, as the opposite of love. Such an individual is indifferent, lacking in passion and emotion, uninvolved, detached and unrelated, with little will to do anything about it. The energy body is so contracted that it is unreachable and ineffective. In relationship, such a person no longer cares to fight or even engage in any way; both meaning and hope are lost and there is no motivation to change. In an apathetic relationship, partners may go about their daily routines in an effective way, but utterly without passion. Because they do not fight, others tend to see their relationship as ideal.

On the other hand, a person experiencing boredom is filled with energy, with a restlessness and a desire to change. Although there may be little interest in the person or task at hand, the self has a strong urge to find something or somebody in which to develop an interest. Too often, bored people blame something or someone else for the feeling of boredom ("they are boring" or "it is boring"), thus keeping themselves as victims in a state of helplessness. In fact, it is those people themselves that produce the boredom by not engaging their interest.

To take ownership of the feeling of boredom means assuming the responsibility to do something about it, using the will, initiative, courage and creativity to make necessary changes. In relationships, revealing feelings of boredom to one another is important, as the problem is a shared one that requires shared solutions. It is at this point that a review of the Communications Model would be helpful, stressing ownership of one's feelings and ruling out all blame. Remember the dictum that *there are no boring people—there are only bored people!*

Most people assume that boredom arises from a lack of interest in the subject or person. Many times this is so, in which case it would be interesting to pursue an investigation as to why little energy is being invested there. People should consider attempting a trial interest for a limited time before abandoning it altogether. In some instances, boredom is actually an active *defence* against becoming involved. Such might be the case of a churchgoer who is bored with pornography, or a pornographer who claims to be bored with the church. In intimate relationships, it is worthwhile to consider the possibility that boredom is only masking a fear about intimacy; the greater the emotional charge related to that boredom, the greater is the possibility that it may be a defence.

The Interior Landscape

Within each person, all of the feelings exist as in a huge landscape—here is a cool valley of tranquility, there a desert of despair, while in this area are the expansive fields of openness, over here the mountains of exhilaration and joy, close by the frightening cliffs of risk-taking, over there the gentle rains of sadness, here the steamy jungles of desire. While in the midst of any of these areas of your inner geography, you will tend to believe that that's all there is. You will tend to forget that you have merely brought into the foreground that particular feeling with which you are now in touch. All of the other feelings—the other aspects of your landscape—are still present, even though they are presently in the background. You can be sure that you will move on to the other areas at another time. Remembering this will provide you with some perspective when you feel irretrievably stuck in a part of your inner landscape of feelings. Remember the peaks when you are stuck in the swamps. While you are visiting your joyful mountaintops, keep in mind that your deserts are not far away, so that when you slide down into them, you need not despair. Keep your compass and your perspective!

Notes

1. Willard Gaylin, *Feelings, Our Vital Signs* (New York: Harper & Row, 1988).

2. George R. Bach, *The Intimate Enemy* (New York: William Morrow and Company, 1969).

3. Rollo May, *Love and Will* (New York: W.W. Norton & Company, 1969).

From Object to Person

Objectification

The early human experience is largely one of objectification.[1] Infants are physiological beings capable of physical survival only through being taken care of by another—any caretaker who is prepared to feed them, clean them up and keep them warm. In our view, humans at birth have only have a potential of a Self; thus, early experiences are as one impersonal object to another—as child to parent, not as person to person. In this primary paradigm, no person is necessary; at the beginning, babies merely need beings that are prepared to play the roles of provider and protector. For this, "parents" are ideally suited. Motivated by some primordial urge to procreate and care for the young—an urge that is encoded in the genetic code and mediated by a complicated system of endocrine and biochemical imperatives—parents respond to this task with relish. Neither the child nor the parent has any idea who this other person really is; nor does it matter at this beginning stage. It is an object-object ("objectified") relationship of great importance to the human race—but one in which neither party is privileged to see the real person behind the object.

This condition has a complex set of parameters that operate to ensure the safety and health of the developing child-being whose Self has yet to be born. Roles, expectations, a sense of entitlement, obligations, morality and taboos, guilt and pride all are a part of this objectifying experience. With ever-growing consciousness, the Self of the child is finally hatched, with the *potential* of flowering and developing into a whole person. Only after this hatching occurs does the possibility exist of having some person-to-person interaction. Unfortunately, for most people, that will be a rare occurrence!

Some, like Daniel Stern, say that the Self is present from the beginning, as a "prestructured emergent entity."[2] In the contrasting camp, object relations theorists maintain that the birth of the Self is somewhere toward the end of the third year of life. Until that time, the young person has been mostly living in an objectified world. This disagreement has given rise in psychological theory to what Morris Berman refers to as "murky territory." Berman maintains that this dispute is "not amenable to scientific verification."[3] Certainly, infants seem little capable of recognizing the concerns and interests of those around them;

and until about three years of age, children are good at following rules, but not adept at being considerate of the feelings and experience of others. In this book, you can see that we tend to believe, with the object relations theorists, that the Self is only a possibility at birth, and develops in interaction with other humans.

Most children are raised by a process of training rather than one that encourages personal development. They are taught appropriate behaviour, they learn whom they can depend on, they learn how to distinguish right from wrong, they know what it means to be grateful and guilty. But no one provides them with the manual of how to become a person. They do the best they can, struggling to become perfect as successful objects playing socially acceptable roles (they become "good" children, then later "good" students, husbands, wives, citizens, and business people). Such striving works for most of their lives, providing them with a meaning for life, especially if they succeed. However, later in life (even if they succeed), many begin to wonder what it all has been for. Feeling some lack of a sense of fulfilment, they may come to realize that they do not know themselves as persons. All they know well are their roles—their objectified self! How has this happened?

Mirroring

Developing the Self as a person rather than as an object is a complex process, in which *mirroring* and exercising the use of *boundaries* play important roles. As the child-as-object is being cared for, the infant looks searchingly into the caretakers' eyes for reflected messages about who the child is. Because most parents see their children as possessions and objects to be trained, *that* is what is contained in the reflected message. Most parents serve as *distorted* mirrors— seeing their children as either more (convex mirroring) or less (concave mirroring) important than they really are; rarely do parents see their children as the *persons* they actually are (*direct* mirroring). Thus, most children develop their self-concept through their roles, and see their parents in the same way. This parent-child relationship is mainly an object-to-object one, rather than person-to-person. To become more personal, the parties of the relationship must provide direct mirroring for one another. Because children have little experience or authority to do so with parental figures, such a process must begin with the parents. Parents themselves have had little practice with their own parents, so they likely will learn it with peers. This is one of the main functions of intimate relationships.

Boundaries and Walls

In a previous book, we wrote about boundaries and walls.[4] A boundary is the *felt* interface between the Self and other; it is flexible and in constant motion, moving outward to reach for experience, and contracting to protect the Self from experience. Contact at this boundary stimulates an excitation within the Self, motivating movement toward contact or away from it; these directional excitations are the feelings of interpersonal communication. An individual's feelings depend upon that person's interpretations of the quality of contact.

In playing a role, the Self must abandon or repress those impulses that arise from the Authentic Self, and defend the Self from vulnerable contact. In doing so, the Self builds walls to contain itself and control others. Unlike boundaries, walls are inflexible and unchanging, full of "shoulds" and rules, with little ability to adapt to changing conditions. Within these walls are the major defence mechanisms that are used to maintain distance from others, but they also contain all of the socially acceptable training that provides people with social acceptance and financial reward. Because walls are thick and impermeable, they are unresponsive, possessing little sensitivity to those outside of them. Walls are like grand castles that have been erected for looks and defence—impressive and useful for keeping out enemies, but cold and difficult to live within.

Walls can only be changed from the inside. In intimate relationships, the Self can lower the moat, and open the doors and windows to reveal what is going on inside. Taking your partner on a tour of the walls is to acknowledge where, how and why you are defensive and controlling, providing information about your inner world and offering a vulnerable state of intimacy. When you are secure enough with your partner's visits into your inner world, then you can begin to dismantle your walls and *replace them with boundaries*. Many people who have had walls for a long time get too enthusiastic about getting rid of them when they find an appropriate partner—they tend to want to *merge* with the other, which is another way of losing the Self. "Give thyself, but give thyself not away."[5]

Boundaries are established by first recognizing that you are fully responsible only for yourself, your own feelings, and your own behaviour; there are no grounds for blaming others. Then you can see all of the options that are open to you; in choosing any of these options, be prepared to accept the consequences of that choice. The choices that are made at the interface between the Self and others create the boundary; remember that the choice can be a "yes" as well as a "no." With boundaries, you can change your mind so long as you keep others informed of such changes. In this way, boundaries remain flexible and are in less danger of solidifying into walls again. To become boundaried is to become human. Persons live fully with boundaries between them in intimate relationships; objects (i.e., objectified persons) are separated by walls and are only capable of familiarity at best.

To encourage the development of the person in their offspring, parents must always acknowledge the perspective of the child. "It's your bedtime, go to bed now!" expresses a rule without regard for the person. How different it would be if the parent could say, "I know it must be difficult to stop your current activity (acknowledging the person), but to get enough rest for tomorrow's activities (consequences), you'll have to get some sleep now (boundaries)." Rules are shortcuts to control behaviour, but they have the unfortunate consequence of building walls and making objects; boundaries, on the other hand, strengthen the development of the person. Permissiveness is an abandonment of both walls and boundaries that arrests development of the person; often, children will interpret permissiveness as lack of caring (which it usually is!).

Political vs. Personal

We define "political" as being related to power; generally, the political is involved with domination and submission. "Personal" has to do with the unfolding development of the human being, without any reference to power or domination or submission. From the vantage of the political, the person is not valued; in the personal, humanness is of concern. As people acquire power, they lose touch with their authentic nature; they become powerful, but out of touch. When people become more authentic, they manifest "strength" in being in touch with themselves and others; although they might have little power, they are present in themselves.

Most educational systems are authoritarian in nature, promoting objectifying behaviour that will ultimately lead to financial security. Usually, people are taught to develop *power* over others; in this way, education tends to become *political*, and its concern is in dealing with the other objectified beings in the external environment. Only a few schools (such as the Waldorf schools built on the concepts of Rudolf Steiner) attempt to reach and teach the person to grow with an inner *strength*.

Most people have had this politicized education at home and at school, "for their own good." When they enter into relationship, they usually do so with an objectifying ("political") attitude, concerned with the power to control or to be controlled, to own or be owned.

The Garden: From the Political to the Personal

For a relationship to serve as a garden that promotes growth, partners must agree to weed out all political interpersonal behaviour by identifying it when it emerges. A basic principle is to reveal and acknowledge all ways in which each person attempts to control the other. Once political behaviour is identified, the focus should then shift to sharing the feelings underlying that political behaviour—is there some hurt or fear in that person? When the relationship remains political, the atmosphere is like a police station or courtroom, with partners trying to determine who hurt whom, or who really said what, or who really is to blame for the mess that has been created. When a relationship becomes personal, both parties stand revealed and vulnerable; they both acknowledge responsibility for their own feelings, and are willing to share them. In such an atmosphere both individuals can grow in strength.

The objectified self serves the Self very well; it is worthy of being honoured rather than reviled. It is only when people wish to create an intimate relationship that they will find themselves wanting. With an understanding partner, these skills can be learned and developed. Hopefully, people will be able to choose their appropriate modus operandi in each situation. Again, to repeat, *nothing is ever right or wrong*; some behaviour is ineffective, or inappropriate to getting what you want or to where you wish to go.

Incorporating Objectification into Intimacy

In intimate relationships, much passion can be created by objectifying the other and playing power games. Such is the nature of sexual excitement; such is the pleasure of dependency. Most sentimentality is based on objectification; our most popular love songs announce "I can't live without you" (i.e., I have shifted my centre into you), "You hurt me when you left" (i.e., you are to blame for my pain), and "Nobody knows the trouble I've seen" (i.e., a full attack of objectifying self-pity). Life without these objectifying experiences would certainly be dull! Hopefully, in intimate relationships there can be some agreement to allow partners to feel and express those feelings to one another, *so long as they do not control one another!* A productive agreement would allow partners to play with those feelings, expressing them for limited times and in designated places. Then these potentially destructive elements become more like movie theatre experiences—they can be enjoyed thoroughly for the moment, without controlling the direction of the relationship. We summarize it this way: *Feel, but ultimately get real!*

Opportunities for Becoming Personal

In everyday life, most interaction occurs on a political level of power and control. The political occurs when people want to get control in nasty ways; it happens when they take care of one another in nice ways. It happens in shrewd ways in the business world, and in what may initially seem to be altruistic actions in the church world. It happens in the playgrounds of the very young and in the dance clubs and bars (the playgrounds of the older kids!). It happens in family homes and on the mountain slopes of ski resorts. Whether buying clothes or groceries, airline tickets or hardware, interactions are mostly all political.

Becoming personal offers an experience of intimacy. This is threatening for most people; if you offer this in public, you will be judged to be immodest, inappropriate, crazy, or dangerous. Judging you and rejecting you will assuage most of the anxiety within the breasts of the more conservative. So whenever you step out of the confines of being an object, you will immediately face your fear of rejection and the extent of your field dependency. That is why few people risk becoming personal in the public domain. But the fears are even greater in the private domain, because with loved ones the fear of rejection takes on even greater significance.

Sharing Anger

Examine your preparedness to show anger in public. Although this is not easily done, there is considerable public acceptance to express such feelings in restaurants or across retail counters when it is apparent that you have been wronged in some way. Usually that anger is expressed in a blaming, intimidating way that most people will understand; at worst, you will be judged as a boor, and dismissed as such. But you will not have been vulnerable. In a similar fashion, you may rage and blame in threatening ways at home. If you are loud enough or big enough, you will likely get away with controlling others; such power-based activity often succeeds.

But if you and your partner were more interested in growing, you would share your anger in a more vulnerable and personal manner—perhaps just as loudly, but without blame and intimidation. After your initial reaction of anger, you would then be committed to "sweep up," to own up to your immature ways, to acknowledge any underlying feelings of hurt or fear, to share in a curiosity about the origin of all this feeling. You would be vulnerable and offering intimacy—a glimpse into your depth. This would be far more risky than your actions in public, because if your intimate partner is whom you love the most, you likely have more fear about being abandoned.

The Reward for Being Personal

Even though it may be risky, the act of moving outside the walls and defences of an object position has many potential rewards. Here is the ideal situation to finally learn how to become a person—beyond depersonalizing rules, obligations and expectations!

It is through the development of an intimate relationship in a Relationship Garden that people finally discover themselves beyond the limitations and encumbrances of their objectified roles.

> The basic word I-You can be spoken only with one's whole being. The concentration and fusion into a whole being can never be accomplished by me, can never be accomplished without me. I require a You to become; becoming I, I say You. All actual life is encounter. —Martin Buber[6]

Notes

1. B.R. Wong & J. McKeen, *A Manual for Life* (Gabriola Island, BC: PD Publishing, 1992), pp. 87–91.

2. Morris Berman, *Coming To Our Senses* (New York: Bantam Books, 1990), pp. 32–34.

3. Ibid.

4. B.R. Wong & J. McKeen, *A Manual for Life* (Gabriola Island, BC: PD Publishing, 1992), pp. 25–29.

5. D.H. Lawrence, *Aaron's Rod* (Harmondsworth: Penguin Books, 1950), p. 200.

6. Martin Buber, *I and Thou*, trans. Walter Kaufman (New York: Charles Scribner's Sons, 1970), p. 62.

Developmental Stages
of Relationships

The bird a nest, the spider a web, man friendship. —William Blake[1]

Introduction

Any relationship proceeds through a series of stages in development. Just as the individual grows and changes in an evolving process of life experiences, so too does a relationship undergo a developmental process. Although we outlined the relationship cycle in an earlier book,[2] we have now evolved these ideas more thoroughly. The discussion in the following pages will serve to show our current thinking about the evolution of relationships.

There are general principles that apply to all relationships. These are most easily seen in male-female adult relationships. However, the same stages, principles and motivations apply to parent-child relationships, to same-sex pairings, to friends of either sex, and to work relationships.

Purpose of Relationships

In relationships, people are attempting to satisfy deep motivations; there seems to be a basic drive to associate with others and to establish ongoing ties with them. Often, people seek others to compensate for their own limitations and to overcome infantile fears. Many times, people select partners in order to deal with their inner feelings of emptiness (angst, existential anxiety) and loneliness. By becoming obsessed with another person, they attempt to convert existential anxiety into neurotic anxiety, to make their emptiness manageable.

Commonly, people use their partners to justify themselves. They either crave the agreement of a like mind, in order to feel more secure; or they want a scapegoat to blame for their troubles. At first glance, righteousness and morality seem useful to make life dependable; if people dedicate life energy to being "right," there is little time left to feel basic anxieties and insecurities. However, they also feel much less of themselves, and are walled off from their partners.

To risk becoming vulnerable and revealed to one's partner opens up the possibility for self-discovery, and for learning about self and other through intimate dialogue. Any two people who have good will, intention and endurance can proceed through the stages of relationship, deepening their awareness and acceptance of themselves and each other in the process.

The Five Stages of Relationships

The five stages of Relationship (Romance, Power Struggle, Stability, Commitment and Co-Creativity) were first used by Susan Campbell in her book *A Couple's Journey.*[3] Although the stages were originally enunciated in a vertical list, we believe this process is more of a circle, a repetitive cycle, not a straight-line list. There is remarkable similarity between the evolving process of relationships and the dynamic energy states of the Chinese Five Stages of Change.[4] Because of the confusion engendered by the term "Stability" (which seems to imply some kind of static condition), in this book we have replaced that word with the term "Integration." Furthermore, we now see that a closed circle does not adequately describe the phenomenon of human development. Every turn of the wheel involves a return with more experience and more degrees of freedom. Hence, the arrow from Co-Creative to Romance does not return to the original Romance, but extends into the space outside the Romance phase, indicating the opening of a spiral. Life, energy and relationships evolve in ever widening spirals.

In a relationship garden, the movement is from objectification to subjective knowing of the self and other. The early stages (Romance and Power Struggle) are characterized by much energy (passion, obsession, sexual excitement, and anger), whereas the later stages are more calm and fulfilling. In the earlier stages, partners have very little knowing of each other. A developing closeness is characterized by increases in knowing of self and other. As knowing increases, so also the possibility for intimacy grows; with revelation, vulnerability, curiosity and commitment, a mature and stable relationship can be established.

The Process of the Relationship Cycle

These stages apply to all relationships—husband/wife, lovers, parent/child, siblings, other family relationships, business partnerships, and friends. All people

Developmental Stages of Relationships

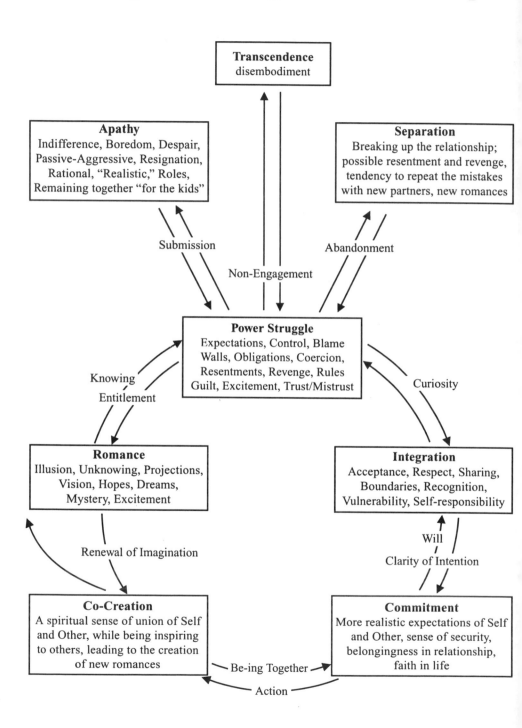

can potentially go through these phases of relationship. The progress through the stages is from imagination with little experience in Romance, to the turmoil of the Power Struggle, to getting to know one another in Integration, to mutual willed activities in Commitment, to creativity in the Co-creative phase. People can learn the principles of the process in any kind of relationship; what they have learned in one relationship becomes applicable to all of their other relationships.

In proceeding through the stages, power, control, entitlement and isolation tend to diminish. As these are in decline, humanness, knowledge, and self-awareness grow. There is also steady development of responsibility and strength. A sense of aloneness increases; strangely, this is accompanied by a sense of being connected to others and to life. Strength, passion and humility increase. One's capacity for intimate contact steadily grows. There is less caretaking and more being in touch with the other person.

The earlier stages of Romance and Power Struggle are characterized by high energy and excitement. Integration and the phases that ensue have much more fulfilment, with less of the frantic drivenness of the earlier phases.

In the following chapters, we will go into detail about the various unfolding stages and their characteristics.

Being in Different Stages in Different Phases of One's Life

It is possible to be at different stages in different phases of one's life. For example, an individual might be in Romance with her newborn infant, while she is in a Power Struggle with her spouse, in a state of Integration with her older children, in Commitment with her community work, and Co-creative in her art projects.

Two different people can be at different stages in the same relationship. The wife might be in Integration with the husband, because she accepts him; meanwhile, he may be in Romance with her, because he refuses to see her beyond his image projections. This does not mean the relationship has to end. Indeed, in most relationships, there can frequently be periods where the partners are at different stages. By learning to acknowledge these differences without defence and to appreciate the viewpoints of both partners, the relationship can continue to grow. When couples use this difference in phases to blame and criticize, the whole endeavour is reduced to a power struggle!

The Deviations from the Cycle

The states of Apathy, Transcendence and Separation are not stages in the developmental cycle; they occur when people step off the circle. These deviations will be outlined more thoroughly (see "The Power Struggle Stage," p. 63).

Stages Within Stages

Just as in the Chinese Five Stages of Change, where every stage contains the others, every stage of the relationship cycle contains every other stage. So, there is a Commitment in every stage; there is a kind of Power Struggle at every stage (for example, the struggle to create together or to share ideas); there is a Romance (a dream) that fuels every stage; every stage has its own capacity for Integration; a Co-creative possibility exists in every stage (for example, there can be a Co-creativity of sharing romantic fantasies).

Partners are rarely in one stage to the exclusion of the others. Commonly, a couple who is largely in Integration Stage can readily revert to a Power Struggle in times of stress. Certain situations will provide a trigger for the re-entry of earlier stage behaviour; for example, when he buys her a special gift at Christmas, she might well re-enter the Romance Stage with him for a time.

Images for the Stages of Relationships

For those of you who like visual metaphors, the following images for each stage might stimulate some associations.

Romance	a movie theatre
Power Struggle	a battlefield
Integration	a lush garden
Apathy	a desert
Separation	a single figure under a street lamp
Transcendence	a cold cathedral
Commitment	a drawn bow with stored, constrained potential energy
Co-Creative	the artist's workshop

Intentions in Relationship

In each of the five stages, the following are useful questions:

"What do I want?"
"What do you want?"
"What do we want?"
"What do we choose to do?"

Another useful question is "What is this all for?" The answer could be "for happiness," "for excellence," or "for security." The answer people give determines how they will proceed through the various stages of relationship. If they are after excellence, their relationship will have a very different texture than if they are after security, or power, or sex, or some other aspiration. These queries involve the notion of will and intentionality; in our Communication Model, this is the aspect of intention, through which people decide what actions they will take.[5]

People define their position first through their attitudes, and then through their efforts. In living in relationship, partners can come to know themselves more fully, and thus they can move increasingly in harmony with self and other. People pass through the various stages by a mutual interaction and sharing. They tend the garden of the relationship through the various seasons; their success in dealing with the contingencies that each phase requires is dependent upon how much mutuality and sharing they have together.

Notes

1. William Blake, quoted in Thomas Moore, *Soul Mates* (New York: HarperCollins, 1994), p. 43.

2. B.R. Wong & J. McKeen, *A Manual for Life* (Gabriola Island, BC: PD Publishing, 1992), p. 96.

3. Susan Campbell, *A Couple's Journey* (San Luis Obispo, CA: Impact Publishers, 1980).

4. D. Connelly, *Traditional Acupuncture: The Law of the Five Elements* (Columbia, MD: Centre For Traditional Acupuncture, 1979), p. 22.

5. B.R. Wong & J. McKeen, *A Manual for Life* (Gabriola Island, BC: PD Publishing, 1992), pp. 6–10.

The Stage of Romance

Q. What do most people do on a first date?
A. On the first date, they just tell each other lies, and that usually gets them interested enough to go for a second date.—Martin (age 10)
A. Many daters just eat pork chops and french fries and talk about love.
—Craig (age 9)[1]

Introduction

The first phase of any relationship is based upon the imagination; in this "Romance," very little is known about the other. The relationship is a dream, a story, involving hopes and expectations; partners have little experience of each other. Because the individuals do not know each other, they first relate to their mutual image projections—their objectifications of each other. This is not limited to the traditional male-female Romances of "falling in love." Indeed, the first phase of any relationship is a Romance, in that the parties do not know each other; this is equally the case with budding friendships, the Romance of having a new child, or in a fledgling business enterprise. Hopes and dreams are strong, and the sobering influence of experience has not had the opportunity to modulate feelings.

Thrilling, But Not True Closeness

The period of Romance is a most stimulating time in any relationship. The world seems brighter, and people in love feel more energetic, with more sense of purpose and zest for life. They are willing to consider unusual things, and every moment seems fresh. Indeed, Romance is the spice of life!

In the Romance stage, and in the objectification of sexual charge, people tend to feel important and close to each other. Yet, on closer examination, we can see that they are actually only obsessed with each other's image. What they feel is a simulacrum of true closeness; in their objectification, they are disconnected from the cosmic energy, and thus are actually separate, even though their experience is one of being close and connected (see "Sexuality and Relationships," p. 154). They are excited, but they are not resonating. They have a charge, but they are not intimate.

56

This excitement and strong interest in each other also occurs in the early stages of nonsexual relationships. At the beginning, people generally do not relate to each other as persons; instead, they relate to each other's images.

Romance with Children

New parents have a Romance with the new infant in the household. They are full of enthusiasm for buying baby clothes and planning the future for this little being. The dreams, the imaginings, are very stimulating, and provide an energy of engagement that is nourishing to both the child and the parents alike.

Romance in Friendship

At the beginning of a friendship, people are enthusiastic about their newfound ally. They have energy to talk together, to discover areas of common interest, and they often pursue many stimulating activities together. They are in the Romance phase, as they don't really know each other yet.

Romance in Business

The beginning of business ventures is also a Romance. Initially, the whole project is a dream, undampened by experience. The excitement and enthusiasm at the beginning is similar to the beginning of a courtship. In both cases, the individuals are eager to get together, to talk, to plan, to dream. The air crackles with excitement as they imagine what will be in their future together. Whether they are talking about how wonderful it would be to have a little cottage together with children and pets, or a giant factory pouring out widgets to the world, the state of enthusiasm—the romance—is the same.

The Root of Romance: Infantile Insecurity

The first Romance occurs in infancy with parents or protectors. To infants, parents seem larger than life, wise, strong and ever capable. This is the fabric of the child-parent Romance: children have an unrealistic view that their parents are all-powerful and can protect the child at all times. For the infant, this objectification and inflation of parental potency helps them to cope with their insecurities; yet it constitutes a denial of their basic state of anxiety. This dependency upon an external object to provide protection and security becomes the paradigm for all subsequent relationships—a search for "someone, out there" who will make everything all right.

The Pattern of Being Pleasing

Children establish relationships of pleasing their parents, in order to avoid being abandoned. In the infantile logic, if they are pleasing, the parents will want to stay with them, and thus their protection will continue. This theme is adopted as a basic pattern, and is carried on throughout life. In later relationships, people continue to try to please others, in order to establish the security of a relationship (someone to help and protect them), to deny their basic existential aloneness.[2]

Following upon the relationship with their parents, children seek to please friends and teachers; as adults, they have romance with partners and spouses. Then, later in life, people pursue romance with their own offspring, and even later with grandchildren. This theme of wanting to please others continues in these later relationships. This is based upon a denial of basic insecurities, and involves a desperate dependency upon someone else.

Objects, not Persons

Q. *What exactly is marriage?*
A. *Marriage is when you get to keep your girl and don't have to give her back to her parents.*—Eric (age 6)[3]

In Romance, the other is not a person; the other is an object, who can take care of anxiety and needs. This perspective is rooted in the objectifying experiences of early childhood. For infants, this objectification is normal; they learn to relate to the outside world by objectifying it, dividing it up into "objects" and learning to interact with these objects in their field. The early relationship objects (generally the parents and other siblings) are seen as protectors and caregivers. This becomes the prototype for later objects of choice for relationships.

In parent-child relationships, this objectification occurs equally on both sides. Parents do not know their children at first. The children are little objects, projections for parental imaginations and desires. Indeed, infants have scarcely developed, and there is little of a "personal" nature to know. Also, the child does not know the actual personhood of the parent; the parent is largely an object: to fulfil desires, to protect, and to minister to needs. Many people do not outgrow this romantic view of their parents, and later in life, when the parents want to establish a more interpersonal relationship, it is often the children who refuse to shift from calling the parents "Mom" or "Dad" into using their given names.

Many people do not move far beyond this state of objectification in relationship, even as adults. They continue to relate to objects, rather than people, by operating within roles, and expecting others to do the same. Obviously, the relationship at this stage of objectification (the Romance phase) is not personal, as neither individual knows the other. Because there is little knowing, there cannot be any true acceptance of the personhood of the other.

The Basic Problem: Underlying Insecurity

In the Romance phase, people project their concept of the perfect partner onto the current individual of choice. Children do this with their parents to cope with insecurity; parents do this with their children to have an object of meaning; dating couples do this with each other; and the same projection occurs in business relationships as well.

People select someone for relationship who has specific attributes, consistent with an internal image. In short, people have a codified notion of who will be a perfect partner, and they are attracted to someone who fits this image. They believe that if they can make a relationship work with this ideal person, then the shortcomings and insecurities of their life will be solved. The problem is that in looking for someone else to fulfil their romantic wishes, people place their centre outside themselves; hence they remain weak, unknown to themselves, and incapable of caring dialogue with others. In relationship, their partners are objects to possess, not persons.

> Q. What is the proper age to get married?
> A. Once I'm done with kindergarten, I'm going to find me a wife. —Bert (age 5)[4]

The Microdot

Robert Stoller, in his book *Sexual Excitement*, describes the concept of the "microdot."[5] This is a term that was used in World War II by the experts in espionage.

Basically, vital information was photographed and the picture was reduced repeatedly in size, until all the information was contained in a small dot (the microdot), the size of a period at the end of a sentence in a book. Then, a period was punched from a designated page in a book, and replaced with the microdot—the encoded reduced information. Someone could then carry the book across a dangerous border, delivering it safely into the hands of collaborators, who simply had to turn to the proper page, and have the microdot blown up, to see all the information. In a similar fashion, the attributes of the "perfect partner" are condensed and encoded; when people meet someone, they can subconsciously check off that individual's attributes against the checklist of the internal microdot. This explains the specificity of the sexual charge (see "Sexuality and Relationships," p. 154). It also explains the very exact elements that go into whom individuals find attractive for relationship.

To the child, whose world is insecure, the idealized parent figure has many features of the "saviour," who will make life safe and meaningful. At the beginning, the elements of the saviour are quite vague and generalized. As people grow and gain experience, they commonly stay with the infantile theme of looking for a parent or saviour figure to take away their pain and insecurity. As they develop relationships, they continue to look for the microdot saviour, who has the qualities that will overcome their internal struggles and discomforts. The underlying theme in Romance is that *someone out there is going to protect me, help me, save me.* The romantic story becomes increasingly elaborate, and the characters in the story begin to fill out, and have very definite characteristics. These characteristics are not only physical; they might also include a certain tone of voice, a predilection for certain authors or subjects of interest, or particular mannerisms. These elements that are part of people's Romance are encoded in their personal microdot (the detailed romantic image of who will save them).

Desperateness in Romance

Romance is an attempt to deal with fear of nonbeing; hence, underlying Romance is a desperateness. Romance actually involves a great deal of control; the theme has been developed in order to reduce the insecurities of life. In D.H. Lawrence's brilliant novel, *Women in Love*, a young man tries to save his girlfriend from drowning; she pulls him down in her attempt to cling to him, and they both perish.[6] This is allegorical of how people's Romance tends to drown the selfness of both parties in their desperate clinging attempts to avoid reality. In a relationship at the Romance stage, there are two unconscious robots in operation, with no actual persons visible. Sometimes, there is an eerie deathlike quality lurking under the fervour of Romance—the desire for it is so strong, it is so unreal, and the people seem so lost and desperate in their obsessions with each other.

Hope and Disappointment

Hope and faith are different.[7] Whereas faith is self-affirming and accepting of life as it is, hope involves a dissatisfaction with self and present circumstance, and is dependent upon external events or people to provide change. People hope that life will be different, or better, or fuller; their hoping involves a lack of acceptance and a thrust toward change. In the Romance phase, hope is a common underlying theme. Dissatisfied with their basic insecurities, people commonly hope that a newfound romantic partner will solve their problems, and that life will become better.

Hope involves a basic lack of acceptance of self and other. Indeed, in the Romance stage, awareness of self and other are so clouded by the romantic dreams and projections that people have insufficient information to actually accept anyone or anything with any validity.

Disappointment is the other face of hope; like hope, disappointment is based in a discontentment with the present. The Romance phase is generally destined for disappointment, because the things people are trying to change probably will not alter at all; once they emerge from the swoon of Romance, they are once again faced with their basic insecurities, and their hoping flips into disappointment.

Romance is Exciting

The stage of Romance is an exciting time. There is some degree of romance in any relationship. Because people do not know each other at the beginning, they have to depend upon their intuition and their past experiences with other people, which they project upon their new partner. In the Romance, they imagine what could be.

There is nothing wrong with Romance. Indeed, this is a very energetic phase. Imagination is high, little is known for certain, and much is possible. There usually is much enthusiasm and vitality in this stage.

In Romance, the world can change. When we imagine, and then try to realize the romance, we are recreating the world afresh. This is the projected possible. Although the purpose of the original infant's Romance was to overcome pain and uncertainty, later in life, Romance can be for excitement—the stimulation of doing something new.

Notes

1. David Heller, *Growing Up Isn't Hard to Do If You Start Out As a Kid* (New York: Random House, 1991).

2. E. Becker, *Denial of Death* (New York: The Free Press, 1973).

3. David Heller, *Growing Up Isn't Hard to Do If You Start Out As a Kid* (New York: Random House, 1991).

4. Ibid.

5. Robert Stoller, *Sexual Excitement* (New York: Pantheon Books, 1979).

6. D.H. Lawrence, *Women in Love* (Middlesex, England: Penguin Books, 1960), p. 212.

7. B.R. Wong & J. McKeen, *A Manual for Life* (Gabriola Island, BC: PD Publishing, 1992), p. 60.

The Power Struggle Stage

Q. When is it OK to kiss someone?

A. You should never kiss a girl unless you have enough bucks to buy her a ring and her own VCR, 'cause she'll want to have videos of the wedding.
—Allan (age 10)[1]

Romance Fades: Enter the Power Struggle

The Romance phase persists by limiting information—when the image projections can be maintained by low lights and sensual diversions. When couples are dating and can go home to their individual respective abodes to dream about each other, the Romance is maintained. When they move in with each other, they find it more difficult to maintain the projections of their romantic images of each other. As partners become more familiar, they gradually accumulate evidence of the true nature and behaviour of each other. There is nothing like seeing one's partner's personal habits on an ongoing basis to have reality insistently begin to impinge. In such a state, one might say, "This is not my handsome prince (beautiful princess) after all! This is a person who has qualities that I find quite objectionable! However, all is not lost! I can devote my efforts to changing my partner into the perfect being that he (she) could be." This marks the entry into the next phase of relationship—the Power Struggle stage.

This dawning of awareness of the true nature of the other occurs in all relationships, given time and experience together. The Romance of finding a perfect partner fades into a realization that one is living with someone with particular foibles, desires and habits. The Romance of having a baby is eclipsed by the weariness that comes with night-after-night experiences of a crying infant. The Romance of a new job soon gives way to the recognition that this occupation is not going to fulfil all one's dreams.

Gentle Beginnings

Generally, the maneuvers of the Power Struggle stage begin with quiet admonition, urging the other to change slightly. "Dear, you would look so much more handsome if you were to comb your hair like this" actually means "You would more perfectly fit my ideal man microdot if you were to alter your appearance." People buy each other gifts of clothing to wear and encourage behaviours that suit their image projections. Of course, their partners never fully get the message, and they insist upon remaining the persons they are. Thus, people are thwarted in their desire to turn their partners into the perfect object of their romantic desire, the saviour who will take away all discomfort and cravings.

This Power Struggle goes on in every relationship, regardless of its nature (husband/wife, parent/child, siblings, business associations). The Romance fades with the recognition of the limitations and specifics of the other; when this happens, people usually try to control their partners into conforming to the image they believe the partner could be. Partners become dissatisfied and try to change each other, to satisfy hidden security needs. They often think that their motivation is for the benefit of the other: "You are not fully the person you could be, but I can help you; it's for your own good!"

The Gloves Are Off!

The subtle "nice" hints gradually give way to more overt forms of control and conflict. Subtle reminders become repetitive chiding; sweet requests become whining demands. People want their partners to change, and they are desperate to accomplish this mission. They are driven in this project, in order to hide from themselves. People don't actually want to know their partners for themselves; rather, they want their partners to conform to images they are projecting. They want partners to fit into their script (which they began to develop in childhood). If people actually could succeed in changing their partners into the perfect object of their romantic image, they would then be relieved of so much discomfort—they would have a saviour! The lurking anxiety and discomfort of existence would be relieved if people could gain full control of a perfect object.

Motive for the Power Struggle

Many times, people are trying to undo unhappy experiences from their pasts. For example, if someone were beaten or abused as a child, she might be seeking someone to protect her; she thus continually attempts to control her spouse's outbursts of frustration or anger (for fear that he might become like her abusive father). Her motive for control is to find some security for herself; she is trying to control the present because of past experiences. However, this is quite illusory and fraught with trouble. In trying to control her spouse, she has objectified him, and relates to him as if he were actually her abusive father. There can be no security in such a situation; of course she cannot really control her father from the past, and she does not relate personally to the actual person who is married to her. Such objectification often lurks beneath the surface of people's attempts to control one another in relationship.

War is Declared

As partners remain together, the subtle forms of control are replaced by repetitious patterns of conflict. Sometimes all-out war is declared. Rather than accept the uniqueness of their partners, people often persist in their efforts to have them conform to the image that they think will satisfy their inner insecurity. They blame and complain, and try to move the partner into the role they have designed. In the Power Struggle stage, partners actually know more about each other; however, because they are not willing to accept what they know, they persist with attempts to control rather than face the possibilities for intimacy that could occur with acceptance. The partner is still being used as an objectified image; this is the same process that children use with parents in an attempt to overcome basic insecurity. Instead of the dialogue that could occur, partners in Power Struggle are invested in the clashes of attack and defence. While defences are high, intimacy is impossible. At this stage, partners retreat behind roles and obligations, and fuel the conflict with guilt and blame and defensive behaviours.

Expectations

The Power Struggle involves expectations of the other and of oneself. If partners adopt a moral stance, then their expectations are mixed with righteous allegations. There is nothing wrong or destructive about expectations in themselves; indeed, relationships can grow very solid through mutually agreed-upon expectations. The problem occurs when one partner tries to control or dominate the other with expectations.

The Power Struggle Is Exciting

Most couples do not get beyond the Power Struggle stage. Still, they can find much stimulation in the back-and-forth conflicts and mutual controls; they can persist for years in blame, withdrawal and game-playing. Indeed, for some this is a satisfactory existence. In the play *Who's Afraid of Virginia Woolf*,[2] George and Martha, a middle-aged couple, talk with each other after an evening of intense, alcoholic fireworks and conflict; in apparent friendship and in conspiratorial tones, one talks to the other tenderly. The young couple who had witnessed the earlier fighting had gone home in dismay at the intensity, the cruelty, and the relentlessness of the games that their hosts had displayed to them. What the young couple did not understand was that the bickering, sarcasm, shouting, and abusive behaviour were all part of a well-executed script that the two had worked out over years of Power Struggle stage together. They were willing combatants, and actually enjoyed the fight!

Sexuality and the Power Struggle

As we will further discuss (see "Sexuality and Relationships," p. 154), sexual charge is rooted in infantile insecurities; the theme of domination and submission in charged sexual fantasies can be an attempt to overcome earlier inadequacies, to feel power through sexual activity. Thus, within highly charged sexual interaction—and within highly charged power and control issues—often lurks a history of insecurity and unresolved childhood inadequacies. People attempt to dominate their partners in the present (either sexually or in other forms of conflict) in an attempt to bolster themselves up, to prove themselves powerful; all this is to make up for a time when they felt powerless.

The motif in the Power Struggle stage involves domination and submission and control; hence the disagreements can be sexualized. In sexual relationships, the charge can be very high indeed in this phase. With conflict comes tension, and the release can take the form of explosive sexuality. Fighting and making up typically precede sex play in this stage. The misery of conflict is balanced by the sexual charge that is maintained.

Guilt and Blame

The Power Struggle is maintained by a moral stance. In this attitude, there are definite rights and a wrongs. When people blame their partners, they are saying "You are wrong, and you should change." Similarly, guilt also involves a moral process; instead of saying "You are wrong," the guilty partner is saying "I am wrong." The result is the same. Guilt and blame are the coinage of interaction of the Power Struggle.

The Power Struggle stage is inevitable. There is nothing wrong with it. Indeed, it can be exciting; to struggle with another can be a stimulating experience, one that encourages strength. In the Power Struggle, partners can begin to see the differences between themselves; they just don't like or accept these differences at this stage. During this period, partners prefer the security of roles and walls, rather than the insecurity of authenticity and self-reliance, through which personal boundaries could be created.

In the Power Struggle, partners are caught up with the Ideal Self.[3] Guilt and blame are attempts to create and maintain images. With blame, one is trying to mould the partner into an idealized image; in guilt, one is trying to conform oneself into an image of perfection. In this way, intimacy is limited; partners are caught up in objectification, both of themselves and each other.

Symptoms and Illnesses in Power Struggle

In the Power Struggle stage, people often experience physical and emotional symptoms. Headaches, back pain, depression, and other psychophysiological complaints commonly accompany the frustrations of trying to control oneself or one's partner. This stage is highly charged and volatile, with much tension and anxiety; frequently, partners succumb to illnesses that express the turbulence of this period.

Turbulence Precedes New Order

At the Power Struggle stage, partners should commit to stay in for the conflict, rather than withdraw, abandon, or attempt to overpower the other. In conflict, new information can emerge, and each can learn a great deal. The fights seem so disruptive; however, if couples do not fixate in repetitive control struggles, they can learn more about themselves and each other. Struggles such as these can be a stimulus to challenge fixed ideas of self and other. Indeed, without some disruption, there can be fixation of attitude and activity. In chemistry, no molecular change occurs without disruption; much work has been done in science in the area of "dissipative structures"—the orderliness in which disruption occurs.[4] In chaos theory, turbulence involves hidden patterns of order that can unfold into unforeseen possibilities. In the turbulence of interpersonal conflict, there can be revelation of self and the other.

Evolution is chaos with feedback. —Joseph Ford[5]

Indeed, when partners are willing to face the new information that emerges, they can use this to proceed to the next stages, where more intimacy is possible. Because the Power Struggle is so universal, and has so much energy involved in it, we recommend that couples really come to know their Power Struggle, and find a field of activity to share conflict that is mutually agreeable, as well as safe and respectful. Instead of throwing china and hurling insults, partners can engage in energetic competitive athletics, card and board games, or intellectual thrust and parry. Instead of avoiding or denying the strife, partners can come to actually enjoy it and to learn about themselves and each other. This period calls for presence on the part of both partners; when people succumb to non-presence, they enter the deviation of Apathy, which we will describe below.

Entitlement

To repeat, there is nothing problematic or wrong about the Power Struggle itself; difficulties arise when one or both parties remain stuck and fixated in moralistic, combative positions. One common factor in remaining stuck is the phenomenon of entitlement. When partners believe they have a "right" to specific behaviour from the other, they become fixated in blame, guilt, and control. Once people face and deal with their feelings of entitlement, they are able to unfixate, and they can open themselves to the curiosity that will help carry them into further stages where intimacy and authentic sharing are possible. When partners relinquish the position of entitlement, they also become free of the prison of being invested in the Power Struggle. At this point, they can relinquish the battle, acknowledging their disagreements and their attempts to control; the path is then open to move beyond righteousness into further and deeper dialogue.

Deviation One: APATHY

If one submits to the will of the other, giving up the power struggle, one can enter a state that looks quite peaceful compared to the turbulence of previous conflict. Suddenly, one is calm, and there is less turmoil. This is the deviation of Apathy, in which people step off the relationship cycle, and enter a lifeless state.

Apathy can be mistaken for the stage of Integration: it looks superficially the same. However, they are quite different in that the Integration phase has much life and acceptance, whereas Apathy is lifeless and resigned. In Apathy, one simply decides that the fight is not worth the trouble, and closes off. There is no longer any argument; the apathetic person is actually giving up, moving away from the life dynamic. Apathetic individuals have less passion; calmly, but lifelessly, they conform to the forms of relating, without any actual investment or vitality.

Some couples spend many years like this, and then just separate; others remain under the same roof, and live their days in a semblance of togetherness, but without love and passion. Socially, these Apathetic couples don't make any bother and look good together (albeit somewhat dispirited). Often people are very approving of them, and even hold them up as models to emulate. These people play the role of relationship, and live and work together—but without passion!

> Apathy is the withdrawal of will and love, a statement that they "don't matter," a suspension of commitment.[6]

Apathy involves numbing of feelings; apathetic individuals are walled off, out of touch with themselves and others. In Apathy, people can turn to numbing behaviours to avoid the turmoil of the Power Struggle. Often they are simply depressed, remote from their feelings for themselves and others. They might become addicted to drugs or alcohol, in an attempt to maintain a semblance of quiet. Sometimes, people who are addicted to work or other activities, who appear so vital and energetic during the day, sink to a quiet resignation in the evenings at home with their partners; their driven activity is an addiction, to fill the emptiness of the Apathy. These people laugh rarely; or when they do, the laugh can have a hollow ring. Often a symptom of Apathy is the loss of a sense of humour.

Illnesses can occur: with Apathy can come psychophysiological illnesses, depression, and other symptoms of being closed off. People with allergies sometimes have submitted, and have not defined their own boundaries; hence they acquire an illness to make defensive walls when they do not make life-defining boundaries. Other signs and symptoms of Apathy include compulsions, addictions, weakness, tiredness, boredom, ennui, and the currently popular chronic fatigue syndrome. These states involve numbing of the self.

Because people in Apathy don't make trouble, they don't bring much attention to themselves. Others believe that they have an "ideal relationship," as no one ever sees them in disagreement. Often people are shocked when a couple suddenly separates after many years of marriage; they seemed to be such an "ideal couple," but they were walled off from each other. This ideal couple had been in a state of peace; but they have not had the mutual respect and acceptance that occurs in harmony. Sometimes people discover their Apathy after the early demands of relationships are satisfied. When couples have young children, their time can be filled, and they don't have to face the distance between them. Then years later, when the children all leave home, they are alone together in the home, with the dawning realization that they don't know one another and don't have much feeling at all for one another!

The way out of the death-in-life of Apathy is to re-enter the Power Struggle. Because apathetic people are not present, they need to come back to presence. Often in rekindling a Power Struggle, people rediscover a degree of presence that is lacking in the Apathy state.

Deviation Two: TRANSCENDENCE

Rather than simply submit to others, one can leave the field of endeavour altogether, and become interested in nonphysical planes of being. In Transcendence, people rise above the day-to-day concerns of relationship, and simply attempt to become uninvested in interpersonal interactions. Some spiritual teachers advise rising above the behaviour of oneself and one's partner, to "disidentify"; such leaders teach "You are not your body" and "You are not your behaviour."

The partner who remains is often frustrated with the superior, condescending, "holier than thou" attitude of the transcendental one. The transcending one can become quite defensive and righteous, albeit in the "higher" language of spiritual truths; yet, hidden within this dismissive attitude is non-acceptance of the other, and a devaluing of the life process in relationship. In short, in transcending, the individual has risen above the concerns of the personal relationships.

To us, this is neither human nor personal nor spiritual. In the guise of a spiritual rise, the person has abandoned the field of relationship to pursue investments on other planes. For us, true spirituality involves finding meaning in daily activity, high or lowly. Transcendence converts spirituality into a religious dogma of superiority and condescension, where the physical, day-to-day struggles of humans are devalued or reviled.

Certainly, transcending is a possible life choice. However, there is no possibility for an ongoing interpersonal engagement, where partners can grow authentically in genuine dialogue. Basically, the transcending one prohibits interpersonal deepening, as that person values the spiritual practice more than the relationship itself. Often people can experience peace in transcendence; the tragedy is that this peace is accomplished by denial of the physical being, the relationship, and the partner.

After all the years of our relationship project, we have continued to value interpersonal processing. One of us (Jock) certainly did his best to explore the realms of transcendence.[7] Now, for us, our spiritual practice is the Communication Model. We are interested in *transformation* (working through all the issues that arise in dialogue, and growing through progressively and repeatedly accepting these issues).

> *As we become transparent, revealed for exactly who we are and not who we wish to be, then the mystery of human life as a whole glistens momentarily in a flash of incarnation. Spirituality emanates from the ordinariness of this human life made transparent by lifelong tending to its nature and fate.* —Thomas Moore[8]

Deviation Three: SEPARATION

Often, partners decide to give up, and walk away from the Power Struggle. Wishing to avoid further fighting and disagreement and disappointment, they abandon their partners (and themselves) and break off the relationship. Generally, they find themselves searching for a new Romance, and enter the cycle of expectation again, with rekindled hope that someone outside will provide the solution to their life difficulties. Sometimes partners can separate and come to new Romance with the same person; others separate from one person and find a Romance with another one. In separating, people are often showing their field dependence, searching for solutions to their problems outside of themselves.

Certainly, in an abusive relationship, where a partner continually crosses stated boundaries (for example, with violence or repeated addictive behaviours), separation is sometimes the only solution. When separation is accomplished without resentment or rancour, people can find more of themselves in the process, and then can approach a new relationship with deeper self-awareness, rather than blindly seeking a new Romance to ease their pain.

If partners do choose to separate, we advise them to stay long enough to process through the pain, grief, guilt, anger, and resentment, so that they can leave the relationship at rest, and not carry the conflicts into the next one. If people are going to separate, at least they can learn from what they have done, so that they don't recreate similar fixations and destructive behaviour in the next relationship.

> One feature that distinguishes humans from other animals—perhaps as characteristic as speech or upright posture—is the fact that we find so many ways to oppress and exploit one another ... "Power" is the generic term to describe the ability of a person to have others expend their lives to satisfy his or her goals.
>
> —Mihaly Csikszentmihalyi[9]

Notes

1. David Heller, *Growing Up Isn't Hard to Do If You Start Out As a Kid* (New York: Random House, 1991).

2. E. Albee, *Who's Afraid of Virginia Woolf?* (New York: Pocket Books, 1964).

3. B.R. Wong & J. McKeen, *A Manual for Life* (Gabriola Island, BC: PD Publishing, 1992), pp. 15–19.

4. I. Prigogine, quoted in J. Briggs & F.D. Peat, *Turbulent Mirror* (New York: Harper and Row, 1989), p. 138.

5. J. Ford, quoted in J. Gleick, *Chaos: Making a New Science* (New York: Penguin Books, 1987), p. 314.

6. Rollo May, *Love and Will* (New York: W.W. Norton & Company, 1969), p. 33.

7. B.R. Wong & J. McKeen, *In and Out of Our Own Way* (Gabriola Island, BC: PD Publishing, 1995), pp. 34, 35.

8. T. Moore, *Care of the Soul* (New York: Harper Collins, 1992), p. 262.

9. M. Csikszentmihalyi, *The Evolving Self* (New York: Harper Collins, 1993), p. 89.

The Stage of Integration

Q. *Is it better to be single or married?*

A. *It's better for girls to be single, but not for boys. Boys need somebody to clean up after them.* —Anita (age 9)

A. *It gives me a headache to think about that stuff. I'm just a kid. I don't need that kind of trouble.* —Will (age 7)[1]

Introduction

The Power Struggle has a life span of about five to seven years. After this period, couples tend to come to some new ground with regard to their differences. Often they stop fighting, or have more of a sense of humour about going through the same old routines over and over. When the turmoil of the Power Struggle settles, couples enter a period of calm that many find disturbing. When they are no longer fighting, they find that the excitement they expect seems to have gone. In this phase, couples who are in a sexual relationship often find that their sexual charge has diminished. Many times couples separate at this time, thinking that something is wrong. Often, something is very right!

Indeed, after partners have endured the illlusions and disorientation of Romance, and have weathered the storms of the Power Struggle, they often find that they have a solid relationship that has much flexibility and endurance. Having arrived at some stable knowledge of each other, they are capable of embarking upon a new adventure—the journey into a deepening intimacy. For them, the Romance and the Power Struggle were tests and proving grounds, wherein they worked through and past many blocks, in order to be able to witness each other with more receptive eyes and hearts. They are ready to enter the advanced phases of relationship, beyond illusions and defences, beginning with the Phase of Integration.

The Seven-Year Itch

The so-called "seven-year itch" reflects the tendency for the Power Struggle to quiet down. As their relationship calms, people invested in having a constant charge with their partner will tend to look elsewhere for stimulation, believing

73

that the relationship has gone dead. Commonly, this is not so. The partners might have achieved a level of awareness of themselves and each other, and might have diminished their investment in proving the other to be in the wrong. If people are field dependent, and expect that a charge is the only measure of vitality, they might begin to look for an affair, or for a brand new relationship to find the stimulation of a charge again. This seeking of a new Romance is the deviation of Separation mentioned previously (see "The Power Struggle Stage," p. 63).

Couples who accept this, and begin to share with each other, often find that they are actually feeling very warm and close with each other, now that the charge has diminished. They are actually beginning to become intimate!

Beginning to Learn Together

In the Power Struggle, both parties are more invested in being right; thus, they stay remote from themselves and each other in the charge of conflict and defence and blame. They don't come to know each other more deeply, because they keep themselves and each other objectified in the conflict. They don't know the personhood of their partner, who is more the object of defensiveness and blame.

With a shift in attitude, partners no longer try to control, change or blame each other. Instead, they begin to listen, with genuine interest and curiosity. In the Power Struggle Stage, partners have had the information to come to know the other; however, they generally have used this information in order to keep distant in conflict. In the Integration Stage, they become curious to know each other; with this attitude, they begin to listen and question rather than defend. The relationship deepens, and the partners come to know each other and themselves. As they come to accept what they discover instead of resisting it, the flower of intimacy opens.

Curiosity and Communication

Curiosity is the catalyst to proceed from Power Struggle to Integration. By using the Model For Communication,[2] people can become more accepting of themselves and each other through a process that we call "The Four A's" (Awareness, Acknowledgement, Acceptance, Action). Through curiosity, people become *aware* of what they are doing in any situation. By *acknowledging* their position, they can move to a further *acceptance* of their attitudes. In this process, they begin to know themselves and their partners more fully; rather than being defended and unaware, they are learning with each other. This awareness can be translated into *action*, where further self-development and relationship enhancement can take place.

For example, the action that might emerge from a process of awareness, acknowledgement, and acceptance might be like this: "I am aware that I tend to blame you when you are late, and I acknowledge that I just did it again; I accept that I tend to do this, and I also am curious about your perspective on why you have arrived home at this time. Will you tell me more of what has been occurring for you? The action I wish to take is to sit down and talk with you about this, rather than just storm out in a rage and break off communication."

Weeding the Garden

Just as an established garden requires maintenance and periodic labour, the Integration stage involves work to deepen the relationship. We recommend that partners devote a period of time each day to sharing their perceptions, thoughts, feelings and experiences, to keep up to date with each other's world. In this way, they can gradually come to know themselves and each other beyond the limited viewpoints of their idealizations and objectifications. Each time the partners acknowledge a moralistic fixed belief about the way things are, they are able to move through the limitation into a process where they can gain increasing awareness of themselves and each other.

Partners Can Disagree

In Integration, partners can disagree without fighting; they are not invested in being right, they can accept differences, and they can stay together with someone who has quite different viewpoints. This process involves progressive acceptance of both self and other. With this growing acceptance, intimacy deepens. Partners find more self awareness and more awareness of each other. The Relationship Garden now is in a rapid stage of growth; the partners (the plants in the garden) are maturing and ripening in their development as individuals together. The process of harmony is evident (see "The Harmonious Garden," p. 200).

People gain strength in recognizing themselves and their partners for who they are, without any necessity to change. They are visibly more calm, secure, and stable in other phases of their life, too. They are moving past being dependent upon someone else for the security of their existence into becoming more self-reliant. They don't need their partners to be a certain way in order to solve their existential dilemma. They might say, "I am OK and you are OK, and we can each be together, accepting our separateness, and our differences. And we can love each other."

In Integration, the couples are *not at peace*, which occurs in the deviation of Apathy noted previously (see "The Power Struggle Stage," p. 63). Rather they share in a *harmony* of differences. They each can sing their own note, without having to move to the melody of the other; in this mutual acceptance and acknowledgment, their melodies will harmonize with growing intimacy and depth of interaction.

Sexuality in the Integration Stage

Although the sexual charge tends to diminish in Integration, it can be rekindled if people want, by coming to a deeper understanding of how the charge is generated. In couples who are willing to share sexual fantasies, the possibility exists to find new levels of sexual charge through playing with objectification. This sharing requires mature stability from each partner, to avoid the guilt or blame that might be generated in the Power Struggle stage.

Finally—They Are Personal!

In the Integration stage, both partners are for the first time personal; in previous stages, both were objectified roles. Now in Integration, each person is valued, accepted, and acknowledged. With the sharing and witnessing of each other, they both are revealed. As partners open to themselves and to each other, they become more substantial as individuated persons and as relationship participants.

What begins as an interpersonal sharing moves into deeper, more spiritual domains. Partners come to know each other in depth, and witness the life process revealed in each of them. This is the opening of true dialogue; the relationship moves beyond "I-It" to "I-Thou."[3]

Integration Is Rare

This stage of Integration rarely occurs to much degree. Most people remain mired in the conflicts of the Power Struggle, and the heady illusions of Romance, and do not fully enter the domain of Integration. When partners do find stability between them, they can still have power struggles and romance; but they acknowledge them for what they are and don't take them seriously. In short, in Integration, people have moved their centre from outside of themselves into the centre of their own beings; they are now increasingly self-reliant, and hence more sensitive and aware of both themselves and each other. They are no longer attempting to overcome their existential condition through the mirages and facades of romance and objectification; they possess the ready certainty of individuals who are growing strong in their own autonomy and self-directed purpose, while remaining sensitive to their partners.

The Courageous Life

The emptiness and meaninglessness that lurks at the centre of existence provides a challenge for people to grow and develop and become stronger in themselves. In relation with another, people face the dread of nonbeing when they do not succumb to the illusory objectifications and images of the Romance and Power Struggle stages. When they face their insecurities and share them, they can accept themselves and their partners as they are; they then know themselves to be alone, without a definite meaning provided for them.

Although meaning is not given, it can be created; emptiness can be filled with one's own actions, consistent with one's own values. Daring people who have reached the Integration stage are in a position to create their own personal meaning and fill the emptiness by courageous acts of intimate sharing and openness with themselves, and with their partners. In relationship, the project of self-becoming is enhanced through the mirroring of dialogue. Partners gain both knowledge of themselves and each other; as they open, revealed to each other, they also become open and revealed to themselves.

Integration and Anxiety

For people in the Integration phase, anxiety diminishes as they progressively accept their own separateness. When they do experience deeper levels of angst, they rise to the occasion with a further confirmation of faith. Such people even acknowledge their own despair and face the challenge with a further acceptance of even the darkest aspects of their beings:

> *The acceptance of despair is in itself faith and on the boundary line of the courage to be.* —Paul Tillich[4]

Such individuals can go through their dark periods without closing off, or abandoning themselves or others; they continue to operate in courageous dialogue with their partners, and with life itself. Their spirituality is grounded in a profound acceptance of themselves and their partners; in so doing, they embrace life, with ever-growing feelings of participation and reverence.

People in Integration accept the existential condition of aloneness and separateness. In so doing, they are open to experience the fulfillment that comes with sharing with another separate being. They come to celebrate themselves, their relationship, and their interactions with all of life, with courage, strength and dedication.

Humour

Humour and periodic light-heartedness are characteristic of the phase of Integration. The intensity and seriousness of righteousness, guilt and blame give way to spirited teasing and self-aware laughter. What previously were heavy subjects now are simply more things to face, with equanimity and with pleasure. Partners begin to celebrate their everyday life together, with all its challenges, tribulations and joy.

Honesty and Responsibility

Honesty is of paramount importance; it is a required tool to deepen interchange. By the time partners have reached some Integration, they have come to recognize that one person cannot hurt another's feelings; indeed, their attitude is that one person cannot make anyone else feel anything (see "Feelings and Closeness," p. 34). The attitude that one person can hurt another leads to protection, defensiveness, secrecy, and diminished intimacy—characteristics of the Power Struggle. When partners acknowledge that each is responsible for his or her own feelings, a sense of openness and freedom arises; no subject is taboo, and they can face any situation, willing to communicate and learn together.

Sharing

In the Integration stage, people are prepared to share more and more of themselves, in dialogue with each other. Anything shared can enhance the intimacy that comes in the unfolding honesty of the Integration phase. Indeed, when the elements of the Power Struggle (jealousy, guilt, anger, blame, etc.) are shared, they become useful information for the Integration phase. When partners accept these elements in themselves without trying to use them for control, they become interesting items of curiosity, useful for growth and enhancement of the relationship. When they are shared, previously disruptive elements become the ground substance for the stable relationship.

Flow

Whereas people tend to become stuck and fixated in repetitious righteous fighting in the Power Struggle stage, partners experience movement and flow in the Integration stage. They are becoming persons, beyond the objectifications that they have experienced from themselves and from others. They come to know themselves and each other. In this movement, they enter the flow of life, and experience greater degrees of freedom. They readily shoulder the increased responsibility that accompanies this freedom.

Csikszentmihalyi has described the qualities of people in the "flow experience."[5] These people tend to have clear goals, to act decisively, and to be single-minded, capable of focus and concentration, possessing a sense of control; they tend to experience loss of self-consciousness and a feeling of participation in something greater than themselves. For them time passes faster, and they find enjoyment of experiences for their own sake. Partners in the Integration stage often show the characteristics of the "flow experience." They are involved and present, with themselves and each other; hence, they experience themselves as participating in life, and they find they have a sense of belonging to something greater than themselves.

Continual Renewal

Couples who have achieved the stage of Integration can maintain their dynamic relationship through continual renewal. They cannot rest on their laurels and expect the relationship to take care of itself; indeed, the relationship is the vehicle through which they continue to grow and develop, together and separately. In order to continue to grow together, they need to find new things to share. The following are some key issues to maintain an ongoing Integration, and prevent a slide into self-satisfaction or boredom.

1. *Frequent dependable contact* keeps the partners aware of each other and the life process. Having coffee together as a routine, or sharing a favourite television program together, brings an ongoing organismic awareness of each other.

2. *Daily clearing* time is important, in order to keep each other informed and aware of thoughts and feelings and experiences that have come to each partner. This can be in the early morning, before the day begins, or later in the evening, to recap events of the day.

3. *An ongoing project of mutual interest* brings a focus to the relationship. This can be tending a garden together, or researching some topic, or collaborating in business. Partners that have projects together have a natural inclination to interact with each other.

4. *Reporting of individual interests* keeps both partners informed and involved in each other's lives. For example, when one partner is interested in jogging, and the other one likes to stay at home to read, they should ask each other how the individual experiences of the solitary activities were for each of them. This way, independent interests can be shared, to avoid them becoming elements that introduce distance.

5. *Novelty and experimentation* help to keep a relationship bright and vital. Trips together to unknown places or experiencing new foods or artistic performances together can provide fresh subjects for discussion and sharing. As the experiences accumulate, the partners discover an ongoing sense of challenge and enjoyment within themselves and with each other.

6. *Learning together* brings new dimension to the relationship. Whether couples decide to informally research a topic together, study ballroom dancing, or attend a class at a community college, the act of learning together helps to deepen their interaction.

7. *Renewal of romance* through affectionate gestures and rituals brings a feeling of warmth and specialness to the relationship. Couples can have their own little private jokes and signals, which mean that they are special to each other.

Loving

In the Relationship Garden, loving blossoms in the Integration phase. Partners begin to know each other; there is more reality and less fantasy. Perhaps the period of Integration is not as exciting as the tumultuous periods of Romance and Power Struggle; but, for the first time, these people are able to experience true fulfilment, with themselves and each other.

Individuals in this stage are very responsible. They tend not to blame their partners; nor do they indulge in the self-blame of guilt and regret. In the Integration phase, partners have moved beyond the limitations of morality; instead of seeing situations in terms of right and wrong, guilt and blame, they tend to see possibilities for curiosity and learning.

They accept their Actual Selves, and in the process, begin to forge an authentic relationship with each other. In this intimacy, they are involved in issues of strength, not power. The process of dialogue enhances the growth and development of both persons, at the same time as the relationship is deepening.

> For one human being to love another human being: that is perhaps the most difficult task that has been entrusted to us, the ultimate task, the final test and proof, the work for which all other work is merely preparation. —Rainer Maria Rilke[6]

Notes

1. David Heller, *Growing Up Isn't Hard to Do If You Start Out As a Kid* (New York: Random House, 1991).

2. B.R. Wong & J. McKeen, *A Manual for Life* (Gabriola Island, BC: PD Publishing, 1992), pp. 6–10.

3. Martin Buber, *I and Thou* (New York: Charles Scribner's Sons, 1970), p. 14.

4. P. Tillich, *The Courage To Be* (New Haven: Yale University Press, 1952), p. 175.

5. M. Csikszentmihalyi, *The Evolving Self* (New York: Harper Collins, 1993), pp. 178–79.

6. R.M. Rilke, quoted in E.H. Sell, *The Spirit of Loving* (Boston, MA: Shambhala Publications, 1995), p. 47.

The Stage of Commitment

Integration is the Precursor to Commitment

Once partners achieve a degree of stability in the Integration phase, they are engaged in active meaningful dialogue. Each is a person, not merely an objectified role. Their knowledge of themselves and each other deepens, and they become stronger, both in themselves and in the relationship. Now, there is no requirement for anyone to change (a good thing, since this is fundamentally impossible!). Instead, they are progressively more aware and accepting of themselves and each other. Once this process of Integration is well-established, the partners are ready to enter the next stage, Commitment.

The Commitment Stage

In the Commitment stage, partners know each other very well—both in their authenticity and in the games and power plays that each can play. They communicate their thoughts and feelings readily, and in this way continue to deepen their awareness of themselves and each other. They are more and more engaged with life, with each other, and with themselves. Now they are ready to make an informed commitment, with full knowledge of themselves, and the other with whom they are committing.

Because partners know each other well at this stage, they do not commit out of the illusions of Romance or the obligations of the Power Struggle. Instead, with awareness, they commit with free choice.

They do not commit to each other; indeed, they affirm their commitment to life and to themselves. In this process, they are willing to make agreements to share a commitment, to embark upon projects together with mutual expectations and decisions.

Having Children in the Commitment Stage

This is the best stage at which to have a baby. Too often, couples decide to become pregnant in the Romance stage, without knowing themselves or their partners adequately. Also, many children are conceived in the Power Struggle, when the partners believe that bringing another life into the relationship will help to ease the tension and struggles that occur as a consequence of their projected objectifications of each other. Children born in the early stages are faced with parents who are not aware of themselves and whose energies are invested in struggling with each other. More stable parents will be aware of themselves, each other, and their motivations and desires; such individuals will naturally be aware of their children, and can be clear in setting boundaries with their partners and their children. In this environment, youngsters can have the experience of a strong relationship matrix in which to grow and develop into authentic personhood.

The Evolution of Commitment

Commitment matures and changes as the partners change. There actually is a commitment required at each stage of relationship. At the Romance stage, commitment is to a dream, an ideal; when people marry at this stage they frequently promise to "love, honour and obey" someone they don't even know. At the Romance stage, couples should commit to staying together long enough to get to know each other. In the Power Struggle stage, partners should commit to being present with each other, in order to work through the conflict; if they succumb to non-presence, they move off the developmental cycle, and enter one of the deviations—Apathy, Transcendence, or Separation. In Power Struggle, people generally have an unconscious commitment to win, to overpower the other (which obviously works against developing of intimacy). Most commitments in Power Struggle or Romance are ultimately life restricting; such inclinations tend to limit the relationship, or even terminate it.

After partners achieve some degree of Integration, they are more capable of a solid, informed Commitment of mutuality. Having developed honest, dependable communication and curiosity in the Integration stage, partners can put plans and imaginings into action. Such commitments are not whimsical or naive; they proceed naturally from informed knowledge of both self and other in the Integration stage. By now, partners are individuating, unique and strong within themselves. With knowledge of themselves, they are able to commit with assurance, and dedicate their wills to whatever they choose. In relationship, when these partners commit together, they can depend upon themselves and each other. At this stage, partners can embark upon a solid commitment, for life, both separate and together. They do not need each other; but they have the assurance that they can depend upon themselves and each other.

Will and Willfulness

The Commitment stage involves the use of the *will.* Note that *willfulness* is a characteristic of the Power Struggle stage, and generally involves objectification and defence; clear expression of the will is an aspect of a mature personality, and is important in developing advanced functions, such as dedication, dependability, industry, responsibility, and purposeful, responsive action. The will is used to work *for* a purpose; willfulness operates *against* growth and thus often leads to fixation. Willfulness serves the purposes of pride, righteousness, security, and walls—thus interfering with intimacy. Clean use of the will supports the growth functions of the Relationship Garden, while willfulness tends to grow like a weed, suffocating tender new growth.

Care and Maintenance of a Relationship

Relationships are like old houses; they need maintenance and care, or they tend to settle into dysfunction. With a commitment to deal with any situation that comes up with sharing, honesty, and openness, the relationship can be kept in a healthy state. Just as a garden constantly needs weeding, watering, and fertilizing, a relationship needs the constant care and maintenance that mutual commitments can bring. Where there is genuine care and curiosity for the other, and sharing of the self, there is revelation of both partners; this revelation brings renewal to a relationship through time.

Commitment is to Oneself

One should not commit to another; one commits oneself, dedicating one's life to designated activities or purposes. Each person's growth is enhanced, and develops with the discipline and restraint of commitment. Instead of the impulsiveness of youth, where one cause or position is abandoned for the next whim, partners in the Commitment stage can weather the storms together and continue to grow, develop and deepen through time. With commitment, focus becomes possible, and the partners are increasingly capable of managing large projects, and growing with increasing challenges. The use of the will in commitment permits the evolution of strong, mature, individuated selves. When such selves commit together in relationship, they each grow, and the relationship grows.

Deep Roots

In the Relationship Garden, committed people are like deeply rooted plants. Knowing themselves, they can remain in place, and dedicate themselves to the life of the garden without requiring special attention or excessive care. They reach deep into the soil, and nourish themselves to the centre of their beings, in harmony with nature and their surroundings. They are strong enough to endure temporary hardships and challenges, and can grow in harmony with the other strong plants in their garden.

Teaching Children About Commitment

The ability to commit is a developed skill, and grows by diligent repetition—just as athletic practice develops the muscles and the endurance that accompany increasing prowess. A child learns self-discipline by committing to small projects. Children's self-acceptance and self-esteem grow as they learn that they can commit themselves to anything and follow through, sticking to what they set out to do. Children become more secure in themselves as they learn that they can depend upon themselves to do what they intend.

In this way, children can learn to depend upon themselves and become self-reliant. For example, by learning to budget their money, spending only a little of their allowance and saving some for later, young people can learn how to maintain their resources. Thus, children can very early develop good financial sense, and grow in the knowledge that they can increasingly manage their own affairs.

Commitment Together

I do not commit to you; I commit myself to whatever I choose. In relationship, my commitment involves what I offer to the relationship. When you offer to commit as well, we are able to be together in relationship with expectations that are not demands, but mutual agreements. The more I value you, the more I will commit myself with you, and the more expectations we can have with each other. This is the root of dependability; when people are dependable, their roots grow deep and strong, and the changing tides of events cannot disrupt their lives. When partners learn dependability together, they and their relationship can grow to become strong and sturdy.

Limited Commitments

Many people who are commitment phobic can dedicate themselves for a limited period of time. If people are afraid of the immensity of commitment, they can probably accept a limited one—for example a month-by-month commitment, or a three-month period. When they agree to the time, they can devote themselves to the principles of relationship without worrying about it being forever. As they learn that they can live through a short period of commitment, a longer one does not seem so impossible. We recommend to people who are reluctant to commit that they build up in realistic increments.

In our own case, Jock cured his phobia about commitment when he found that he could save money on an extended subscription to *Time* magazine; he elected to stay with Ben for the longer period to economize—his Scottish blood won out over his fear when he could save a few dollars![1] In the same manner, by committing together to a financial responsibility, people can learn that they indeed can last through the vicissitudes of circumstances, and feel stronger in themselves for it. For example, buying a house together can be a very fulfilling proposition; we now say that people mature when they are willing to take on a mortgage!

Practising Commitment in Workshops

In our long-term residential programs, we conduct a Relationships workshop to which people can invite spouses, parents, children, business partners, or siblings. If participants do not invite any of these significant others, they pair themselves with other unpartnered participants, and they have a relationship for the weekend. Any relationship goes through the same stages, and follows the same principles; hence, even in such a limited commitment as this, people can learn about relationships. People can use what they learn in one relationship to further understand other relationships that they already have, or might have in the future.

Commitments for Different Relationships

In relationships of different types, different commitments are needed. For example, business partners need perhaps only a few minutes each day to keep their business enterprise on track. For friends, a commitment to spending an evening a week together permits them to develop the relationship adequately. For partners in a primary relationship, we recommend a minimum of a half hour per day devoted to sharing, clearing, and focusing on feelings and thoughts with each other.

For long-standing relationships, we recommend that couples re-evaluate their commitment from time to time; often, they discover that they have acquired a taste for commitment, and like the strength that longer commitments afford.

In our own relationship, we summarize our commitment as follows:

> Our commitment is for life. The commitment could end tomorrow, if the life went out of the relationship. This is not a time-based commitment; rather, it is a life-based commitment. But then, we are also committed to work through all the details of ending a relationship before we would separate; so, we likely would not leave each other, since we likely would find new life in the stimulation of finding out about the issues of separation. Both parties are free to choose to stay in or leave. We stay because we continue to find life together.

Commitment is the Basis of Life

In Commitment lies the key to a great secret. In Taoist philosophy, when human beings direct their wills in creative, life-enhancing pursuits, they participate beneficially in the larger will of life itself. This is the secret of manifestation. People who use their wills in commitments of mutual concern can shine in brilliant illumination; their endeavours together become numinous. The will of life is expressed in the human action; the word is made flesh.

> Until one is committed, there is hesitancy, the chance to draw back, always ineffectiveness, concerning all acts of initiative (and creation). There is one elementary truth the ignorance of which kills countless ideas and splendid plans: that the moment one definitely commits oneself, then Providence moves too. All sorts of things occur to help one that would never otherwise have occurred. A whole stream of events issues from the decision, raising in one's favour all manner of unforseen incidents and meetings and material assistance which no man could have dreamed would have come his way. Whatever you can do or dream you can, begin it. Boldness has genius, power and magic in it. Begin it now. —Johann Wolfgang von Goethe[2]

Notes

1. B. Wong & J. McKeen, *In and Out of Our Own Way* (Gabriola Island, BC: PD Publishing, 1995), p. 131.

2. J.W. Goethe, translator unknown. Original German quoted in *Goethe's Faust, Gesamtausgabe* (Frankfurt am Main: Insel Verlag, 1976), p. 142.

The Stage of Co-creativity

The final stage in the cycle is Co-creativity. When partners have achieved the stages of Integration and Commitment, they proceed with knowledge of each other and themselves. They know their strengths, their weaknesses, their desires, and their dreams. Being dependable in their commitments, they can join in the mutuality of genuine collaboration. When they are together, any task they choose becomes a creative endeavour. There seems to be a field of originality and vitality around such pairings. When they dedicate themselves together, whatever they touch seems to become infused with life and light, and is inspiring to others around them. The creative partnerships in the world of the theatre illustrate the fine-tuned sensitivity and great work that emerges from such interaction—the musical collaboration of Rodgers and Hammerstein is a good example.

In this Co-creativity, partners' efforts harmonize with each other. There is a flow that seems tangible when they are together. Whether they are joined in a pas de deux, or are just washing the dishes together, their movements and interchanges are fluid and possess a simple grace. Their very interaction serves as an inspiration to those around them.

When partners have moved beyond the moralizing of the Power Struggle, have achieved the awareness of self and other in the Integration stage, and have learned to team up with their wills in the Commitment stage, they find a multitude of possibilities opening up before them. Some report an aura of life and love around such people; even their most mundane pursuits have a spiritual life to them. They manifest the Zen spirit of life in every moment—together, yet distinct, separate, individuated, and authentic. The word is made flesh. Spirit, in its imaginings, infuses the human body and the material world. This is true incarnation.

With their capacity to acknowledge and share all aspects of their beings, co-creative partners can make use of what were earlier seen to be negative or destructive aspects in the relationship. They can convert differences into creative challenges rather than fighting over legalistic points. One partner's negative aspects can be used positively: the stingy partner can be the one who does the bookkeeping, and the partner invested in control can do the scheduling and planning. Elements in their personalities that were originally developed for defence can be used creatively in the service of the relationship and in projects together. By acknowledging and accepting character traits, nothing needs to be seen as inherently negative.

The Cycle Regenerates

Freedom abounds, and life is full of possibilities; in this phase, people are strong, with full capacity to actually manifest their dreams and desires. Because there is less fixedness, these people are ready to entertain new ideas and imagine novel approaches to situations. In short, they are open, and ready for entering the next phase, which is a return to the domain of Romance.

Because these people now have the accumulated experience from the learning of the previous stages, this is a *more informed* Romance. Hence, this return to Romance is not shown in our diagram as a circular return (see "Developmental Stages of Relationship," p. 50); rather, it involves a spiralling, expanding into life and further creativity. The imagination reopens into a new Romance; people enter new territory they do not know, with much anticipation of what is possible. With this enhanced view, people can see further ranges of life, love and relationship, which they can pursue. Soon, the partners enter into further learning, with new Power Struggles; now they are capable of moving more quickly through to new Integration, with ever-increasing awareness of themselves and each other. And so on they go, through further Commitment and more Co-creativity. This is indeed the cycle of life, lived out in relationship.

When Fritz Perls wrote his famous poem in the 1960s ("I am not in this world to live up to your expectations, and you are not in this world to live up to mine"), many people believed that the way to grow was on one's own, and that relationships were counterproductive to growth. The following answer to Perls provides a relationships perspective:

Beyond Perls

If I just do my thing
And you do yours
We stand in danger
Of losing each other
And ourselves.
I am not in this world
To live up to your expectations,
But I am in this world
To confirm you as a unique human being
And to be confirmed by you.
We are fully ourselves
Only in relation to each other;
The I detached from a Thou disintegrates.
I do not find you by chance;
I find you by an active life of reaching out.
Rather than passively letting things happen to me
I can act intentionally
To make them happen.
I must begin with my Self, true;
But I must not end with my Self
The truth begins with two.

—Walter Tubbs[1]

Notes

1. Walter Tubbs, "Beyond Perls," *Journal of Humanistic Psychology, 12*(2), Fall 1972.

Chaos and Relationships

Chaos Theory

Chaos theory proposes a still state referred to as *equilibrium* in which energy is in its lowest state of activity and is largely predictable. On the other extreme of a continuum is *turbulence*; in turbulence (chaos) energy is organized, but the patterns are so complex as to be unpredictable.[1]

Consider a stone that is rolled uphill. The further away from equilibrium it is moved, the more unstable it becomes; it stores more energy and is increasingly more precarious, ready to roll back to its state of equilibrium. Hence, the greater the distance from equilibrium, the greater is the possibility of turbulence, or unpredictable behaviour.

Viewing human life and individual development from this perspective, people move a certain distance from equilibrium as they face the demands of living. If that distance from equilibrium is small, the person remains still and close to death; if it is further away, the person is more tense and uncertain, but also more alive. Maximum growth is possible at what we refer to as the *Zone of Optimal Integration* (ZOI), a kind of plateau beyond which turbulence (experienced as anxiety) becomes too great for a person to handle. The more turbulence a person can manage, the greater the distance from equilibrium that person can move. With increasing distance from equilibrium, the opportunities are greater to discover and experience more of life.

As a growing and developing person handles new situations, the Zone of Optimal Integration expands; when that person is at rest, or retreating in face of threats (real or imagined), the ZOI contracts. This pulsatile process of expansion and contraction is characteristic of healthy, live organisms—the greater the range of pulsation, the greater the flexibility of movement and the fuller the experiencing of life.

Chaos is not disorganization; rather, it is patterned but unpredictable complexity. The further the distance from equilibrium that a person moves, the more turbulence and complexity is encountered. In such chaotic situations, it is common for individuals to contract in fixed ways, narrowing their range of experiencing by drawing in their boundaries and walling themselves off from contact; this is the *neurotic* solution to turbulence. Such persons not only diminish the size of their Zone of Optimal Integration, but they also rigidify their boundaries into thick, defensive walls that prevent them from feeling alive, fulfilled and whole. The more that this rigidification happens, the more the ZOI tends to slide toward equilibrium (this equilibrium is what existentialists identify as a "death in life").

Neurosis is a narrowing and fixation of the life process as a means of controlling the uncertainty of chaos. Anxiety occurs with a threatened loss of that control. People are afraid that in loss of control, disastrous things will occur; in the extreme, they fear that the loss of control can result in either criminal or psychotic behaviour. People who fear experiencing the full expansion of life with all its complexity (chaos) develop an interest in power and control, which provides some semblance of security; by controlling themselves and taking power over others, they hope to avoid the perils of chaotic expressions.

The Self in Context

The figure "The Self In Context" (page 94) illustrates the relationship between equilibrium and chaos as it applies to human beings. At the centre is *equilibrium* (stillness), where there is no movement, no growth, no change; events here are predictable and certain. The farther from the centre, the greater the tendency to unpredictability and chaos (turbulence). The movement from equilibrium into chaos occurs in three zones: the *Spiritual*, the *Training Camp*, and the *Relationship Garden*. In the Training Camp, chaos is controlled and resisted through socialized repetitive behaviours and attitudes. In the Relationship Garden, chaos is transformed through dynamic acceptance of it. In the zone of the Spiritual, meaning is given to chaos.

The Training Camp

In life, people gradually encounter increasing amounts of chaos, and learn to deal with it. Most early training and schooling involves learning standard approaches and tools to deal with unpredictability. Indeed, language, roles and rules of conduct embody the conventions that help society to keep order in the midst of unpredictable chaos. The more successful the training, the more predictable and socialized a person will be; unfortunately, this involves fixation of life force energy, and the individual's creativity and sense of vitality are stifled.

The trade-off involves suppressing one's authentic life force energy in order to fit into the constraints of the social order. This is the project of the Training Camp.

Children learn to adopt the behaviours and concerns of their parents, and through mimicry to become more socialized. The parents give approval as their youngsters become more trained into the ways of the parents. The children feel more comfort as they fit in; at the same time, there is less spontaneous life and anxiety to feel. By a process of externalization, children learn to turn the focus of their attention from within to seek the approval and attention of outside referents ("authorities"). At first these outside referents are people (teachers, parents, siblings); later, they are more abstract rewards from the culture at

The Self In Context

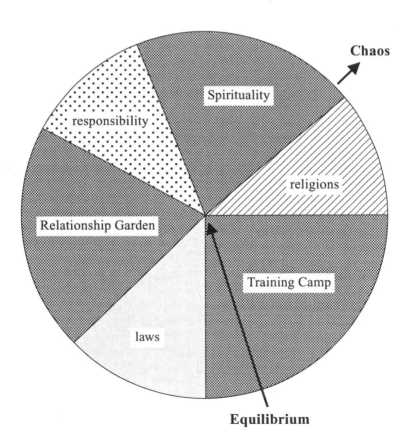

large (reputation, titles, etc.). Thus, the Training Camp teaches control of in-appropriate impulses; in the process, people lose touch with the Authentic Self in pursuit of the Ideal Self; this results in an objectifying, depersonalizing externalization of energy.

The Relationship Garden

The attitude in the Relationship Garden is one of accepting chaos and working with it. Instead of trying to control and suppress chaos, the individuals in a relationship garden will welcome the unpredictable events as sources of new-ness and creativity. When unanticipated events occur between them, they will tend to share their anxiety rather than try to diminish or ignore it. Hence, the energy of turbulence becomes available for interaction, communion, and personal growth.

In this process of intimacy, sharing, and acceptance, both parties become more fully themselves and more fully engaged with the authentic personhood of the partner. With the revelation of their internal process, they come to know both themselves and each other better. Thus, they can experience growth and increasing autonomy. Whereas in the Training Camp the participants *react* from fixed attitudes and patterns, in the Relationship Garden they *respond* to each other as sensitive persons. In the Training Camp, participants are *objects*, relating on an "It-It" basis; in the Relationship Garden, they become *people* with an "I-You" orientation.[2] The Training Camp is characterized by roled individuals who moralize and erect walls; the Relationship Garden involves responsible people who develop boundaries with interpersonal sensitivity, and who thus can apply their personal ethics to each novel situation.

Thus, the Relationship Garden fosters freedom of expression, while remaining sensitive to self and other. This facilitates the discovery of the Authentic Self. People in the Relationship Garden are less ideal, but they are more responsive, more vital, and more personal.

The Spiritual

Chaos provides a challenge to find meaning. The Spiritual is the domain where this occurs. By facing the emptiness and unpredictability of chaos, people can learn to contend with emptiness by filling it with their own meaning. In the Spiritual, there are no constraints; hence there are neither walls nor boundaries. The Spiritual involves *eternity* (timelessness) and *infinity* (spacelessness).

The Interface Regions

There is an interface between each domain. *Religions* are developed in the interface between the Spiritual and the Training Camp. *Responsibility* occurs between the Relationship Garden and the Spiritual. *Laws* (structured relationships) occur between the Training Camp and the Relationship Garden; this is where social rules, obligations, roles, and conventions reside.

The Zone of Optimal Integration

The Zone of Optimal Integration (ZOI) is where integration of chaos is possible without undue strain. There is a ZOI in all three facets (the Spiritual, the Relationship Garden, and the Training Camp). In the ZOI of the Spiritual, the individual is not overwhelmed by emptiness. In the ZOI of the Training Camp, conventions and rules are not so strong as to overwhelm the life force entirely. In the ZOI of the Relationship Garden, individualism will be balanced with sensitivity and awareness.

Being in Synch

The greater the distance from equilibrium, the more important is the relatedness to context.[3] When people move into greater chaos, they need to be more related to the context in order to maintain themselves, while remaining sensitive to others. This *phase locking* (also called "slaving") at a distance from equilibrium occurs in a jazz group, when the musicians progress farther and farther from conventional melody lines; the drummer sets the context through the rhythm, and the other musicians become increasingly dependent upon the drummer's context. Although the other musicians are very dependent upon the drummer's rhythms, they have great freedom within these constraints. They become "in synch" or "in the groove" with each other (in our terms, they are "in harmony" or "in resonance.")

This relatedness to context occurs in each of the three domains (the Spiritual, the Relationship Garden, and the Training Camp). Slaving need not be excessively limiting; rather, it occurs when people are in harmony, responsively relating to each other. Slaving involves being self-reliant, not dependent upon externals and yet remaining sensitive to one's environment. This appropriateness arises from autonomous inner sensitivity, rather than obligatory behaviour dictated by rules from without. When people learn to respond to their context without ignoring or resisting it, they can come to know more deeply their unique place in resonant harmony.

Freedom and Chaos

People lose their freedom by externalizing, becoming field dependent. In the Training Camp, people learn to fit in, in order to limit chaos; in this trade for security, they lose their freedom. In the Training Camp, when people obey the dictates of an authoritarian figure, they lose their autonomy. In the Spiritual, people might be tempted to follow a guru in a Training Camp manner, and hence lose themselves in adopting their meaning from the external. When partners lose contact with themselves or each other, they become isolated, lose their place, and hence become unfree.

Boundaries and Walls

Boundaries are related to the Relationship Garden, because there is acceptance and sensitivity to self and other that embraces unpredictability and turbulence. In the Training Camp, *walls* are erected to maintain defensive controls over self and other. In the Spirituality domain, there are no walls or boundaries; there are only universals.

Peace and Harmony

Peace involves tolerance, rather than true acceptance; people learn to negotiate temporary peace in the rules and structuring of the Training Camp (see "The Harmonious Garden," p. 200). Thus, the Romance and Power Struggle stages involve peace and conflict (which is lack of peace). Apathy or Separation occur with the restrictions of peace, or when the failure of peace breaks into battles.

Harmony involves acceptance, and occurs in the Relationship Garden. Couples manifest harmony in the stage of Integration; they can accept themselves and each other, even in face of disagreement. Whereas peace involves tolerance and requires agreement, harmony can embrace differences without strain.

The Spiritual involves oneness; hence there is neither agreement nor disagreement.

In order to find one's place in the infinity of being, one must be able both to separate and to unite. —I Ching[4]

Romance and Chaos

In the Romantic phase of relationship, the imagination of possibilities breaks through the rigid confines of each person's neurotic walls, resulting in the heady release of pent-up chaotic energy called being "in love." This condition is usually valued as a positive experience, even though it is similar in many ways to a temporary psychotic state; the *excitement* of Romance is deemed to be desirable, even though in other circumstances the same feelings would be called *anxiety* and would be negatively valued.

The surrendering of control that is so much the experience of Romance becomes possible because the imagination provides an illusion of safety and security, with the belief that the loved one either will be possessed or wishes to possess. Hence, walls and boundaries are dissolved in the promises of mutual concern and control, and the persons feel glad even in the midst of much turbulence. In this phase, as in all neuroses, the relationship narrows all consideration of the problems and turbulence that exist outside of the relationship. At this time, there is very little intimacy (by our definition of really *knowing* one another); however, there is a great deal of discovery of one another's world of imagination (which is no small feat in itself!).

Power Struggle and Chaos

When couples begin to know one another past their romantic versions, their protective bubble bursts to reveal the threats of harsh reality. This heralds the expression of each person's typical patterns of control—control of one another as well as of the relationship—to handle the hitherto denied turbulence. Most people become possessive, attempting to narrow their world to manageable proportions, walling themselves off from the rest of their social contacts. Control through bribery, jealousy, caretaking, guilt, placating, and blackmail are all too common symptoms of this process. If the controls are successful, the relationship may appear stable; nevertheless, under the surface the relationship becomes rigid and suffocating. The relationship's Zone of Optimal Integration ceases to pulsate, losing its vitality to all of its walls and regulations, and begins to slide toward equilibrium, carrying both parties with it. Inside the relationship, each person's own Zone of Optimal Integration also narrows, rigidifies, becomes walled and less pulsatile, contributing toward both parties becoming bored and apathetic, even while they remain secure. Personal growth becomes greatly restricted as each manages to contain turbulence within the walls and controls; creativity and learning both suffer. The spiritual sense of aliveness is replaced by a strict adherence to moral judgments and righteousness. Such a relationship ceases to be a garden for growth and becomes a prison for security.

Integration

If the Power Struggle is handled with sensitivity, care, understanding, and acceptance, the relationship enters a phase of Integration that progressively moves a further distance from equilibrium. The Relationship Garden expands to promote the growth of each of the individuals (which may include children) within it. Dealing with the turbulence of new ideas, novel experiences, travel to distant places and cultures, and deeper questions about spirituality and religion provides a kind of fertilizing effect on all of the inhabitants within the garden, as well as on friends and any others operating within this couple's sphere of influence. By integrating new insights into their everyday life, these kinds of relationships continue to expand the boundaries of each individual so that increasing amounts of turbulence can be encompassed.

Although control is frequently used to manage the chaos and differences in the Power Struggle, turbulence and diversity are welcomed in this phase of Integration. Being responsible for their own feelings allows partners a wider expression of who each person is. Instead of seeking compromise, each seeks to expand the range of understanding and acceptance, even though it may mean having to face jealousy, hurt, and insecurity. In this way, the Zone of Optimal Integration incorporates new life and greater growth.

The mind operates within the context of a body, which lives in an environment; the mind "couples" or associates experiences in these realms. For example, children that have been physically abused by parents would likely experience fear inside their bodies in the presence of authority figures. The mind has "coupled" the traumatic parental experience within the body; the body becomes set in this attitude, and is preconditioned to have similar reactions in similar contexts in the future. The very same process operates within all of those persons' encounters, sometimes having profound effects in their most intimate relationships.

The revelations of these coupled, often walled-off, experiences can sometimes become the central issue in the Relationship Garden, which affords a unique opportunity for healing and growth. In an atmosphere of understanding and acceptance, old coupling patterns can be challenged, unearthed, examined and tested in this nutritive, safe context that offers the possibility of a new contextual coupling. This is what therapy attempts to do with patients. In the same way, couples can learn in the dialogue of intimacy to uncouple their old habitual patterns of relating, and embrace new styles of interaction and mutuality.

A relationship that moves a further distance from equilibrium creates an environment of exploration and creativity. In this kind of "garden," each person supports the other(s) in uncovering old habits and discovering new things about themselves. When partners enter this zone of increased intimacy, many find it helpful to make a commitment to remain in relationship through what may become very difficult revelations. Couples can reach a plateau of comfort where they are able to accept much turbulence; this becomes an exciting milieu for sharing growth.

Notes

1. Dean Black, *Inner Wisdom* (Springville, UT: Tapestry Press, 1990), p. 42.

2. Martin Buber, *I and Thou* (New York: Charles Scribner's Sons, 1970), p. 14.

3. Dean Black, *Inner Wisdom* (Springville, UT: Tapestry Press, 1990), pp. 119, 120.

4. Richard Wilhelm & Carey F. Baynes, translators, *The I Ching, or Book of Changes*, 3rd ed. (Princeton, NJ: Princeton University Press, 1967), p. 17.

Understanding the Power Struggle: Some Useful Concepts

Understanding can permit shifts in perspective that allow people to move beyond the limitations of fixed attitudes and beliefs. Exploring relationship in the Integration phase often challenges people to *uncouple* their previous beliefs and assumptions and learn fresh viewpoints (see "Chaos and Relationships," p. 92). Besides the practical tools that have already been mentioned, people often find much use in concepts that can help them to understand and clarify their relationship issues. This section includes ideas that many have found important in understanding and working through the Power Struggle into further Integration.

Any Two Bozos

We take it as a dictum that *any two bozos can create an intimate relationship.* As a corollary, we maintain that it is easier to do this with some people than with others. As long as both parties are willing to reveal themselves to each other, to be honest, and to dedicate themselves to ongoing mirroring and feedback, their intimacy can deepen. This can involve people of the same or different sex, and applies to people of the same or different age. The important factor is that both people want to explore and be honest with each other, so they can work through the issues of the Power Struggle.

Why Exchange Charge for Intimacy?

Often sexuality interferes with intimacy. Usually, people find intimacy easier with a friend who is not a sexual partner. Although it is possible to develop intimacy with a sexual partner, this is not so easily accomplished. Usually, the sexual charge remains most intense with people whose intimacy is limited, while people who explore intimacy find that their sexual charge diminishes as the closeness increases. This dilemma will be further discussed (see "Sexuality and Relationships," p. 154).

As our cultural ideals have emphasized the importance of charge, why would someone want to move away from an exciting relationship into a more stable one? In moving through the Power Struggle stage, the tendency is for excitement between couples (sexual excitement included) to diminish over time; this occurs because the partners become more familiar with each other, and the excitement of the unknown objectified other is lessened.

Why not look for hedonistic satisfaction, more sexual excitement, or another obsession somewhere else, instead of trying to move into a growing intimacy? The answer is that sensual pleasure, sexual excitement, and the charge of romance are time-limited and tend naturally to diminish. The sensual pleasure of having someone minister to us has a short half-life; after a time of pampering, we want to get on with something else. So it is with the excitement of sexuality or obsession; they too have a half-life, and to maintain the level of excitement takes increasing demands on time and personal resources.

A growing intimacy does not decline in this way—it builds on itself, like a self-seeding perennial flower. Partners experience feelings of strength, security and an ever-expanding sense of fulfillment with the growing knowledge of one another. Excitement is a phenomenon that is doomed to decline; intimacy tends to grow to ever greater levels of order and satisfaction.

The satisfaction of intimacy is different from that which arises from the satisfaction of a power drive. Capturing another person, either in a romantic endeavour or by a sexual conquest, provides a sudden flush of achievement that does not last. Almost immediately, the uncertainty begins to creep in, and people try to maintain the control of the other. In sexual games, one has to prove oneself over and over again. In romance, more and more gifts seem required to provide the assurance that the beloved will not lose interest. And of course there is a natural tendency for partners in such games to lose interest over time and drift into the pursuit of some other person or activity. In sexual games and in romantic pursuits, people want to *capture the other's consciousness*; as Sartre wrote, this is doomed to failure from the beginning.[1]

Sliding Toward Intimacy

Earlier theories in psychology maintained that the basic human condition was separation, and that people would naturally default to isolation. We now propose that the original position is connection, and that the natural inclination is toward closeness (see "Resonance," p. 11). By being together, people all tend to slide to intimacy, just as if they were at the top of a slippery hill. If they let go, they will inevitably move by gravity toward becoming closer.

Most of us carry unconscious fears of intimacy ("I'm afraid if you know me, you'll leave me" or "If we get close, I might dissolve, or lose my sense of myself" or "If I let you get close, you might annihilate me"). Out of this fear, people generally offer resistance in the form of walls and defences, to prevent the slide toward intimacy. Ironically, these blocks, which people think serve to preserve them, are what prevent them from becoming whole, fully developed, and authentic.

Good Will versus Legalism

People's basic intent sets the tone for all their interactions. This applies to all relationships—family, friends, lovers, spouse, and business partners. *Many people would rather be right* (legalistic) *than happy* (vulnerable and intimate). In being legalistic, people are trying to trap their partners into a Power Struggle rather than sharing in the vulnerability of a revealing intimacy. With good will, people can take ownership of their own experience and, hence, avoid inflicting blame or guilt; they can share with honesty and curiosity, to develop an intimacy.

This involves the *spirit* of an interchange, rather than the content. If the basic intention is to be legalistic, the people will become snarled in a Power Struggle; if they intend to work through to Integration by way of vulnerability and sharing, they can say the same things, and the end result is quite different!

Staking a Claim

There is a difference between trying to control one's partner and staking a claim. The latter situation involves a declaration that one has made the partner important and is committing oneself to this particular relationship. When prospectors stake a claim on a particular mine, they dedicate their efforts to mining in that location, and remove their focus from other potential sites. Staking a claim in relationship is tantamount to saying "I will dedicate my time to you, and I am requesting that you do so too." In so doing, people establish a primary location in their relationship. They *claim their position* with their partner; they do not claim the partner's life.

I claim you, in the way I claim my lawn and garden at home. In so doing, I am indicating that I will maintain the garden of our relationship; I will put my efforts toward building ongoing interaction between us. I am not saying I own you; I am saying that I dedicate myself to living with you and growing with you. I claim a particular position with you.

Difference Between Claiming and Control

It is important to draw boundaries and to stick to them. And it is worthwhile pondering the difference between being able to claim what you want or need on the one hand, and trying to control on the other. Only the wisest of people can tell the difference beforehand. After the fact, it is easy. In separation, if it has been control, people feel wasted, hurt and resentful. If not, they will feel free and grateful for the experience, even though they may experience sadness; they are able to continue to honour all that they have created during their time together.

Coffin Nails

Any time a conflict in the Romance or Power Struggle stages is left unattended, the intimacy is threatened; a little of the life goes out of the relationship each time partners fail to communicate. When people choose to hold back, their energy becomes fixated; their life vibration is dampened, and they become less present. Increasing non-presence accompanies the slide into apathy or separation.

These fixations are like little deaths, and a relationship can withstand only so many of them before it dies altogether. Each unresolved issue is like a coffin nail that further limits the relationship. Because it is impossible to know how many coffin nails are needed to completely take the life from the relationship, wise partners deal with each issue as it comes up, no matter how painful it is to do so. This prevents the threat that could come with untold secrets or holding back information.

Prejudices and Fixed Beliefs Limit Intimacy

Prejudices (literally "pre-judgments") are simply interpretations that are deter-mined ahead of time. They are not true, nor do they accurately represent each specific situation; they are simply short-form instruments of prediction that are constructed by codifying past experience. They offer a convenient way for an insecure or immature person to understand the world, but they prevent knowing another as a person. Prejudices are guesses, approximations, that people can use to roughly align themselves with someone; they designate the thoughts and feelings that the judging person will have with that particular individual. However, if people accept their prejudices as true, they will never come to know the genuine human nature of the other. Rather than simply maintaining prejudices, people can share them with each other, and invite the perspective of the other; when this is done, dialogue re-opens. When people share that they are operating from feelings that represent their prejudices, they become revealed, open to new possibilities with themselves and others; this opens the gate to growth and intimacy in the Relationship Garden.

Ghosting

Closely related to the notion of prejudice is the concept of "ghosting." People do not know each other; they know their impressions of one another, which they generate within themselves, based upon interpretations of their sensory input, and synthesized with their memory of past experiences. The feelings one has for another are based on feelings for people previously known who have similar qualities. Often, one partner will relate as if the other were a parent figure, or a person from the past. So, when people are being defensive or argumentative, or trying to control, maybe it is not their partner that they are actually trying to dominate; often, they are trying to compensate for experiences with people in their past. For example, when one partner is afraid of sexual activity because of painful past experiences, that partner is "ghosting" a previous assailant upon the present partner. In this process, the other is objectified, and the relationship becomes fixated in the political struggles against the ghosts of the past.

If people are unwilling to acknowledge ghosting, the relationship remains stuck in Romance or Power Struggle. When this occurs, people maintain the image projection, and remain unaware of further possibilities of knowing themselves and their partners. They turn themselves into helpless victims of circumstance.

To move beyond this ghosting requires courage, dedication and honesty. When people acknowledge the ghosting, they are beginning to move past the limitation of the objectification; often both parties will have feelings to process. The person doing the ghosting often will feel resentful, then afraid, then guilty, then embarrassed and ashamed, as the acknowledgment steadily deepens. The person who has been objectified might feel hurt, enraged, indignant, sad, or compassionate. In the sharing of the feelings that accompany the objectification, both have the opportunity to know themselves and their partners more fully. Once again, this is a theme that is common in working through the Power Struggle—to share objectifications affords the possibility to open into new vulnerability, openness and interpersonal dialogue.

Doomed to Repeat

People are attracted to enter relationships to work out unresolved issues from childhood, and tend to project patterns and impressions from earlier times. The stages of Romance and Power Struggle are characterized by this projection of past experiences upon the partner. People are drawn to relate to a specific type of person, to fulfil cravings, desires and unmet needs. When people abandon the Power Struggle and go into Apathy or Separation, they are often just avoiding the lessons they could learn by sharing the underlying patterns and tendencies with their partners. Separation never solves the problem, because the unexamined patterns will simply show up in the attraction to the next partner. So people might as well work out their issues with the current partner; if they leave one relationship, the tendency is strong for them to simply find someone else of the same type again.

People are doomed to repeat their repetitive compulsion patterns in subsequent relationships until they know themselves and their choice of partners better. Only then are they free to relate with someone of a different type, or to choose the same type of partner with a more open-eyed interest in learning. What they don't learn in this relationship is still there to be addressed in the next one.

Afraid to Love

Some people say they are afraid to love, because they fear losing the person. They are afraid of the pain and grieving when the loved one eventually leaves. So they don't open, remain paralyzed, and don't experience their caring feelings. Then they feel empty, because they have closed off to what they want. Love involves risk and daring. If you don't dare to open the window, the breeze of love cannot enter. When people become more certain of their own autonomous loving, they are more free to feel for themselves, without the concern that the love object might be lost. Indeed, they could never have possessed the love object in the first place. You cannot keep the ones you love, but you can keep your loving.

> The deepest lesson you can ever learn in relationship is that you can't possess anyone. —David Fitzpatrick[2]

Alone and Lonely

As people become more individuated, they become more aware of being alone in their own skin. In relationships, the closer one gets to another, the more the separateness is apparent. People can share this aloneness as part of a genuine dialogue of intimacy. When people do not accept being separate, they feel lonely. *Feeling alone* involves self-acceptance; *feeling lonely* involves non-acceptance of self and life, with a yearning for circumstances to be different from what they are.

Some are afraid of intimacy because they fear facing aloneness; they involve themselves in power games (such as sexual promiscuity) or become dependent, as a means of *avoiding themselves* and their aloneness. Many of the issues of the stage of Romance and Power Struggle arise to avoid this feeling; amidst the illusions that characterize these stages, people often still feel quite lonely. In trying to fulfil an image of being joined to others through enmeshment and dependency, people feel isolated, because they are out of touch with themselves and their partners.

Guilt as Control

In guilt, people are refusing to look at themselves honestly. Instead, they objectify themselves as bad, and they punish themselves with guilt. No self-awareness comes this way, and the guilty person is often trying to control the partner by being guilty. How can the partner be angry at someone who is feeling so bad? So guilt can be a ploy to diminish the other's expectations. Self-recrimination is a convenient substitute for self-investigation, self-awareness and sharing.

In this way, guilt works against intimacy—*unless it is shared.* Sharing anything can enhance intimacy. The guilty partner could say, "I'm feeling insecure, and I recognize I'm afraid to look at myself. Thus, I'm busy feeling guilty instead of looking at my actions clearly. I want to tell you this, so you don't get wrapped up in trying to appease my guilt. My guilt is an attempt to manipulate you, and to prevent myself from looking at myself." Guilt shared in this way can be clarifying for the partner, and can open a door to intimacy and self-awareness again.

Possessiveness and Nonpossessiveness

In Romance and Power Struggle, people attempt to hold on to each other as possessions. The other becomes "my boyfriend" or "my child." In possessiveness, people maintain an objectification of the other. As people become more self-reliant, they are more willing to see others as separate persons. They can acknowledge the desire to hang on and own the other, and can share this as a way of letting go of possessiveness. As people become more stable in their relationships, they tend to celebrate their interaction with their partners, without having to possess them. One of the attributes that people in the Integration stage tend to prize is each other's freedom.

Becoming nonpossessive can look like not caring. Nevertheless, the most profound caring occurs when partners relinquish their ownership of each other and enjoy a relationship in which each is autonomous. They are then free of obligation or demand, and can choose to be together or not; this is the basis of the stage of Commitment.

Velcro Theory of Relationships

In life, people can make one another significant and special, and thus develop a consistent, ongoing relationship; when people fail to make another important, they remain isolated and their potential is not challenged. At the same time, people also have the capacity to become autonomous, and learn to let go of dependency on others; this letting go is especially poignant when a loved one dies, or in divorce.

In growing and maturing relationships, people need to learn both *to attach* (to bond, and make another important), and *to let go* (to relinquish infantile dependency and grow into increasing autonomy). A worthwhile gift for a young child would be a piece of velcro, with the instructions that the child should learn all about getting the velcro to stick together, and also how to take it apart.

Expectations

In the humanistic movement of the late 1960s, expectations got a bad name. By the ethic of those days, people followed Fritz Perls' gestalt prayer ("I am not in this world to live up to your expectations, and you are not in this world to live up to mine"). The "free spirits" who followed this ethic did not develop ongoing relationships; instead, they moved from one person to the next. The Perls poem was sometimes interpreted in a selfish and puerile fashion: it was taken by many to mean that they did not have to consider anyone else, and could proceed on their own solitary, uncaring way.

For a relationship to persist and deepen, expectations become important. People can gauge their distance or closeness by how many expectations they have. It is easy to love all the world and have no particular expectations of specific individuals. When people become closer and want to live in harmony, they find they tend to develop expectations of each other. Sometimes, expectations are the currency of intimacy. The closer people are, the more expectations they are likely to have of each other. Certainly, to use expectations as controls is very limiting; however, it is realistic to expect more of people who are the closest. Ultimately, after making a person important in your life and having acknowledged expectations, you must be prepared to feel emotional pain.

There is no justification for blame, or inviting guilt from the other, when an expectation is not met. People have expectations because they choose them, not because they have an inherent right to them. People certainly can have expectations; but they should be responsible for them, recognizing that they are generated within the person doing the expecting. Partners can agree to meet each other's expectations; but this still does not give them the right to have them fulfilled. Expectations involve a contractual arrangement, not a right.

Resentments are rooted in expectations. If people had no expectations, they would not resent anything; an easy way to reduce resentments is to lower expectations. Whenever people find they are resenting another, they could simply lower their expectations; however, with intimate partners or family members, this might become problematic, because the lowering of the expectations produces a greater distance.

The degree of expectations is related to how intimate one person is with someone; the more that is expected, the more special that person becomes. To have very high and very detailed expectations is a way to set a relationship apart from other acquaintances. The closer people are, the higher will be their expectations of each other. Often, pain and disappointment occur in both parties when an expectation is not met. The one with the unmet expectation feels abandoned, while the one who has not met the expectation feels remorse. One possibility when expectations are not met is for one or both to re-evaluate the agreement to be present together. Many times they choose to continue with the expectation, which represents a challenge for both to grow and develop.

Expectations can be negotiated. In a relationship, the fact that one partner continually fails to meet expectations that have been agreed upon is not a cause to resent or blame. This is a time to re-evaluate the expectations, and decide if both still want them. Perhaps one person wants to lower expectations, and thus have more distance (the other becomes more like everyone else). This has a consequence: in lowering expectations, the specialness that comes in being able to depend upon each other is lessened. Perhaps the person who has not been meeting the expectations decides to strive to do so, in order to maintain the level of closeness that expectations bring. Such issues are ongoing in the dialogue of intimacy.

Investment

Investment is a concept related to expectation. By investing in their partners, people dedicate interest and energy to the relationship with that person. The investment represents how important they have made the other—the less investment with someone, the less importance that has been assigned to them. This can be a rocky shoal to navigate. If people have no investments, they don't care very deeply; if they invest heavily, they will be prone to continually enter the Power Struggle.

The level of expectations indicates the degree of importance people assign to someone. With people to whom little importance is assigned, it is easy to have little expectation. If a casual acquaintance does not live up to an agreement, one can let this pass with very little concern. However, if a primary partner does not live up to even a small agreement, the other is likely to become quite upset, because of the degree of importance assigned to that person.

When people care, they invest; when they invest, they experience pain when hopes and expectations are not met. There is nothing wrong with investment; problems arise when people are not willing to face the discomfort that sometimes accompanies investments.

In the Romance and Power Struggle stages of relationship, people tend to complain over unmet expectations. Later, with more experience and maturity, they come to see that investment is a natural correlate of caring about someone else. In an intimate relationship, people can share disappointments without blame; blame limits intimacy, while sharing increases the feeling of closeness.

Trust

To trust someone else fosters field dependency and maintains the impotence that lies beneath the Romance and Power Struggle stages. Instead, people can learn to *trust their own evaluation of others.* If someone else wants to trust you, you should ask for a definition; if you are being trusted to do something you can't do, don't agree to it. Many problems in relationships could be averted if couples did not trust each other but, rather, clarified their expectations of each other.

In place of trust, couples can clarify their expectations of one another, define their boundaries and bottom lines, and enunciate the consequences that would result from any breaking of the agreements. Trust in the other is unnecessary. However, each person must be prepared to exercise the consequences of broken promises and generally to accept any accompanying pain without blame.

React or Respond

A *reaction* is a fixed behaviour pattern that expresses a closed attitudinal position. Hence, a reaction likely indicates a political stance. When partners are stuck in the Power Struggle, they tend to react in knee-jerk fashion, not to the person, but to an objectified other.

A *response* is a process of involvement that is personal. In responding, one is curious and considerate of both self and other. With response, one listens with interest, considers, ponders, attempts to see the merits in opposing views, and tries to learn in the situation, rather than simply "dealing with it."

Often, fixed reactions are habits from early life. Many times, especially at the beginning years of a relationship, partners find themselves reacting to each other from old prejudices and attitudes. As they become aware of this, they share these patterns; in being curious, they become more intimate with each other. In time, the reaction patterns become known, and one or the other can note that a reaction has just taken place, and invite a dialogue into the responses that humanize the interchange.

For example, if the husband arrived home later for a dinner the wife had prepared, her reaction might be to flare in anger, blaming him. Her response might be to become curious at how important she had made his coming home at a particular time, and search for the underlying meaning. As she probed, she might discover that she was feeling insecure and housebound, and she was afraid that his being late means that he might be less interested in her, and might be considering leaving her. So, in sharing her fear, she might feel sad and embarrassed. If he were not defensive, he could appreciate the vulnerability that she was offering.

Reactions maintain the Power Struggle. Responses are the royal road to personal interchange and growth through increasing Integration.

Pride

Pride limits intimacy. Whenever people become invested in their pride, they are more concerned for their image than in sharing themselves. They would rather be "right" than happy. Pride tends to feed a Power Struggle. In become vulnerable, people relinquish their pride and become more revealed as their genuine selves.

Contempt and Arrogance

Contempt involves elevating the self and devaluing the other in disdain. In contempt, one objectifies, devaluing the other person and life itself. Indeed, in this process, people also devalue themselves and their feelings; to be contemptuous, people step back from life and are out of touch with themselves as well as others. Contempt is usually a defensive posture that masks underlying feelings such as insecurity, fear, or pain. Hence, contempt is often a self-protective posturing. When people want to become closer, they can share their contemptuous feelings, and search for the underlying meaning that maintains the objectification.

Unlike *contempt,* which devaluates the other, *arrogance* overvalues the self in relationship to the other; the word is related to "arrogate," which means "to claim to oneself unduly" (from the Latin *arrogare*—to appropriate to oneself).[3] An arrogant person claims superior consideration or privileges, much as a child would. The positive aspect of arrogance is that it can be a step toward the establishment of high self-esteem when a proper perspective is learned in relationship to others. Although arrogance is often seen to accompany contempt, the consequences of each in relationship are very different; contempt always involves negative energy, but arrogance can further growth.

Indulgence

Indulgence involves an excessive involvement with a particular activity or thought or experience. To indulge in an activity means that the activity takes precedence over other people and situations; in this process, the person is often compulsively stuck in repetitious behaviour. This interferes with a relationship, because the indulgence takes precedence over interaction, and curiosity for the other is lost.

Most experiences are worth having for a limited period. However, when they become indulgent, they occupy more and more time, and the person becomes less present. Obsessions, jealousy, grieving, sexuality, work, food, self-hate, guilt—these are all delicious morsels that are attractive for indulging. Whenever self-hate is expressed for more than two minutes, be alert to the possibility that you are indulging!

Hope and Faith

To be in a state of *hope* interferes with intimacy. Hope anticipates a better circumstance in the future; hence, it is rooted in a dissatisfaction and non-acceptance of the present situation. In relationships, to hope for something different is to fail to contend with the situation as it is. By contrast, *faith* has a profound acceptance of how things are. In faith, people acknowledge and accept themselves and their partners, and are open to interchange.[4]

When a relationship reaches an impasse, as it frequently does, people who rely upon hope will focus on the future when things will be different. Too often, such people become passive and helpless, tending to freeze action while waiting for a favourable turn of events. On the other hand, when people in relationship have faith, they stay present to address themselves to the issues at hand with the assumption that they can make some positive adjustments; they know that no matter what happens, they have confidence in their capabilities to handle all difficulties.

Sulking and Pouting

People hurt when an expectation is not met. One can be responsible for one's hurt, realizing that it comes from one's expectations. Then the person would be vulnerable, and the hurt would be something to share.

To *sulk* is to hang one's head in dejection; to *pout* is to thrust one's lower lip in defiant displeasure. Sulking and pouting are self-pitying posturings that are used for control; often a sulk or a pout is a reaction to a hurt that the person does not want to feel. Besides the self-pity, the sulk or pout is often heavily laced with blame toward the partner for not providing what is expected. To move from Power Struggle to Integration, people can acknowledge that they are sulking or pouting, and become vulnerable by opening to share the hurt that the posturing is covering, without any investment in getting what they want.

Self-Centred is Not Selfish

To be self-centred is to have one's centre within oneself, rather than outside; this is a necessary condition for self-awareness and personal development in the individuation project. In being self-centred, people can remain aware of their own feelings while being sensitive to their partners; hence, they are responsive and open for contact.

Many people confuse *self-centredness* (which facilitates intimacy and Integration) with *selfishness*, which is a closed, power position. Selfishness is short-sighted. In selfishness, people are related to the image of themselves, and are out of touch with genuine feelings for self and other. Pride and indulgence are phenomena of selfishness, not self-centredness.

Selfish people move their centre from within themselves to place it in the other; the focus then becomes what the other person can provide, because selfish people, lacking a centre, cannot do things for themselves. Relationships then become mired in objectifying control for personal gain.

Self-centredness is not selfishness. Selfish people indulge in their own self-importance and fail to establish dialogue; self-centred, autonomous persons can be quite sensitive and responsive to others. Selfishness is objectifying; self-centredness permits intimacy. "Selfish" is a moral word; "self-centred" is a location word. They are not the same.

Field Dependence and Self-Reliance

In *field dependence*, the centre of focus is outside of the self. Children are taught to pay attention and obey their parents; they generally do, because of the insecurity of the infant position. This pattern of external dependency, watching for pleasure and displeasure in the field, becomes the prototype for later inter-actions. People learn not to pay attention to themselves; instead, they become increasingly concerned with whether or not others are pleased with them. When people are caught up in their partner's approval and disapproval, they are not self-directed, and remain inwardly weak, infantile, and undeveloped. This atti-tude of field dependence underlies the Romance and Power Struggle stages in relationships.

To become *self-reliant* means to acknowledge one's externalization and field dependence, and to take responsibility for it. In this process, people can shift their centre back into themselves, becoming *self-centred* (but not selfish!). Then, they are in Integration with themselves, and capable of engaging in intimate contact with another.

Dependence, Independence, Interdependence

Independence and dependence are flip sides of the same coin; they both in-volve having one's centre outside of oneself. Interdependence occurs when two autonomous people share without leaning on each other. Our own develop-ment has been most important to both of us:

> In our relationship, we started out as two ferociously independent people, afraid of clinging, or depending upon anyone else. As we opened to each other, we found we had unfulfilled desires to cling and be clung to (an early stage of loving, from the early childhood experience). Thus, we explored dependence. Not wanting to regress to mutually limiting forms, we agreed upon short-term excursions into dependency. As we became more comfortable with our depend-ence, we found we could share both our independence and depend-ence; hence, we entered a phase we call interdependence. In this, we are both autonomous, but willing to be vulnerable and share our own thoughts and feelings, while being open to appreciate those of the other.

Big Deal

What is a big deal for one partner isn't necessarily a big deal for the other, and vice versa. Both should remember that what one finds very threatening or chal-lenging might seem very small to the other. For example, if one person is afraid of heights, the partner might not understand his reluctance to go somewhere that she finds so easy. In the development of empathy, one learns to see the world as the other sees it. Often a wife expects her husband to be soft, warm and affectionate (a big deal to him because of his violent nontouching family history, but no big deal to her, from her touching family background). The same husband expects the wife to be compliant sexually (no big deal to him, but a huge effort for her, because of her history of trauma and abuse). To get past this, people need curiosity, compassion, empathy, and a willingness to see beyond their own entitlement and fixed perspectives. If people fail to see each other, they remain in the Power Struggle; in acknowledging each other's differences, they can move into Integration.

Humour and Intimacy

The early life struggles to achieve success are serious indeed. In striving for perfection, people grit their teeth, and have little room to enjoy the process. Indeed, under the strong thrust for achievement lurks self-hatred and self-doubt. In this driven pursuit, people do not open to themselves or others. Such people remain objects to themselves, and play roles to satisfy their intense striving. Hence, intimacy and self-awareness are both restricted.

As people gradually relinquish the goal of perfection in exchange for the increasing ease of self-compassion, they relax internally. They begin to enjoy the process of increasingly knowing themselves, drawing ever closer to their authentic nature. These people become more available to be known, and hence are more capable of forming loving intimate relationships.

When people become more comfortable with being revealed to themselves and to their partners, the seriousness of the goal striving is replaced by a hearty humour. As partners advance into growing Integration, Commitment and Co-Creativity, they find more humour and an increasing sense of play in life, loving, and relationships. The whole ridiculous affair is fun! Perhaps this is what the fabled Zen monks of old were laughing at, as they went about their daily existence with full hearts.

Grieving, Sadness and Depression

Grieving and sadness occur as part of a relationship when there is a loss—through divorce, or death, or when a beloved friend moves to another location. In both grieving and sadness, one is letting go of investment in the other. The greater the investment, the more extensive will be the sadness when that person is lost. Grieving is more complicated, as it involves incomplete feelings (such as anger, resentment and even love) that have been unexpressed in the relationship.

You do not grieve the person; you grieve your image of the person. What you are relating to in grieving is the store of held memories related to the experiences you have shared with that person. Partners who process through disappointments and disillusionments as they proceed in relationship will experience sadness and "missing" feelings, but relatively little grieving, when the person actually is actually gone, physically or emotionally. If one does not face up to one's investments at the time, they will have to be faced when the relationship ends. When people do not acknowledge their investments as they proceed, they remain tied to their partner after the person is gone. Partners who are responsible for their feelings and investments throughout the relationship will actually be experiencing sadness as they proceed, rather than storing feelings to grieve later.

In grieving, there is a mixture of anger, hurt, love, and sadness. The anger that people experience emanates from infantile attachments to the other as a possession—inevitable in any relationship of depth. In the grieving process, people are expressing blame of the departed one for leaving. So, grieving fully, with vocalized expression of emotions, is important in order to let go of the departed one. This proceeds more easily if the individual will acknowledge the resentment, disappointment, love, anger, and hatred directed to the departed. The feelings associated with grieving will wax and wane. In grieving, people must go through two aspects of anger—anger at themselves and anger at the other. They are angry at the other for having left, and angry at themselves for having entered into the relationship in which they have ultimately been left.

Underlying a *depression* can be incomplete and fixated grieving. Unexpressed feelings that are stored can become stuck in a chronic state of contraction that is experienced as depression. The person's emotional energy remains tied to the inner image of the other—indeed, there is none available for investing in other relationships. In such a state, the person being missed is held in internal (and possibly unconscious) memory and does not have to be released.

Grieving can be *sentimentalized*; public ritualized forms of grieving sometimes interfere with the genuine expression of grief and loss, which is personal and often private. In personal grieving, people often find deeper resources in themselves, and open themselves to new levels of loving, even after their partner has gone.

The price for a meaningful relationship is pain; there is no free trip. This inner pain cuts new channels into the bedrock of the soul; the person who will invest meaning in the other can mature and deepen. Paul Zweig has said that a person reaches a level of maturity, and can embrace the art of living, when they reach the age of pain.[5]

Notes

1. J.M. Russell, "Sartre's Theory of Sexuality," *Journal of Humanistic Psychology,* 19(2), 1979, p. 41.

2. D. Fitzpatrick, personal communication.

3. N. Webster, *Webster's Collegiate Dictionary* (Springfield, MA: G. & C. Merriam Co., 1947), p. 60.

4. B.R. Wong & J. McKeen, *A Manual for Life* (Gabriola Island, BC: PD Publishing, 1992), p. 60.

5. Paul Zweig, quoted in R. Bly, *Talking All Morning* (Ann Arbor: University of Michigan Press, 1980), p. 177.

Working Through the Power Struggle: A Practical Guide

In moving through the Power Struggle into the stage of Integration, some common roadblocks arise. This chapter includes a variety of topics which people have found useful in working through difficulties.

The Jerk

In relationships, each party holds a trump card. With the inevitable slide toward intimacy (see "Understanding the Power Struggle: Some Useful Concepts," p. 101), people will try to limit the intimacy by defensive behaviours. When all else fails, they pull out the trump card—*the jerk*. Everyone has a particular jerk. For some, it is an offensive jerk, who drives people away by churlish behaviour. Others use an addictive jerk; still others have a violent jerk. The selection of possible jerks is rich and varied: the pick-a-fight-and-then-leave-indignantly jerk; the victim jerk; the "I'll get sick" jerk; the blamer jerk; the guilt tripper jerk; the super-reasonable jerk; the leave-and-go-on-a-trip jerk; the go-into-alternate-realities jerk (crazy jerk); the "I'm too tired" jerk; and so on.

To develop a relationship, it is helpful to know which jerk(s) you have available, so that you can see what your defences against intimacy are. If partners can have good humour and are willing to share these defences with each other, they can facilitate their movement toward intimacy.

Secrecy Opposes Intimacy

Often partners are unwilling to share information, because they are afraid of the consequences—that the other might not accept the information, or that they could be ridiculed. When partners keep secrets from each other, they also keep hidden from themselves; intimacy is limited, and there is a much stronger tendency to objectify.

Intimacy flowers in the light and degenerates in the dark. For a relationship to deepen in intimacy, information must be shared. Many people maintain that a relationship will not tolerate all this honesty. They believe they have to hold back hurtful information to protect the partner. But when information is held back, there is an accompanying distance. Indeed, the entire attitude is objectifying, displaying a belief that the "weak partner" could not take such information.

We reject the view that people should keep some things back for fear of hurting one another. Being honest involves a respect for the capability of both partners. Furthermore, we believe that it is impossible for one person to hurt another's feelings; people's hurt is an expression of their own self-generated tightness, based on their own interpretations of events (see "Intimacy," p. 17).

The motive for sharing is also important. Some people provide information in order to try to hurt the other in retribution; even though this is impossible to do, people still might have the intent to hurt their partner. This is quite different than sharing the same information with the intention of having it in the open, so that the intimacy can deepen.

The price of such honesty is frequently pain; however, the reward is the stability that comes with having all the information available.

Resolve It Now

Any impasse in relationship is an expression of fixation of energy. Often a similar impasse had been reached previously with nuclear family members, and the same pattern is being replicated with the current partner. An intimate relationship is a unique opportunity to resolve issues from the past, so that people can become free from the tyranny of their fixations. If parents clear up issues in their primary relationship, then they will be free to raise their children without unconsciously indoctrinating them into the same fixed patterns. What the parents don't resolve themselves will be passed on down through the generations.

We recommend that people stay in dialogue to resolve issues, even if they are ultimately going to separate. Thus, they can become aware of their patterns of fixation, so that they will not get snarled up again in the next relationship. If they choose to stay together, they can become increasingly familiar with the limiting patterns, and can share their awareness about them, rather than blaming the other, and staying stuck.

Updating the Past

Many people have had trauma in the past and are now afraid to open to new experiences, because they think the old pains will be reproduced. They carry prejudices from the past experiences, and do not come fresh to the present. In one workshop we conducted, a middle-aged woman became stiff and frozen when she was invited to do an exercise with her beloved partner, which involved him tenderly opening her physical position from tightness into a relaxed open stance. Although she knew that he was a loving, sensitive soul, she had a flashback of a previous husband who had violently torn her open in the mornings to have sex against her will; when she embarked upon the exercise, she flashed back to her violent abusive husband, and went into the body memory associated with her fears of previous events. She was not responsive to her sensitive, loving partner. By succumbing to her body memory, she treated the new partner as if he were the old one. She knew her new partner was different, but reacted as if he were her previous husband, because she had a fixed association to the activity of opening.

This is the task in relationship—to update bodily and emotional responses to others.[1] With a developing intimacy, people can become aware of fixed reaction patterns and can acknowledge them, rather than unconsciously succumb to them. Thus, even though people might be afraid of touch because they had unhappy experiences with touch in the past, they could acknowledge that fear, and accept the touch in the present, recognizing that the motivations of the current person could be different from people in the past. Many times, a fearful person will need a code word and a definite agreement that the partner will stop an activity if the body memory becomes too much. When the partner demonstrates dependability, people can overcome even the most intense associations to the past.[2]

Clinging to Romance Prevents Growth

People can so easily lose themselves in an unrealistic pursuit of someone else, hoping to relieve anxiety, pain and loneliness. Although the fairy tale stories of the handsome prince rescuing the beautiful maiden are virtually impossible to realize, people are desperate to live out such fantasies. In Romance, people yearn to find someone special, who will relieve all the disappointments and discomforts in life (see "Developmental Stages of Relationships," p. 50).

In relationship, people are reluctant to give up their dream of a perfect Romance; instead, they impose all their (often unconscious) unmet hopes and desires onto the partner, and expect that the relationship will solve all problems. People are often miserable when they do not have a Romance; and they continue to be miserable when they discover that the partner is not living up to previous hopes.

Such individuals will continue to be unhappy until they accept that they are responsible for their own lives, and that no one else can solve the basic issues of their existence. When people come to know themselves more fully, they are usually more prepared to experience the pain of separation and aloneness—to give up the Romance, and enter day-to-day reality.

Entitlement Limits Intimacy

Early life experience is often one of entitlement. Children tend to think that they are entitled to their parents' attention and love. Parents often believe that they are entitled to their children's gratitude and time; they are amazed when their children would rather spend time with their friends than be at home with the family. If family members remain entitled, repetitive battles and disappointments will ensue.

When parents are entitled, sometimes their teenagers stay home out of obligation, rather than going out with their friends; in playing the role of good children, the young people often tend to resent the family, and can become distant. In a similar way, parents often experience the burden of their children's expectations for attention. Thus, family members who have fixated expectations of themselves and others can limit the intimacy that is possible within the family. In a similar fashion, husbands and wives can objectify one another, and become invested in roles and behaviours of themselves and each other.

To move through this requires acknowledging entitlements and sharing them without a demand that expectations be met. When people share in this way, they are revealed to each other, and can be close. As soon as control is imposed, the opportunity for intimacy fades.

Blame and Symptoms

Blaming produces much stress in the blamer. In order to make others wrong, people tighten and withdraw. Such moralizing constriction can produce diverse physical symptoms such as headaches, abdominal distress, arthritic pain, or heart problems, as well as a host of others. One individual who became stressed in his workplace described the evolution of his cardiovascular symptoms:

> *I am the heir of several generations of men who held back their intense judgments, and instead became ill with high blood pressure, strokes and heart attacks. When I am displeased with someone else, I can feel my blood pressure go up, and my chest tightens. I can see how, in a few years, I could develop this withholding of judgments and blame into a full-fledged myocardial infarction. The way out is to own the blame, and to share it with friends, and to breathe, instead of holding back the experience.*

When people are aware, their symptoms can be used as flags, warning them that they have become righteous or defensive. When people see their symptoms as signals of declining intimacy, they can share their experience with partners and friends. Instead of the blaming stance of "You make me so uptight!", it is possible to investigate the meaning of the symptoms with a question like the following: "I notice my symptoms are getting worse; I wonder how I am holding on and perhaps blaming you; have you noticed any clues that I might be carrying some unconscious resentment?"

In this way, instead of becoming barriers, symptoms may then be used to open into deeper dialogue.

Bottom Lines

The term *bottom line* is commonly used in business to indicate a limit or a basic requirement for a process to continue. For example, in a business enterprise, a bottom line might be profit; if the bottom line were not met for an appreciable period, the business would fold.

In relationship, the bottom lines indicate limits that people have with themselves and their partners. There are usually very few absolute bottom lines in a relationship. When a bottom line is not met, there is a consequence. For example, an absolute bottom line for some people might be that they would not stay in the relationship if they were struck physically.

Honesty might be a desirable bottom line; yet it might not be an absolute one. For example, if one person is inadvertently lying, and is unaware of this, the partners might discuss this rather than separate.

We recommend as a bottom line that neither partner tolerate violence (which we define as the crossing of boundaries). What constitutes violence is particular to each person; what is judged to be violent for one person and circumstance might be acceptable for someone else. For example, some people seem not to mind wrestling with their partner, while others will not even tolerate verbal chiding. This must be defined by the individuals; what is seen to be acceptable vehement verbal interchange to one couple might be judged as abusive by another.

It is not necessary that both partners have the same bottom line, although it is important for both of them to be aware of each other's limits. One partner might have a bottom line of growth, and the other might have a bottom line of security; they could still live in harmony if they were aware of these bottom lines. Bottom lines can shift; thus, they need periodic updating.

A bottom line can be used for intimacy or for control. Intimacy occurs through sharing the bottom line, and setting out the consequence if it is not met; control occurs if the intention is to threaten and limit the behaviour of the other, rather than simply to provide information. On the surface, these situations both look the same; the difference is in the intention (to get close through sharing information, or to gain control by threats).

Sharing Resources

People often become mired in conflict over who is providing more resources to the relationships. This is especially acute when one partner has more money to provide than the other. The superficial glance says that this is not equal, and that one partner should be acknowledged for the greater contribution. This misguided viewpoint is based on a reifying thought process that sees resources only in terms of finances—under this limited perspective, the balance sheet tells all.

Indeed, resources and offerings take numerous forms. There are basically four domains of resources:

1. Money
2. Time
3. Energy
4. Knowledge

Indeed, knowledge *is* energy. More specifically, it is the organizing principle, the pattern that contextualizes energy. Energy takes on form and becomes functional through the resource of knowledge and organization. When people have experience, they are able to direct and harness energy in synthetic and creative ways; it is their knowledge that takes disparate materials and organizes them into a structure that has definite function. For example, appreciating patterns and contexts is important in the construction and maintenance of a bridge; knowing the tensile forces and behaviours of the materials, one can build the bridge to withstand the challenges of nature. The more knowledge one has, the more efficiently and creatively energy can be utilized.

It is possible that equal partners in a business enterprise might not put in equal money. Perhaps one partner in a venture has lots of capital (money), but has little time to devote to the new business. To acknowledge the second partner's time and energy, the second partner could own 50% of the business on the basis of "sweat equity."

In marriages, often one person stays at home and devotes time and energy to raising the children and maintaining the household. The other partner devotes much less time to the home, and instead brings home the majority of the money. These partners might be entirely equal.

Sometimes, people are able to offer their wealth of experience (their knowledge). Their perspective, from having lived and experimented, can provide contextual offerings that make or break a relationship venture. Thus, the time and effort they have put into learning are resources that are available to the relationship. Many people misunderstand this perspective as patronizing the elderly, or simply rewarding people for past labours. What this limited attitude does not see is that the knowledge and experience—the context—is a resource, and many times a vital one. In a business enterprise, sometimes outside directors or consultants are paid handsomely to offer the resource of broad-based experience and sage creative process, which they have developed over years of dedication to their field.

Sometimes a younger partner provides the excitement and creativity of seeing things for the first time. This younger person might also do more of the physical labour in a partnership. The older person might be providing more experience and wisdom; this is equal to the offering of the young person, but quite different.

Couples become involved in a Power Struggle when they insist that each person contribute equal amounts of the same kind of resource. On the other hand, this awareness can be used to slothfully not pull one's load; just because one partner is well endowed with a particular resource, this does not mean that the other should not contribute whatever is possible. When people do have equal amounts of a particular resource, they should contribute this resource equally. Basically, in order for both persons to put into the relationship their full effort and dedication, they must offer whatever they have.

In one marriage, the wife was making a full salary but did not contribute any of it to the marriage, because her husband had considerable financial resources. The husband paid all the bills, because he thought that the man should do so. She used her money for her own interests. This was a parody of this differentiation of resources—with disastrous consequences. This couple did not stay together; they lost each other in the resentment of not having cleared their expectations with each other. And when they separated, she took most of the physical items from the home that he had purchased with his money!

At the beginning of a relationship, partners should discuss their expectations regarding the various resources, and come to agreements about what each person will offer. These agreements can be re-negotiated when the conditions change; nevertheless, making the expectations clear avoids the possibility of future confusion, disappointment and resentment. Although they don't have to contribute equal amounts of each resource, they should contribute what they can. At the beginning, it is useful to keep score of the contributions, especially in relation to financial contributions.

No Compromise

Generally, our culture wants two people in relationship to compromise, to each give up something in order to find a common middle ground. Such an approach attempts to reduce each person to the *lowest common denominator* so that they become lesser versions of themselves. We find that idea objectionable. In order to learn and grow closer, each person can clarify desires and intentions without having to abandon them. If someone were to ask, "What are you prepared to give up to have a relationship?" the life-giving reply is "Nothing; I'd rather not have a relationship than compromise." In compromise, people give up themselves, and there is less of them to offer. In our own relationship, we will never compromise.

We believe each party must acknowledge desires, and try to attain them. This is not a simplistic "follow your bliss" or "go with the energy" approach, which is irresponsible and insensitive. Rather, partners should respect individual differences, and put their desires on the table. Harmony comes in working out a solution that incorporates these desires, rather than denying them. When one compromises, one submits to the desire of the other, becoming reduced and limited. Generally, this is accompanied by resentment of the other, and often a hatred of the self. In acknowledging desires, one surrenders to one's life and becomes stronger, with more to share in a growing intimacy.

How do I know if I am compromising, or simply being open to the other's wishes? The clue comes with the presence or absence of resentment. If I am happy to go the movie you chose, even though I might have chosen another one, then I have not compromised; I am still aware that I want to see the movie I originally selected, and I probably will see it some time. If I resent you for not coming to the movie I wanted, then I did not choose to go with you freely; I was expecting you to change your mind. So, *no resentment indicates no compromise*; resentment and guilt and self-hatred accompany compromise. Unfortunately, such feelings may be repressed, and thus they might not be available as useful cues.

It is with this perspective that we say "negotiated peaces are impossible." Whenever a peace is maintained by a treaty, both parties have submitted, and have accommodated to gain some end, but have not happily surrendered to the differences. Hence, the peace will only last for a period of time; then the conflict will break out again, with ensuing resentments and blame. The territorial struggles in Europe over the centures give evidence of this phenomenon.

Acceptance of the other's differences without compromise creates harmony. In music, harmony can be between seemingly dissonant notes. There are no bad harmonies; sometimes accepting unusual combinations can give rise to complex and interesting interaction. Very dissimilar partners can co-exist in harmony, even with extreme differences. As long as they remain curious, acknowledging and accepting the differences without blame or resentment, they can live together without having to change the other, or reduce themselves. Instead of compromise or judging one to be right or wrong, the goal shifts to expanding the appreciation of the new ("dissonant") harmony.

Although one should not compromise, often realistic solutions to differences are in order. Once one has acknowledged a desire, one can choose not to follow the desire, without abandoning the self. For example, one person might want to go skiing; however, that same person might decide that he would rather stay home with his partner, who does not ski. He has not compromised; he has made a free choice to value being with his partner more than his desire to ski. This works easily when the situation is one in which the person has little investment.

However, when people feel strongly about something, they might not be inclined to yield on some basic issues. It is possible that transgression of a set boundary might result in strong consequences. For example, if a person has vowed that she does not wish to stay in a relationship where she might be hit, she would leave if her partner were to disregard this and strike her. In this case, she does not compromise her values, which she fervently holds.

Thus parents do not need to agree on how to raise their children. If they are fully revealed in their attitudes and feelings, they can know the differences without compromising. Once they know the differences, they can decide together how to be consistent in raising the child by agreeing to adopt one of their ways as the primary method, with a common purpose and will, without compromising their principles. If they are open and curious, they can move beyond the righteousness of the Power Struggle to find practical solutions to differences. In a harmonious family relationship garden, these differences can be openly discussed with the children who can participate in the decision-making process.

Desire and Choice

To be in relationship means paying attention to desires, while remaining open and sensitive to the feelings of one's partner. When people know their desires, they can choose to share them with their intimate partner, without having to follow them. We object strenuously to the current approaches that invite people to "follow the energy" with no regard for the partner. Couples can inform each other about their yearnings, and then can use this as a basis for discussion as to how both parties can get what they want.

A charged issue occurs when one person wants to sleep with someone outside the relationship. The "follow your energy" approach would have the person simply do that, with no regard for the partner. Often such activities are done in secret, which interferes with the intimacy. We recommend that partners discuss such charged issues openly, and decide together how they wish to deal with it. Most people will not accept the partner having an affair; however, they might accept their partners telling them about their attraction toward someone else, with the assurance that they will not act on it. Only in rare couples would one accept the other having the affair; nevertheless, if this were done with full revelation of the entire events to the intimate partner, they could still stay close. Perhaps instead, the partner could role play the desired object, and the desiring one could have some experience of having what he or she wants. We could summarize the situation as follows:

> *Between your head and your heart, follow your heart, unless your heart leads you into danger.*

Actions Demonstrate Desire

People's actions express their motivations and desires. Denying responsibility for one's actions maintains the Power Struggle; acknowledging one's responsibility for actions invites the dialogue of the Integration stage. Both parties can acknowledge that whatever they are doing, they actually want to do this. Although such desires are often unconscious, there is no room for the ready defence of "I didn't want to do what I was doing." A more revealing statement might be: "I recognize that I was thinking about something else, and didn't listen to what you said; I obviously did not value being with you as much as I valued my thoughts." Although this degree of honesty is challenging, it can help to avoid many unnecessary disputes, and keep the relationship from reverting back to the Power Struggle.

Sexual Charge With Others

Commonly one partner will have a sexual charge for someone not in the relationship. Because the sexual charge is based in objectification, this is quite normal, and to be expected (see "Sexuality and Relationships," p. 154). Many partners believe that they should only have a sexual charge for each other, and that something is wrong when they feel excitement over someone else.

There is nothing in this that needs to be a problem. To acknowledge to the partner that one has sexual feelings for someone else can be an act of intimacy. Because there is such a pressure to suppress such feelings, the sharing can bring new vitality into the relationship; the energy that might be consumed in hiding such information would become available to the partners. Both partners would likely become vulnerable with such a degree of honesty; rather than become defensive or blaming, they could remain open to each other to share the feelings of threat that would arise from such candour.

As mentioned above, it is not necessary (and likely undesirable) to actually act on such desires. But to report the charge to the partner keeps an open line of communication in the intimate relationship. Rather than denying or hiding sexual feelings for someone else, people can share these with their partner, to enhance their intimacy.

Gossip

Gossip is talking about someone when that person is not present. When gossip is withheld, intimacy is lessened. This commonly occurs in families, when two people talk about a third; this limits the sharing and interaction that are possible. Certainly, there is no problem with talking about someone when that person is not present, if what is said is reported directly to that person at the first opportunity. When gossip is kept in the open, families, businesses, and friendships can flourish in the atmosphere of openness.

Sharing Violent Thoughts

Violence occurs whenever there is no consent. Hence, for two friends in a karate duel, there is no violence to being struck, as they both agree to such a physical interchange. On the other hand, there can be violence in caretaking someone who does not want attention. We believe that no person or object should ever be injured; hence to us, it is never appropriate to strike a partner. However, in many cases it might be acceptable to use words to describe violence. For example, some couples might not allow physical blows, but might accept being called names in the heat of a disagreement, in order to express all the energy of the interchange.

Couples can agree to describe violent fantasies about the other—for example seeing the partner hurtling through a plate glass window, or imagining administering pain to the other. Sharing the fantasies permits the energy of the disagreement to be expressed without any real danger. Furthermore, there can be a vulnerability in actually revealing such thoughts, which are usually unacceptable; this vulnerability can work for more closeness when it is respected rather than rejected.

Overcoming Numbness

From time to time, most people find themselves out of touch with their feelings and caring. Even people who are dedicated to the relationship project can occasionally close off and become numb, lacking empathy and losing presence with themselves and their partners.

Curiosity and memory can be used to overcome such blunting of feelings. Sometimes the investigation of how presence was lost brings people into touch with some deeper feeling they were avoiding; breathing consciously and looking for unacknowledged feelings often helps. When people don't feel, they can remember that they have previously had feelings. In recognizing that this is a temporary situation, they are less prone to sink into despair over their current numbness; they can relax while they wait to find their way back to feeling again. Also, becoming curious about the other person can overcome dullness of feeling, and return them to a state of presence. Sometimes, the pain in the eyes of one partner (who is missing the dialogue) can summon the other back to presence.

Time Out

Either person can request a "Time Out" rather than persisting in repetitious defensiveness or explosive uncontrolled behaviour. Both parties should honour a request for Time Out, temporarily halting the exchange. The partners agree when they will talk again, before they leave the interaction. After they have had time to consider the situation separately, they can come back to the interchange—hopefully with fresh eyes and less defensiveness.

Five-Minute Cling

In our own exploration of independence and dependence, we made some unexpected discoveries.

> Jock discovered to his horror that he actually liked to cling like an infant. Having been ferociously independent (he kicked his own parents away when they were diapering him), he opened up to new levels of vulnerability in himself when he began to acknowledge his need to cling and be dependent. Ben's fear was that someone would want to fasten onto him, and thus he avoided situations in which

someone would cling to him. Consequently, they both had some-thing to learn.

The solution to this dilemma was *the five-minute cling.* Jock could hang on like a two year old for an agreed upon time, and Ben would commit to remaining present with him during this short period. This clinging always required an agreement, as Ben possibly would not be available at the time of the request. In living this through, we each have faced our fears, and have come to more acceptance of our defensive avoidances. Jock can now enjoy clinging without demanding prolonged attention; Ben has learned that he can survive in the face of Jock's dependency without being overwhelmed.

We have talked about this in workshops over the years, and now other people have come to use the Five-Minute Cling principle, too. The clinging partner can learn to accept not having a cling on demand, and can sink into the experience of having one when it is possible. The person who is being clung to can face the fear of being smothered or restricted, realizing that the event is time limited. Just because the request for a cling comes does not mean the other is obligated to do so; possibly it is inconvenient at the time of the request. Both partners learn a sensitivity to the desires and boundaries of the other by working out these arrangements. By facing the underlying fears and accepting infantile cravings, the charge diminishes in the situation, and both partners gain more autonomy through the process of sharing.

Checking Out

Checking out with someone else involves sharing one's experience, and then asking questions to find out the other's perspective, rather than merely assuming it. In the process, the initiating person expresses perceptions, interpretations and feelings, and then asks the other person to report his or her corresponding perceptions, interpretations, and feelings. This requires *curiosity,* and the recognition that one's partner can easily have a different viewpoint on a situation.

Checking out one's impressions is one of the most important tools in developing an intimate relationship. In the fixed attitude of objectification, people continually represent others from their own prejudices and background experience; they believe that they know the experience of another without checking it out. If they do not ask about the perspective of the other, they will often be proceeding on limited or invalid information. When people do not check out their assumptions, they persist in the limitations of Romance and Power Struggle.

When they do check out their assumptions, they invite a dialogue with the other, which can lead to intimate sharing and more Integration.

Dumping and Clearing

A dumping is not a clearing. When an individual expresses perceptions, thoughts, or feelings without curiosity about the response or feelings of the other, this is a dumping (like having a bowel movement). A dumping is only an impulsive catharsis of feelings and judgments, without interest in a genuine dialogue with the other. The other is kept as object, and the self remains fixed in habitual prejudices (literally, pre-judgments). Dumping involves blame and guilt, and hence is frequently used in the Power Struggle stage.

By contrast, a clearing includes acknowledging one's intentions, and curiosity about the other; a clearing involves questions to discover the viewpoint of the partner. In a dumping, both parties are objectified; in a clearing, they are experienced as persons.

Clearing can involve past issues as well as present ones. Often, partners decide to become more intimate after they have been in relationship for a number of years with each other; by this time, they have accumulated a backlog of unexpressed impressions, assumptions, resentments and appreciations. In the present, they can clear up issues from the past, and thus become engaged in their mutual impressions of the events, rather than remain fixated in their own individualistic judgments.

Clearing Time Each Day

Just as people can adopt an exercise regimen, they can commit to spending time each day to process and become clear in their relationship. This should be done when there are no distractions, because it demands special time, with sharing and specialness and presence. This is a time for contact and mutual exchange; partners take an interest in the activities, thoughts, and feelings of each other. With regular time for clearing and contact, people who lead autonomous lives can be in touch with each other's process, even though they still have separate interests and activities. Business partners can meet early before the day's work for clearing; family members can agree to meet over a meal once a day; husbands and wives can agree to uninterrupted time together in the evening.

We recommend that partners endeavour to keep up to date, and stay clear with each other, rather than permitting unspoken information to accumulate. Just as some birds continually clean their nest to keep it tidy, when people stay current with each other, psychological refuse does not build up to contaminate their relationship nest.

Status Report

Businesses often function with periodic reviews, to see if they are on track with the goals of the enterprise. In raising a vegetable garden, an intermittent check of the condition of the plot is very useful; this would involve checking the moisture of the soil, looking for parasites, and generally assessing the health and growth of the plants themselves.

At any time, couples can request such a review of the relationship garden in the form of a *status report*. This is a particular use of clearing and checking out, where the focus is on determining the state and health of the relationship itself. By periodic review, partners can keep track of ongoing issues and expectations, and evaluate the development of the relationship garden. An in-depth query of each other would include questions such as the following:

> *"What were we hoping for?" "Are we achieving it?"*
> *"Where have we failed?" "What can we do about this?"*
> *"What are we very satisfied with?"*
> *"Where is there room for improvement?"*
> *"What pleasant surprises have we had?"*
> *"What unpleasant shocks have we weathered?"*
> *"How are we feeling with each other in the midst of our relationship project?"*

This review would also include volunteering information such as:

> *"The things you have done that I have appreciated about you are ...."*
> *"The things you have done that I have resented about you are ...."*

The Positive Use of Power Struggle

The Power Struggle stage, full of passion and excitement, involves the investment of people's life energy. When people learn to *share* the elements of their

Power Struggle, they can come to increasing self-awareness and self-acceptance, moving beyond self-righteous, fixed positions into a genuine curiosity and engagement with others and all of life. In this way, what are usually destructive elements (such as jealousy, possessiveness, control, anger, expectations and blame) can be shared in a responsible, growth-enhancing way (see "Intimacy," p. 17, "Feelings and Closeness," p. 34, and "The Stage of Integration," p. 73). In this way, people can come to know themselves and their partners more deeply in a steadily developing Integration of their lives. The elements mentioned in this chapter provide some of the major areas that people can address in the development of their relationships.

Notes

1. B.R. Wong & J. McKeen, The Walking Wounded: A Way of Life, *Journal of Child and Youth Care, 7*(3), 1992, pp. 79–89.

2. B.R. Wong & J. McKeen, Memories of Abuse—A Call For A Balanced Perspective, *Journal of Child and Youth Care, 10*(3), 1996, pp. 67–81.

Love, Obsession
& Addiction

Love Is Junk

While in private practice, we commonly saw young people suffering from the termination of relationships. Having lost a loved partner, their symptoms included depression, anxiety, insomnia, weeping, low energy, loss of appetite, withdrawal of interest from normal activities, self-doubts, ideas of being worthless and unlovable, and, often, unpredictable episodes of anger and rage. At other times, we were being consulted by young people withdrawing from drugs such as alcohol or heroin (known on the street as "junk"); remarkably, their symptoms were similar to those recovering from separation from a loved partner. It soon was apparent that the people suffering from loss of relationship were behaving just as the people who were withdrawing from drugs—they were all addicted! Whether people are addicted to drugs or people, they all go through common symptoms of withdrawal. How does this happen?

Becoming addicted is easily done. If healthy people were given insulin over a long period of time, their bodies would shut down self-production of this chemical. After a while, the body would lose most of its ability to make insulin, and thus would be entirely dependent upon outside sources for its well-being. A similar phenomenon occurs when people are fed a high sugar diet (quick energy source) for a long time; they lose the ability to mobilize energy from their own metabolism. The process is the same for growing children whose emotional needs are always quickly met and never frustrated. Gradually, they develop a sense of *entitlement*, believing that it is their inherent right to such care. Being constantly "loved" (or more accurately, given too much attention), their own loving generator plant is rarely exercised. They grow dependent upon others—rather than themselves—to take care of their emotional needs. They have become effectively "hooked" to outside sources for these needs.

People who emotionally "hook" (addict) others to themselves do so because of their own sense of inadequacy and lack of real meaning in their lives. In a way, they themselves are dependent upon others depending upon them. This condition is common, beginning when parents "think the world of" their children, rarely allowing them to stray from their sight. Unfortunately for both parents and children, such overly solicitous parenting can be a symptom of *obsessing* rather than recognizing and highly valuing that person; these parents need the affection, attention, and compliance of their children for their own sense of value in life. Sometimes such an obsession (called "love") over the children is a convenient way for a couple to avoid dealing with very real problems in their own relationship. A cartoon in the *New Yorker* magazine showed a middle-aged couple, their arms around one another's shoulders, looking out of their living room picture window, with the following caption: "Well, dear, now that the children have all grown up and left home, it's just you versus me!"

This obsessive parent-child interaction provides much *attention* to the children, but little *recognition*. This attitude frequently results in offspring who are unable to make effective commitments and meaningful relationships. They tend to suffer from a low sense of self-esteem, and worst of all, they can develop high expectations of others and unrealistic levels of entitlement for themselves. When they become emotionally involved with others, they want to control and possess them, and to blame them for everything that happens in the relationship. Unfortunately, these are the kinds of relationships that society has idealized. Love songs (mostly "country") fill the radio waves with plaintive proclamations that "I can't live without you" and "You light up my life" so "How am I supposed to live without you?" Our ideal love stories (for example, *Romeo and Juliet*) would have us kill ourselves rather than face life without one another.

Remarkably, in the subculture of addictions, drug suppliers ("pushers") are sometimes referred to as "mothers" by the addict. Pushers will sometimes offer free drugs at the beginning until the recipient has become dependent. This process is similar to the sugar example give previously. The body's own mechanisms tend to shut down, allowing the drug to take over those functions that variously provide a sense of well-being, excitement, or relaxation. Once hooked, that person requires a regular external source to feel whole. The drug addict and the person addict have much in common. No wonder that their withdrawal symptoms are often indistinguishable from one another!

Once pushers have succeeded in establishing the addictive pattern of needs, they have the ultimate control. If the pusher determines that some of the addicts' behaviours are inappropriate, the threat of withdrawal of love will soon make them conform. Over time, as the addiction increases, the price of supplies can escalate, and the pusher thus has increasing control over the addict's life. As with all addictions, the person's very soul is eroded and the Self is lost. The only recourses the addicts see seem limited and self-abusive. They can threaten to switch pushers, substituting one addiction for another; or they can threaten to suicide, either figuratively or through symbolic self-destructive behaviours (such as accidents, physical and emotional illnesses, job losses, or criminal activities).

The Pie Theory of Love

Many people see their love like a pie that can be sliced and exchanged in a variety of ways—a large slice for my partner, perhaps a similar-sized one for the children, a smaller one for work, and maybe even a smaller one for friends. People who live their lives this way keep a wary eye on the proportions served to each of the parties in their lives and on how much is returned. They become nervous and jealous when they believe that they are not being given their "fair" (meaning "expected") share. They are prepared to barter the amounts, and can go crazy attempting to balance the accounts by the end of the day. As they grow addicted to the slices, they nervously live on the brink of anxiety attacks, in fear of losing the share that they now believe they deserve and need. They seek as much attention as possible (instead of nourishing recognition) to satisfy their craving to fill their sense of emptiness. Their own measure of self-worth becomes tied to the relative size of the love pie that is given to them by their partner, children or friends.

Operating with this theory of love contributes to the creation of obsessions and addiction to others. Such people no longer operate from their own centre; instead, their centre is moved from within themselves to somewhere between themselves and others—or in the extreme, completely in the other person! Their own capability of loving is replaced with a desperate need to be loved by somebody who resembles their "microdot" (see "The Stage of Romance," p. 56). To capture the consciousness of the desired object may require a submission to that person and an abandonment of the self. Once they capture their prey, they must constantly monitor their victims, to ensure that they will not be able to escape. Thus they create an obsessive life style, in the name of love.

Obsessions and Compulsions

An *obsession* is a repetitious thought that one cannot dismiss. For example a student often will become obsessed with the ideas that are studied, and cannot shut off the thoughts to go to sleep at night. A *compulsion* is a repetitious action that is dictated by an obsession; the obsession is the thought, and the compulsion is the action that is linked with the obsession. For instance, one might be obsessed with the fear of germs and contamination; the associated compulsion might be repetitious hand-washing. Often, an obsession is an habitual thought process that provides the security of the familiar; people will often obsess in order to avoid uncertainty. For example, if people devote their time to worrying about the future, they have less time to be anxious in the present. Worry is often a substitute for anxiety.

People become obsessed with another, in order to try to overcome the infantile fear of abandonment. At the root is the existential condition of *aloneness*, and the *angst* of existence. The insecure child becomes obsessed with the parent, trying to *capture* the parent's attention, in order to avoid being abandoned. The pattern of trying to capture someone else in relationship becomes set; as this individual establishes relationships later in life, the desire to capture the partner will still be operative. Such obsessions give rise to driven activities, such as telephoning the partner numerous times each day, just to check; another compulsion is stalking the partner, watching outside the home, to spy on the partner's activities. The obsessor's life activity can be entirely taken up with the obsession. The movie *Fatal Attraction* is an excellent on-screen depiction of the chilling disintegration of a competent person through obsession, and the disastrous results that can occur.

Hunter and Hunted

This desire to capture the other is often seen as love. In fact, it is quite otherwise—this desire to capture is what kills love! Because the obsession aims to capture the objectified other, there is no acceptance of the self or the other—and thus there is no loving. Obsession is a prison for the obsessor; the person is not able think or move freely, or be creative. The relationship cannot develop, as all the activity is directed to controlling the other; this is merely a simulacrum of loving. In movies and television, such relationships are seen to be loving, because the parties devote much *attention* to each other; however, this is not genuine caring, as there is no *recognition* of the other. In this prison, the obsessor is trapped, because the key is lost.

Obsessions and Compulsions are Deadly

In an obsession, one abandons oneself and bargains away vitality in exchange for the security and charge of the repetitious thought process. The reward (or

the aim) for an obsession is twofold: there is the similitude of control and domi-
nance, which provides excitement and charge, and there is temporary relief from
anxiety. Obsessions limit people's lives; when people obsess, they don't have
room for more frightening thoughts and feelings. They don't have to face death
or abandonment or aging or impotence or unimportance; they only have to
focus on the obsessions and compulsions themselves. Even though obsessions
can seem so intense, they are death oriented; people lose themselves and their
vitality, and become consumed by obsessions.

Obsessions involve objectification. The Romance stage is filled with obsession
and compulsions; people fantasize and obsess about an imagined other that
they do not know, and then when they find someone, they devote themselves
to the one they have found. In the Romance stage, the relationship is not with
the person; people are often addicted to the object of an obsession. In the same
way, the sexual charge is a repetition compulsion; in the excitement of pursuing a sex object, people tend towards robot-like repetitive thoughts and behaviours that are diminishing of the person. In this way, romance and sexual charge
are similar to other addictive processes; the person is not present. The pursuit
of the object is deadening, but exciting!

Dealing with Obsessions and Compulsions

We should be master of our obsessions; they should not master us. By becoming aware of the obsessions, acknowledging and accepting them in a process of
sharing, people can find the key to the prison. As people become more familiar
with their obsessions, they can become more free with them, able to enter the
obsessions for a limited time for excitement and play, without having to become trapped in them. Thus, couples can have a romantic dinner with each
other, knowing all the while that the pressures of life still exist; or they can
share a sexual fantasy together without having to make it the raison d'être of
their lives.

When obsessions are not shared, they tend to intensify in the secrecy; although
this might increases the charge (which is addictive), it makes intimacy impossible. As people share their obsessions, the level of intimacy goes up, and the
charge diminishes. The key to overcoming an obsession is to become familiar
with it and its underlying motive of seeking security. As with jealousy, the problem arises when people try to *control* their partner instead of acknowledging
their insecurity. As people become more aware of their obsessions, they can
share these with their partners, acknowledging the motive for the compulsions

that accompany them. Thus, they reveal the underlying process, and utilize the awareness to bring more integration in their relationship.

The Empty Bucket Theory of Love

Another common idea of love that governs parent-child relationships is the "Empty Bucket" theory. In this view, people see their children as coming into this world as empty vessels into which "responsible" (read "obligated") parents must pour their "love." The theory supposes that if parents are successful, they will fill their children's buckets sufficiently so that they will have enough in their tanks to be able to find partners into whom they can pour this "love." If all goes well, they will be able to have children of their own into which they can undertake to do the same.

Because this theory relies entirely on outside sources for the supplies of a commodity—"love"—it sets up ideal conditions for the development of an addiction. The more people depend upon others for love, the less they will generate their own; their love-generator will gradually shut down and they will be totally dependent for supplies from others. In such a way, more love addicts are created. For the pushers, the more they can get others addicted to them, the more secure they will feel in life; they never need to be alone again!

> BEN: When I was in private (psychiatric) practice, it slowly dawned on me how essential I was becoming in the lives of my patients. Many of them could not function without me. To my horror, I realized that once I had addicted them to me, they were only able to separate from me by replacing that addiction with prescribed drugs. At best, I was able to encourage them to become addicted to others, to work, or to religion. Once I realized this, I hastened to encourage them to withdraw their centre from me and return it to its proper place within themselves. Establishing opportunities for them to have group experiences instead of private, individual therapy helped; but it was important not to provide a group support that would encourage further addiction. Consequently, Jock and I always discouraged the idea of a therapeutic or spiritual community.

The solution to such addiction is for addicts to take charge of their own lives and well-being. As people take responsibility for their own feelings and activities, they are less prone to the manipulations of those who would like to hook them into addictive behaviours. The movement beyond the Power Struggle into

Integration involves people becoming the authors of their own lives, thus overcoming their dependencies.

A Wholeness Theory of Loving

Both the "Pie" and "Empty Bucket" theories of love have roots in the idea of dependency in relationships; so they are natural precursors to the establishment of co-dependency and addiction. A more wholesome approach involves the concept of personal responsibility with the self and in relationship; this is embodied in the Communication Model that we teach. Instead of being empty buckets, people are seen to be whole beings that generate all of their own feelings—the hurts as well as the loving ones, in response to what they perceive and interpret. People do not *allow* their "buttons" to be pushed; indeed, they do the actual pushing of their buttons! People are never empty; they are always complete, although they keep much of themselves dormant as unrealized potential. When people meet somebody they like, they are stimulated to generate feelings of loving from within their own centre; if they are self-assured, or wish to become so, they will remain open and vulnerable to share such feelings with the other, in this way establishing an intimate relationship. We propose that people *always* have the capability to generate some loving—even though they might not choose to do so out of fear or insecurity. Often, people choose not to love out of a motivation for revenge and anger—even though they themselves, not others, suffer the most!

Contrary to the "Pie" theory, there is not a finite amount of pie that can be divided among loved ones and friends. Instead, each relationship is a full pie unto itself, into which people are capable of contributing *all* of their current feelings for the other person without lessening in any way their loving for their primary partner or their children. Instead of being diminished and exhausted by loving, people can feel refreshingly expanded. The energy does not belong to the individual, and does not have to be measured out or hoarded; it is universal and ever present as potential that only requires stimulation in order to resonate (see "Resonance," p. 11).

As people develop a confidence about their own wholeness, and are prepared to generate and share much of their own feelings, they find an increasing sense of self-esteem and autonomy. In growing children, this is fostered by parental attitudes that encourage responsible, self-supporting behaviour, providing them with experiences of *recognition* for who they really are as persons, instead of *attention* for what they do in their roles. In such an atmosphere, people come to realize that they are not empty buckets in search of others that are prepared to provide them with love; rather, they are full of the possibility for loving. They only need to be stimulated to kickstart their loving generators, and to learn appropriate people and places where they can express their love in relative safety. Such learning does not come easily; nor are there many role models for them to emulate. The Relationship Garden is one place that can support such an education in life.

An Image

Picture a young, fragile, tender sapling growing alongside a strong, straight, well-rooted oak tree. If the sapling develops by leaning on the stronger oak tree, its roots will stay shallow, seeking nourishment only in relation to the oak; its trunk will be bent from leaning; lacking in robustness, its branches will be short and puny, its leaves sparse and small, receiving little of the bright sunshine. Such a co-dependent relationship fosters weakness in both trees.

On the other hand, picture the oak refusing to support the sapling any more than is necessary, refusing to allow it to lean; the young trunk will grow straight and tall, the roots will be wide-spreading, seeking nourishment from a broad area. This kind of sapling grows in strength, with its branches spreading wide to mingle with those of the oak, its leaves full of colour and richness, dancing with the breezes in the sunshine and the rain. Together, they brace against the storms of adversity, and are cleansed by the gentle rains of compassion. Through the years, they continue to grow in strength and complexity, each fulfilling its own destiny.

Weeding the Garden

In a relationship garden, each person must be true to himself or herself, accepting the nourishment that is there available for all within the garden's boundaries. There are many weeds that need to be identified and removed; the control weed is the most virulent. Control strangles growth, expecting others to become what you want them to be, rather than who they really are. Although there are many obviously negative control weeds (such as manipulation, lying, cheating, withholding, withdrawing, terrorizing, threatening, bribing, blaming, threats of self-destruction, guilt, self-pity, mental and physical illnesses), the more covert ones are the most dangerous because they are more confusing. These covert controls include some apparently positive strategies such as being nice, being helpful, taking care, and being supportive; these all are performed ostensibly for the welfare of the other, even though underneath, they are primarily for the benefit of the caretaker's sense of value.

Before these weeds can be pulled, they first must be identified. This is an important task that can only be accomplished through curiosity and an established agreement between the partners. It is most beneficial when each is prepared to openly acknowledge any attempts at control. Healthy dollops of humour and humility really help, as do self-compassion and the "Four A's" of Awareness, Acknowledgment, Acceptance (of the self as well as the other), and the Action required to move beyond fixations. In such a healthy, open environment each person can be nurtured into growth.

> A complete sharing between two people is an impossibility, and whenever it seems, nevertheless, to exist, it is a narrowing, a mutual agreement which robs either one member or both of his fullest freedom and development. But, once the realization is accepted that, even between the closest human beings, infinite distances continue to exist, a wonderful living side by side can grow up, if they succeed in loving the distance between them which makes it possible for each to see the other whole and against a wide sky!
>
> —Rainer Maria Rilke[1]

Notes

1. Rainer Maria Rilke, *Letters of Rainer Maria Rilke* (New York: W.W. Norton, 1945), p. 52.

The Family Garden

Learning how to relate begins in the family garden, where people establish feelings of security and insecurity that they will carry for the rest of their lives. The child is born into the context of the parents' relationship. Different children in a family can have very dissimilar learning situations depending on what stage of relationship the parents are in when they are born. Each phase in the parents' partnering provides a specific milieu that can either help or hinder the child's personal growth. The best conditions for child-rearing occur when the couple is in the stages of Integration, Commitment, or Co-creativity. Too often children are born while the couple is struggling to know the ground of their relationship; then the children are objectified, sometimes sent away to boarding school or simply ignored at home. When children are born in Romance, they might not learn valuable lessons about the realities of life. The atmosphere for children is most destructive when they are objectified and used as weapons or bribes during a Power Struggle. The milieu is most nutritive when the parents have an interest in their own personal development, and are intimate with each other.

Roles

At the beginning, relationships are object to object, first in the mother-child paradigm, then expanding to include the father-child, then to the brother-sister objects. The project of *intimacy* involves moving beyond these objectifications to practice relating person to person—to shift from the family situation of *familiarity*, dropping roles and walls to discover just *who* the parents and siblings really are! Families often shy away from doing this because they are unaware of the consequences until it is too late; and furthermore, parents often have little experience with being vulnerable themselves. For parents to be vulnerable, they would share with their children their true feelings *without control* (especially guilt). Instead of being *sincere* (doing the ideal, without fault), vulnerability calls for being *authentic* (truly honest).

In the early years, children need the security of the parent-child objectification, but soon they are capable of shifting gradually to more personal relating. A mother could begin by sharing with her children when she is tired, or angry, or frustrated (since they know anyway), always remembering to own her *responsibility* for those feelings, so that the children will not blame themselves. Usually, in families that play roles, children bear the brunt of those parental feelings without realizing the source, which is always the *person* of the parent. Without that link, both the parent and child become embroiled in fostering *blame*. When this condition is acknowledged in open discussion, remembering that *each person is responsible for his or her own feelings*, the child can learn about sharing feelings between people in a responsible and growth-promoting way. In families such as these, the children can learn about intimacy from early days, instead of waiting to clumsily experiment with it with their own future partners or offspring.

Parents often think that they should shelter their children from their own concerns; this is usually because of a family romance or an overall fear of intimacy. Children are able to *feel* the effects of that worry; lacking the information that intimacy could provide, they tend to fantasize about the causes; too often, they take the burden onto themselves. This is a common problem in any relationship where people are playing roles, whether it be friend-friend, student-teacher, or employee-employer. People can only break through these roles into an atmosphere of intimacy when all of the facts are exposed. Hopefully, understanding parents will help their offspring along this path at a early age.

Rules

For the sake of efficiency and safety within the family, rules are necessary. Through rules, a child learns appropriate behaviour and good personal habits that will ensure future social acceptance and success. Unfortunately, rules also promote the establishment of roles and walled defences; although such policies afford protection, they tend to become imprisoning. Regulations dictate the behaviour of interpersonal relating (the social skills), through which the child can practice and learn about consideration of others; when people rely entirely upon these rules, they lose *sensitivity* to others. Rules should be guidelines that do not take the place of responsive interaction with others. The person with boundaries remains cognizant of the rules, but is also constantly aware of the point of contact, remaining in touch with others. Children can learn this, although teaching it requires a greater awareness and expenditure of time on the part of the parents. Instead of shouting a rule ("Don't hit your brother!"), teaching boundaries would involve having a discussion among all of the concerned parties to help everyone understand any particular incident; in this process, all of them could learn how to acknowledge and appreciate one another's feelings.

Children can benefit from having experience with a variety of walls and boundaries. For example, children may be allowed to designate their bedroom as private space for which they are fully responsible, and which others may not enter without permission (excluding the instances when the room may become a fire and public health hazard). On the other extreme, the living room may be a space in which only certain behaviour of decorum and manners is permissible; in the more formal atmosphere of the living room, children can learn about limiting their personal expression in such public spaces as libraries and churches. Other common spaces in the home, such as the family room and the dining room, could be areas with fewer rules than the living room; in these common spaces, children would be expected to respect others' boundaries and privileges, being sensitive to the feelings of others (although not controlled by them).

Hopefully, children can experience a shift from being controlled by rules to assuming responsibility for themselves; then parents will apply rules only when a youngster demonstrates an inability or a refusal to accept such a responsibility. Being in charge of their own feelings and being willing to share them in a responsible way helps to prepare children for intimate relationships, in which personhood (rather than roles) can flourish.

Control

For obvious reasons, children often feel helpless and inadequate. Having a limited array of tools, they soon discover that their most effective ways of getting what they want—to be fed, cleaned, held, given attention—are by crying and expressing hurt feelings; early in their lives, they learn how to control others with such feelings. Because these methods are so effective, people become convinced that they can hurt (and control) others with their feelings, and that others can hurt them. Thus people learn to relate through guilt and blame, leading them to play roles and to take care of one another. These habits are difficult to break later in life, but such attitudes and behaviours must be overcome in order to fully experience intimacy.

BEN: *One day, Jock and I were attending a picnic on the lawn by the beach. Two six-year-old children of our friends wandered a little way down the beach out of sight of the adults. We surreptitiously watched as the little boy gave the little girl a shove, causing her to fall on her knees. Rising to brush off the sand, she looked around to see if any adults were around. We were out of sight, and no others were close by. So in silence, the little girl began to head for the lawn, crawling over boulders and logs to do so. After a matter of many minutes, she finally arrived at a place in her mother's line of vision. There, she stopped dead in her tracks and began to howl as if in great pain, effectively drawing her mother swiftly to her side to minister sympathy and comfort. It struck us both that the child's hurt (physical as well as emotional) was being used to solicit attention more than expressing pain.*

By quickly responding to hurt, parents unwittingly reinforce the idea that feelings can be used to control others. Children must learn that although their feelings will be acknowledged and respected, others will not be controlled by them. They need to hear such statements as "I can see that you hurt ... I feel with you ... you have a perfect right to have and express your own feelings ... but let's consider the feelings of others also."

Children's impulses must be checked so that they can learn to respond rather than react. Responsiveness requires holding back a reaction long enough to consider deeply within oneself what one truly feels and wants to communicate; by so doing, the individual develops a greater capability of self-reflection. According to Ernest Becker:

> *...the child must be blocked in his experience in order to be able to register that experience. If we don't "stop" the child he develops very little sense of himself, he becomes an automaton, a reflex of the surface of his world playing upon his own surface.*[1]

So-called "sensitive" children are usually just opposite to that. Their hurt feelings are used to control the behaviour of others who, fearing that they might be trampling on them, tiptoe gingerly to please them. Frequently, such "sensitive" children manage to control the actions and destinies of the entire family, merely with the threat of being hurt. The net result is the development of strong feelings of entitlement and expectations of others, very little sense of being responsible for the self, and little experience at relating at the boundaries with others. Hence, there is little intimacy. In fact, "sensitive" people are actually very *insensitive* to others, being more concerned with their own control over others in their environment!

An even more dangerous situation is set up when the control of children's behaviour is inconsistent. If youngsters are at different times variously punished, rewarded, then ignored for a certain behaviour, they fail to develop a respect and sensitivity to the wishes of others. More often, they become contemptuous, and begin to dismiss the words of others as being irrelevant. How often do we hear parents yelling ("I thought I told you not to do that! Now, I don't want to have to tell you again!"), only to find themselves repeating the same phrase over and over again, without any consequences. Instead of being controlled, such children learn that they are in control. Later in relationships, they fail to see or appreciate that there are consequences to any of their behaviours.

To teach consequences, parents must always be consistent. First of all, consequences should be realistic and explainable, preferably related to the act involved. For example, no dessert if the dinner is not finished is a natural consequence; having to go to bed early for the same dining infraction is not. In general, children need to have the initiative to make choices, but should be aware of the consequences of those choices, and be prepared to fully accept them. One of the main responsibilities of parents involves teaching their children that there are *always* consequences, to clearly state what the consequences would be for certain actions, and to consistently apply those consequences when necessary.

Sharing Feelings

People's feelings are like internal weather; they fluctuate, they move and flow and change, and are part of the texture of the individual's inner world. They provide texture, colour and meaningful dimension to everyday activities. As such, feelings are a natural part of human life, which needs expression. Just as the weather can be either a source of pleasure and variety or a destructive force to withstand, feelings can be either enhancing or interfering to people and their relationships.

In the family garden, each individual should have the possibility of sharing feelings. When feelings are used for control, the roles and rituals take precedence; when feelings are shared with vulnerability, respect, and sensitivity, all members of the garden can benefit. Parents can share the range of their feelings as expressions of themselves as people; children can learn to express themselves with openness and candour, without blaming or manipulating others. Then feelings become rich soil of interpersonal interaction, which nourishes the growth of each individual in the family garden.

Mirroring and Self-Esteem

The family garden is where people experience their earliest mirroring, which they tend to carry with them for the rest of their lives. Thus, it is unfortunate that most parents give their children greatly distorted mirroring. Believing they are helping their children's self-esteem, parents commonly utilize *convex mirroring*, in which the child's image is reflected back as bigger than the person really is. When the child returns home from school to show the parents the drawing that was done that morning, parents are used to saying exaggerated comments ("How wonderful! That's the GREATEST drawing!"), when in fact it is only a so-so work of art. More accurately, the parent might say something more realistic ("How colourful!" or "How different!" or "Boy, it sure looks like you had fun drawing that!"). Emphasis should be more on asking the child about his or her experience ("How did you enjoy painting that?"), rather than on the parent judging the piece to be a work of art. With convex mirroring, children either will have an overinflated idea of their talents, supporting the belief that they do not have to work at school; or if they disbelieve the hyperbole, they can develop contempt for what the parent says.

Frequently, children are subjugated to *concave mirroring* (such as "Is that all you can do?" or "Why can't you bring home good marks like Sammy does?"). Such experiences contribute towards a pattern of self-doubting, self-hating, and low self-esteem, which can haunt these people for the rest of their lives. If such people are fortunate to acquire a partner later in life who is able to give more honest, *direct mirroring*, they often find difficulty in being open to accept it; they have become fixated in the reduced vision of themselves that came with the parental concave mirror.

This is another challenge in intimate relationships: to learn to give and receive direct mirroring feedback, and thus construct accurate representations of oneself and one's partner in the present. Through this process of direct mirroring, one learns self-acceptance and self-compassion.

Genes and Memes

Genes are biological determinants of structure, function (and possibly behavioural tendencies) that are located on the chromosomes; genetic material is transmitted from parent to progeny, providing given characteristics at birth. A *meme* is a sociocultural pattern that impinges on the being within and outside of the womb; thus a meme is imprinted or learned by the developing child. Among clinicians and theoreticians, much controversy rages around how much behaviour is determined by heredity and how much by learning. We hold the view that the *possibilities* for a particular behaviour were present at conception. Whether or not that potential is converted into reality depends on whether or not it is stimulated and nurtured by experience. Thus, the evolving person never changes—she or he merely transforms from one state to another.

Genes and memes provide the context in which people live and die. They are the parameters that structure human experience. Although the dictates of the genes are relatively fixed (for example, you can do very little about your racial characteristics or sex identity), the memes have much variety of possibility for transformation. The individual can make autonomous choices not to follow the robot-like patterns of inculcated beliefs and rules. Instead, with free will, sensitivity, and choice, people can begin to lead responsible lives of personal participation; in so doing, they can decide not to blindly live out accustomed roles and automatic behaviours. People have the capacity to grow beyond the limitations of fixed beliefs, attitudes, and prejudices that they learned in childhood. For such a daring venture, an ongoing intimate interchange in a relationship garden is a rich medium in which to learn and grow.

For example, there are numerous memes (culturally coded behavioural expectations) around the concept of love. Some of these common memes were discussed previously; comon ones are the "Empty Bucket" theory of loving, and the "Pie Theory" of loving (see "Love, Obsession and Addiction," p. 136). Each person is born with the potential to be loving; whether or not that capability is turned on and developed is dependent on life experiences, first in the family garden, then later in schools and out in society. Rather than giving love to their children (as in the "Empty Bucket" meme), parents can provide stimulation to be able to be loving. If parents merely imprint on their children a formula of loving (such as telephoning home on holidays, or routinely sending Hallmark cards on birthdays), the children have been trained to do so, but they will experience little fulfilment in the performance of those duties. Hopefully, if children are stimulated to be in touch with their sensitivity and loving, they might genuinely come to desire to do some of these things, and feel good about doing them; they would not be fulfilling an obligation, but would be acting autonomously.

The Immortality Project

For many parents, their investment in their children represents their lack of acceptance of their own mortality. This is dressed up in language that refers to "family pride," "family honour," and "what will the neighbours think!" At root, such parents are afraid of facing their own sense of puniness and death; they take comfort in knowing that their children might carry on for them after their demise. For these parents, if the children can do well, and ultimately procreate themselves, then they have hope that their lineage will not die when they do. They are mortal; perhaps the family line is not. In this way, grandchildren are even more symbolic of hope than are one's own children.

Parents Need a Life

In the family garden, when parents devote the majority of their attention to their offspring, they are in danger of giving the children a feeling of undue importance. This becomes a burden to young people when their lives are the chief source of meaning and pleasure for their parents. Commonly, people make their children most important, and often will stay together in unhappy relationships "for the sake of the children." They are prepared to sacrifice themselves, making the family more important than their own personal happiness or growth. This is dangerous to all concerned, because it can breed complaint, resentment, and weakness. One day, these parents are liable to wake up to discover that they do not know themselves or anybody else, that their lives are devoid of meaning, that they have wasted a lifetime of years fulfilling their obligations without any rewards beyond the assuaging of their own guilt. This is a great (and common) tragedy.

The parents' primary relationship should be with one another, in their intimacy is where everything needs to be revealed and shared. When one parent establishes that primary place with one or more of the children, a rift occurs in the family dynamics, with a danger of some child getting control of the family (a control that (s)he both desires and dreads!). To be made primary by a parent is too much of a burden for children. When children are made most important, they do not develop the healthy perspective that the world does not revolve around them. For a child to be made primary to a parent encourages a sense of entitlement, weak will, and a poor sense of self-directed learning. They suffer in the light of convex mirroring. They become spoiled, pampered children, with an inflated sense of their own importance.[2] The spoiled children are "Little Emperors" who often dictate to the parents. This objectifying situation of entitlement threatens to lead to stunted, narcissistic development in these youngsters, who are likely to have unsatisfactory relationships throughout life. When they grow up, they are shocked to learn that their spouse or boss does not beam approval upon them with the same kind of reverence that their parents did. Indeed, when others wish to treat them with fairness and equality, such people lack the tools to properly assess their own performance in relationships.

Whenever we are asked what would be the best thing that parents can do for their children, without hesitation we recommend that *parents should get a life of their own!* By that, we mean that the parents should be primary with one another, and that they should have interests of their own quite apart from the children. All individuals within the family are best served in a family garden that considers and provides for the interests and needs of all members. Everybody in the garden, including parents, deserves the opportunity to grow.

Parents Are Not Perfect

Ultimately, children must leave their original family garden to establish one of their own. Hopefully, they will have learned what worked well in the original family garden, and what actions produced undesirable results, so that they can cultivate an even more nourishing relationship garden. As people create their own, it is important that they acknowledge and appreciate what they have been given. As Judith Viorst writes in *Necessary Losses*:

> There is plenty that we wanted, and did not receive, from our parents. It is time to know, and accept, that we never will...For now that the world belongs to our generation—not to theirs—we see how little power they ever had: To love us perfectly. To understand us perfectly. To save us from sorrow and solitude—and from death. We see how little power they had, and how little we have now, to build sturdy bridges across the gulfs which separate us. Letting go of our vain expectations as parents and children and spouses and friends, we learn to give thanks for even imperfect connections.[3]

With this understanding, it is time to close the gate of this important family garden, remembering all of the important lessons that were learned here—the negative as well as the positive. Close the gate but don't bolt the latch.

Notes

1. Ernest Becker, *The Denial of Death* (New York: The Free Press, Macmillan Publishing, 1973), p. 263.

2. B.R. Wong & J. McKeen, *A Manual for Life* (Gabriola Island, BC: PD Publishing, 1992), pp. 69–74.

3. Judith Viorst, *Necessary Losses* (New York: Simon and Schuster, 1986), p. 234.

Sexuality and Relationships

Q. What exactly is marriage?

A. When somebody's been dating for a while, the boy might propose to the girl. He says to her, "I'll take you for a whole life, or at least until we have kids and get divorced, but you got to do one particular thing for me." Then she says, "Yes," but she's wondering what the thing is and whether it's naughty or not. She can't wait to find out.—Anita (age 9)[1]

Intimacy is Not Sexuality

Although many people confuse intimacy and sexuality, they are very different. By intimacy, we mean a deep knowing and understanding of one another's interior lives that is achieved through vulnerable revelation and a shared sense of closeness and caring. Some intimate relationships have no sexual component to them, and yet partners are deeply close. Indeed, in many sexual relationships, the partners are more involved in charge and excitement, with very little intimacy or emotional closeness. For years, we have proposed that the *sexual charge (sexual excitement) and intimacy are often mutually exclusive phenomena.*[2] When one is pursuing a sexual charge, often the partner is objectified in a way that makes intimacy very difficult to achieve. One can have an intimacy with a friend or colleague by being open and revealed with that person; generally, this openness does not lead to a sexual encounter. This distinction between sexual charge and intimacy flies in the face of the common euphemism for sexual contact, "having intimate relations." To us, an intimate relationship is based upon relinquishing barriers and defences, moving beyond objectification into profoundly knowing one another; usually, there is little or no sexual contact in such a relationship.

Sexual Charge and Anonymity

It is in the beginning stages of a relationship—when people are relative strangers to one another—that the sexual charge is usually the highest. After getting to know one another well (which takes about five years on average), the sexual charge appears to diminish and may even be lost! At a casual glance, it appears as though intimacy breeds sexual apathy! Some recent studies suggest that a neurochemical process might be involved that leads to diminished sexual charge after a time; perhaps nature has designed this to motivate couples to be rearranged within five years, for maximum mixing of the gene pool. For those who are feeling concerned about their sexual lives, we know it is possible to have sexual excitement and intimacy with the same person—but not easily or automatically! Indeed, it takes considerable self-awareness and commitment between couples in order to bring together the sexual charge and intimacy, which naturally seem to move apart from each other.

Sexual Identity and Gender Identity

Sexual identity is biologically based, determined by the chromosomes in one's genetic makeup. A person is *male* (XY) or *female* (XX), except in a few rare circumstances where there are variations in this standard coding. Sexual identity is biologically determined, and unchangeable. Even if people undergo a so-called sex change, they are still the same sex as when they began, because their chromosomes do not change. The genetic makeup determines the secondary sexual characteristics: females have a uterus, fallopian tubes, and ovaries, and at maturity will menstruate and be capable of childbearing. A male will have a penis and testicles, and will at maturity be able to produce spermatozoa capable of impregnating a female. It is these sex chromosomes that determine the body characteristics for males and females: heavier musculature, beard, and deep voice for the male, and softer skin and more rounded form for the female. Within these general tendencies, there are individual variations; some women have larger, more muscular bodies than some men, and some men have more of the female qualities. Yet, biologically, the men still have the organs for the male aspect of reproduction, and at the cellular level, each cell is masculine, as the nuclear chromosomes have XY chromosomes; similarly, at the cellular level, a woman will have XX chromosomes. This is unchangeable.

Gender identity is culturally determined. Both sexes have *masculine* and *feminine* qualities. Culturally, males are encouraged to develop and express the so-called masculine qualities; thus little boys are encouraged to have blue blankets, play with trucks, and learn to be aggressive and play football and climb trees and get dirty. Little girls are given pink blankets and frilly dresses, and are expected to play with dolls and not get dirty. This sets up a dichotomy between the sexes, with culturally expected roles and attitudes. The woman is supposed to wait for the man to take the initiative. Once married, the traditional value is for the male to earn the living and the female to take care of the household and, indeed, to caretake the very relationship.

In traditional Chinese philosophy, human beings have both *yin* and *yang* qualities (yin is soft, feminine, yielding, enveloping and nurturing—"feminine"; yang is hard, aggressive, directed, and initiatory—"masculine."). From a Jungian point of view, all people have both masculine and feminine aspects. The male is taught to suppress the feminine qualities, and to search for a female to complete himself. The situation is similar for females with respect to their masculine attributes.

Thus, people experience themselves as incomplete, requiring someone else to complete them. This is the basis for loneliness, where people are subject to the romance that urges them to find someone special to complete them. They are lonely when they don't have the perfect life partner. This is the main issue in the Romance and Power Struggle stages of relationship; at this period, people have little knowledge of themselves or of others, and they are looking for images to complete themselves.

When people begin to accept themselves and others, they move into the Integration phase of relating. People at this stage are not concerned with being completed by another; they recognize that they are already whole, and find fascination in the ongoing project of discovering themselves and their partners. The project shifts from one in which something wrong needs to be fixed to one in which there is ever-increasing revelation of universal wholeness. Then, people are no longer lonely. Men do not have to look for a woman to complete them; they can search to discover their own feminine nature, which informs the images of their anima projection (and fuels sexual excitement and romances). In the same way, women can experience their wholeness without depending upon a man to complete them. Whereas the Romance and Power Struggle stages are associated with incompleteness and dependence upon externals, in the Integration phase people can experience themselves as whole, responsible for themselves as unique expressions of the entire universe.

When people become interested in delving beneath their habitual roles, they often discover that they have been trying to get their partner to provide what they themselves could offer. In the grotesque fixedness of the traditional family meme (pattern), the man comes home from work and puts his feet up, while the wife is supposed to make the meal, minister to him, listen attentively to his grumbling, and take care of the children, without ever expecting any of the same in return. Thus, the male is stunted in his nurturing ability, and his ability to relate in a responsive, receptive manner. To become more responsible, people must become aware of these gender prejudices and to acknowledge them to their partner; in the process of accepting them, they begin to able to move through and beyond them. This can be very freeing indeed. Many men find they especially enjoy some of the roles usually assigned to the feminine gender—cooking, childrearing and shopping. Many women find a great liberation in taking more of the heavy lifting, and moving into the workforce and contributing to the family finances.

In most relationships, there will be gender prejudices that were learned from families and culture; when these are understood and overcome, people can become full and integrated—both yin and yang, masculine and feminine. Much of this can be discovered in sex play between partners who want to learn. This investigation can be intimidating, sobering, and sometimes very frightening, because it questions very basic self-assumptions. But it can be so invigorating and revelatory!

Dimensions of Sexuality

Q. *What is the proper age to get married?*

A. *Eighty-four—because at that age, you don't have to work any more, and you can spend all your time loving each other in your bedroom.*—Carolyn (age 8)[3]

In our book *A Manual For Life* ,[4] we developed a chart describing the different aspects of sexuality. Our ideas have now been further developed to include a wider variety of experiences that can be seen in the updated chart on page 158.

Note that these categories are not mutually exclusive. Indeed, all of these dimensions are simultaneously possible. In any given individual in a specific situation, there will be varying degrees of expression of these dimensions of sexuality. When a young couple is trying to get pregnant, the biological dimension might be foremost, with them taking great care to have sex at fertile times; in an early stage of a relationship, the sexual charge is more dominant, and later on gives way to the development of aesthetics and romance and spirituality.

The mixture of these elements is like a brewing soup; they are the components of the recipe that can be included in varying intensities. Some soups are heavily laden with garlic; others have a light touch of lemon grass. Some relationships are highly charged, while others are more fragrant with aesthetics or romance. None of the motifs is better or worse than the others. They are simply the components that go into the multidimensionality of a sexual relationship.

DIMENSIONS OF SEXUALITY

	Biological	Sensual-Erotic	Sexual Charge	Romantic	Aesthetic/Mythic	Trans-personal
Location	Physical	Physical	Mental-Emotional	Mental	Deeper Nature	Higher Self
Motivation	Relieve Tension	Relieve Tension	Overcome Helplessness	Relieve Anomie	Emotional Spiritual	Meaningfulness
System	Endocrine	Diencephalic A.N.S. (prim. parasymp.)	Cortical A.N.S. (prim. sympath.)	Cortical A.N.S. (prim. parasymp.)	Cortical R.A.S. (limbic system?)	Higher Self (pineal gland?)
Mode	Ejaculatory	Stroking	Penetration/ Fenestration	Image Management	Meaning Management	Ecstasy
Purpose	Reproduction	Pleasure/ Pain	Domination/ Submission	Control	Meaning Attribution	Union
Means	Organic	Sensory	Symbolic	Symbolic	Sensory/ Symbolic	Ineffable (Inarticulate)
Intimacy	Impersonal	Impersonal	Impersonal	Impersonal	Impersonal	Impersonal

The Biological Sex Drive

In its pure form, the biological sex drive plays an important but limited role in the overall scheme of sexuality. The female's hormonal cycle is very central to her sexual functioning. Her inner world is like the changing seasons, punctuated by the more chaotic daily mood swings as she responds to her inner clock. It is ever changing, full and fascinating, as her hormones prepare her body for reproduction. This is a symphony of feelings—sometimes adagio and sweet, sometimes lyrical and joyful, sometimes urgent and exciting. Some women find this cyclic alteration to be bothersome; nevertheless, it cannot be denied. Once a month, at ovulation, a capsule within an ovary explodes with ripeness, releasing an ovum into the prepared fallopian tubes where the egg could be fertilized. That event is heralded by the release into the atmosphere of a chemical called a *pheromone*, whose scent is a call to action, compelling nearby males to service her sexually so that she can be impregnated.

The male's inner hormonal orchestration is much simpler. His hormonal levels remain fairly constant, rising quickly during adolescence, reaching a peak in his youth, then gradually declining over the remaining years of his life. Their function appears to be twofold—to prepare his testes to produce viable sperm with which he may service the female of the species, and to develop his musculature so that he may be able to capture one of the creatures of the opposite sex when he is called, and to protect her and the offspring when they are most vulnerable. It is a simple yet quite valuable melody.

Thus, nature arranges for the preservation and continuation of the species by this intricate process. In this way, the biological imperative for sexual behaviour occurs only once a month, driven by the woman's reproductive cycle. From Mother Nature's point of view, sexual interest and activity at all other times is *perverse* (from the Latin *perversus*, meaning "turned the wrong way"[5]). This is pure biological activity, which humans share in common with many other creatures. It is *impersonal* and functional; anybody with the appropriate biology will do. In the sex act, the orgasm relieves both parties of the sense of urgency that was created by these endocrines.

Sensual-Erotic Sexuality

Embedded in the genetic makeup and biology of the human organism, the sensual-erotic aspects of sexuality are also impersonal. As with other mammals, the human neurological hardwiring is designed to provide pleasure when the senses are stimulated, independent of who or what is doing the stimulating. Thus people love to be touched, stroked, warmed, and made comfortable. Their vision fills them with pleasure over colourful sights and mood-enhancing candlelight; their ears transmit the pleasurable sounds of melodies and softly spoken words; their lips and taste buds are stimulated by ambrosian foods and drink, and their noses fill with the heady perfumes of flowers and oils. The stimulation of all of the senses is sexual and pleasureful. But as with the biological sex drive, the sensual-erotic experience is limited in scope, having a relatively brief half-life. Being stroked or massaged can fairly soon become irritating, as would too many scents or tastes over an extended period of time. Yet for many people (women more than men), being stroked, held and cuddled is a primary form of their sexual desire.

Aesthetic Sexuality

As the sensual-erotic is pleasing to the body, so is the *aesthetic* impulse pleasing to the mind. People who are stimulated in this way are thrilled with the lines of a body or the particular structure of a face. Graceful movement and transient shadows can also be pleasing in this way. A perfect setting for a meeting, a particular shadow falling across the face, the flickering of candlelight across a bare arm, the tinkling of a deftly played piano—any of these can be sexually stimulating to the person whose charge involves the aesthetic. The meaning that is ascribed to these experiences is derived from some deeper, primordial place within the nature of such a being. Satisfying as it may be, it too is impersonal. Although it may never lead to sexual intercourse, such sexuality could be sufficient unto itself—witness the ecstasy of the saints or the passion of an artist.

Mythic Sexuality

Myths are stories that express universal deep structures of human life. The characters in these stories express the qualities of basic psychological patterns, which Jung called "archetypes." A basic theme involves the eternal interplay between masculine and feminine forces, represented in male and female characters in the myths. The interplay of these masculine and feminine forces, the dynamism, the conflicts and the joining was called the *hieros gamos* (holy marriage) in occult literature. In Chinese philosophy, these eternal forces are known as *yin* (the soft, yielding, feminine) and *yang* (hard, directed, masculine). In Jungian psychology, every male has a deeply buried feminine nature, known as his *anima*; every female has a hidden *animus* (her masculine nature). When men are attracted to women, they are said to be drawn to the projected anima; it is their own feminine nature that they have imposed upon the sex object, and are indeed trying to discover their own nature! Conversely, women are attracted to their animus projection.[6,7,8]

Myths are universal; every society has its myths. Although there are cultural variations in how the myths are told, their basic structure is similar, enunciating universal patterns of organization. They commonly involve stories of infatuation, wooing, and conquest; these are utilized in the creation of characters in plays, movies, art works, and folk tales. There are myths of same-sex friendships (for example, Damon and Pythias), parent-child interactions (such as Oedipus), as well as the more commonplace male-female relationships. In art and literature of the western world, depictions of sex and relationships have drawn heavily from the stories of Amor and Psyche, the rape of Persephone, Leda and the swan, the myth of Narcissus, and the legend of Apollo and Daphne. The universal tale of lovers defying their parents to be with one another is written into Shakespeare's *Romeo and Juliet*, which was taken from earlier folk tales.

The figures in myths enunciate the play of cosmic forces that are expressed in the interactions of gods and humans. These are story representations expressing the deeper structures of the universe, which manifest in the lives of humans. This mythic dimension is not usually directly available to the awareness of couples in sexual interplay. Nevertheless, in their interaction, there are common themes and patterns, which appear repeatedly in stories, folk tales, legends and myths.

Transpersonal Sexuality

With most sexual behaviour, the sexual orgasm tends to play an important role. The sexual drive (for whatever reason it is being created) produces a state of tension that compels the person to seek some outlet, such as sexual intercourse. This tension is increased during the sex act itself, usually peaking with a release that ranges in intensity from an *ejaculation* (only a genital release) through to a full body release called an *orgasm*. As well, there is the possibility of dissolving all of the confines of the imprisoning ego so that the self may completely be joined with the other in a *cosmic orgasm*. All of these three kinds of release serve the purpose of relieving tensions at the levels of the body, the body-mind and the body-spiritual levels. Whatever the kind of orgasm, each may serve as "peak experiences," previews to the ultimate surrender. After orgasm, people settle into their old self once more (and frequently, turn away immediately and fall into a deep sleep).

It may only be possible to reach transpersonal ("beyond the self") states to a more constant degree through means other than sexual. Nonetheless, some subscribe to tantric practices, where sexual energy is channeled toward enlightenment. Many people find romantic appeal in the notion that sexual practice between loving partners may result in mutual orgasms and closer connections between them.

Romantic Sexuality

Most of the preceding types of sexual expression, as well as the following "sexual charge," have been ascribed special status by the process of romanticizing—applying fantasies that provide meaning to the activities. Once people believe that they are finally with "the one and only"—the person to whom they are prepared to dedicate the rest of their lives, the one to whom they have promised to forever "love, honour and obey"—their sexual activity takes on new (and oftentimes immense) significance. Of such stuff are romances created. The colour and odour of roses may be sensually stimulating in themselves. But oh, that they have been sent by *him* makes them symbols of much greater (perhaps even cosmic?) importance! Her body lines and graceful movements may be perfect, but because they are *hers*, aren't they even more than perfect? And although a prostitute would perhaps be more skilled at managing effective intercourse, partners excuse the bumblings and ineptness of their most treasured soul-mate, with whom they would only *make love*, never fuck. In such ways does romance make fools of all, overriding the demands of nature, the pristine spiritual cravings, the body hungering for stimulation and the mind seeking perfect form!

With romance, all is reduced to fantasy and prejudice, expectation and control, hope and heartache. But even the pains of romance are experienced as sweet and desirable! Romance is the adult's sandbox—in which most people would prefer to play, rather than face the stark realities of life. At its best, romance opens up the imagination to new possibilities. As an interlude, romances are refreshingly enjoyable. Unfortunately, becoming obsessed with them puts the possibility of personal growth into the background. One special kind of romance involves the sexual charge.

The Sexual Charge

Although there is certainly some sexual excitement and pleasure in both antici-
pating and participating in the five previously described forms of sexuality, the
excitement and pleasure of the *sexual charge* are of a different nature. Unlike
the languishing swoon of the sensual-erotic, the sexual charge is exciting, ten-
sion-filled and urgent, compelling the person to action and creating within that
person a physiological flooding of blood flow, increased blood pressure and
heart rate, and a hypersensitivity and turgidity of erotic zones in the body. They
are all symptoms of an organismic fight/flight pattern that has become sexualized.
Underlying this biological process is an associated theme of domination and
submission: in subconscious fantasies are themes of penetrating or being pen-
etrated, capturing or being captured.

As children, people wrestle with feelings of inadequacy and helplessness, yearning for the day that they will be able to have some control. They practice the many
ways of seduction and pleasing that are available to them as children, frequently
incorporating any successful gambits into their character structures. In this way,
they develop an armament of control mechanisms in preparation for the day
that they will have the opportunity to be in command! With the rapid growth
of the hormonal system during adolescence, that day finally arrives.

Unconsciously, most people would want the undivided attention of one or both
of their parents. Usually, that desire is thwarted by the demands of reality, but
people never stop wanting. In adolescence, with the sudden growth of their
bodies and a pervasive sense of freedom, they begin to realize that they are
capable of attracting others, or being attracted. To the adolescent, it seems that
this motif of attraction may be able to fill their need for undivided attention.
They crave to be wanted and desired, to possess and be possessed; in short, as
Sartre proposed, they want to *capture someone else's consciousness.*[9] Because the
strongest impulses early in adolescence tend to be sexual in nature, that craving to capture consciousness is easily sexualized, finding expression in the sexual
charge.

Basically, the story line at the root of sexual charge is one of *domination* and
submission, to capture and be captured. The participants of this drama are
objectified to play their parts—hence the appropriate reference to being made
into a "sex object." The excitement of possible capture may even eliminate the
person altogether by condensing the fantasy into a symbol such as a part of the
body (e.g., breasts or buttocks), or projecting it into inanimate objects such as

a shoe or some fancy underwear; in this way sexual *fetishes* are created. Viewing, touching, or possessing these fetishes is frequently more exciting than relating to a person.

People develop an entire panoply of preening and practices, stances and seductions, innuendoes and suggestiveness that are usually acted upon in indirect ways—all in the service of attracting attention and capturing the consciousness of others. The hunt is exhilarating and frightening. Toward this end, much of the commercial market is devoted to providing aids and weapons, as so humorously portrayed by Philip Wylie in *Generation of Vipers:*

> *...innumerable advertisers have printed the head and shoulders or the whole torso of stripped, orgiastic soubrettes beneath the statement that a given product has rendered them more kissable, engageable, marriageable, popular at parties, and in demand for moonlight strolls— or caused them to be okay in the matter of feminine hygiene, breath, armpit and perspiration odour, or made their hair withstand the male test, God save us, of "nasal close-up"—or brought a host of new swains to them because of neater techniques during menstruation—or taken them to house parties where they were, according to serial cartoon illustrations, constantly in the bushes with boys. The products have transmuted ten thousand wallflowers into passionflowers. Various medicaments, pads, pledgets, salves, gargles, girdles, rinses, soaps, douches, rubber devices, elastic undergarments, negligees, cigarettes, automobiles, house furnishings, washing machines, kitchen appliances, cosmetics, deodorants, perspiration arrestors, booklets of intimate advice, dandruff removers, and hangover remedies have dismissed these handsome wenches from states in which nobody paid any attention to them and prostrated them in the illustrated position of copulative thrall, with (or, so far as the reader can discern, without) benefit of clergy. Since the implied purpose of every syllable of such copy and every expression on the face of every such model, photographed or painted, is to startle the woman reader into an inquiry of whether or not her body is thoroughly prepared for nonrancid sex service, the slogan "Are you a good lay?" is the real one.[10]*

Ideal Sex Objects

The elements of a sexual charge are both cultural and individual. Each society has some objectified ideals that are held to be attractive; because they are arbitrary, they vary from generation to generation, from century to century, and from locale to locale. Currently, in North America (and because of movies, increasingly so in many other parts of the world), the cultural female sex object ideals are such things as blonde hair, athletic body, long legs, pouty lips, and well-shaped buttocks—much of which can be found in the reigning movie stars such as Sharon Stone and singers like Madonna. The male counterparts are a well-muscled athletic body, boyish face, shy grin, penetrating eyes, flat abdomen, and a devil-may-care attitude like Mel Gibson. Men and women "turn on" to these stars and emulate them as much as possible. The storyline underlying these characteristics is that "she" is both strong and helplessly child-like, chaste as well as somewhat of a harlot; "he" is both tough and vulnerable, self-reliant and shy. Obviously, our cultural sex object ideals must be an amalgam of opposites.

On an individual level, people's sexual charges are more related to their individual histories. Nobody is turned on to all men or all women. People encode within their sexual charges their unfinished childhood business. Each person has a particular story to tell in his or her specific charges. If someone craved to possess his blonde-haired mother, perhaps he would be interested in a partner with blonde hair; or if that is too threatening to recognize, perhaps he would convert that and become interested in raven-haired girlfriends. For people who did not have enough of father's attention, they might choose the object of their sexual desire to be men with a body or disposition similar to that of their father. Perhaps when they were children their father drank; even though they might have sworn never to become involved with someone who is similarly inclined, they often find themselves unconsciously responding sexually to that very kind of man, sometimes only discovering that fact many years after marriage.

The Sexual Microdot

All of these stories, cultural as well as individual, are coded into the *sexual microdot*. The concept of microdot was discussed previously (see "The Stage of Romance," p. 56). People's life stories are reduced and symbolized into a tiny place within their subconscious, to control the specifics of who and what each person will want to pursue. The object is never a person; it is only parts of a person, or things belonging to a specific kind of person, or personality characteristics related to people in the past upon whom the individual has tended to become fixated. In fact, the sexual charge is a symptom of obsessions and fixations upon objects dating back from early childhood all the way up to the present time.

This explains the wide variety of choices of people's sexual charges—whether the object of desire should be skinny, fat, full-breasted or no-breasted, athletic or wasted, tall or short, tight or slack-jawed, hairy or smooth-skinned, with dirty fingernails or surgically clean, talking rough or with sophistication, dressed in lumbermen shirts or basic black with pearls. The underlying stories are legion.

From across a crowded room, or a little ways down the bar, or on the other end of a pew, people are quickly able to spot the object of their sexual charge, thanks to the silent radar that seems to be attached to the internal sexual microdot. The pulse quickens, and they begin to fantasize scenarios that ultimately lead to pursuit, to make the object their very own! These scripts of pursuit and acquisition are themselves written in the microdot, motivating the unfolding of very specific moves that could lead to a capture. Once the object is captured, people have idiosyncratic ways to relate to the captured object; the particulars of the ultimate interactions will be specific to each individual. Some of these are classical in nature, reflecting the society in which people are raised—such as finding a professional man or woman who could assure a stable economic future together, or an athletic partner with whom one may climb or ski mountain tops together. These common themes provide the story line underlying the laments and pleasures of romance; they stem from the internal microdot, reflecting tastes and predilections, hopes and desires.

Pornography

Once the relationship is sexualized, people are then influenced by their cultural and personal pornographies. Contrary to popular belief, we believe that all relationships have their pornographic components. Webster defines pornography as "obscene literature or art calculated solely to supply sexual excitement."[11] This is close to the legal definition of pornography, which creates so many problems for censorship boards and art galleries. For example, much energy is consumed in attempting to determine if the painter *intended* merely to sexually excite, without any artistic redeeming value. From this chapter's frame of reference, *all* pornography, whether visual (which is primarily a male form) or literature (which, like the Harlequin romances, is primarily a female form)—intends to excite as a means of dominating others through a capture of their consciousness in a submission/domination theme. We tend to agree with Stoller that with pornography there is always a victim, whether real or fantasied; we do not go so far as he does in claiming that *all* pornography is essentially hostile.

> As with all perversions, pornography is a matter of aesthetics: one
> man's delight is another's boredom. Also, as with all perversions, at
> its heart is a fantasied act of revenge, condensing in itself the sub-
> ject's sexual life history—his memories and fantasies, traumas, frus-
> trations, and joys. There is always a victim, no matter how disguised:
> no victim, no pornography.[12]

It is worthwhile to remind the reader at this time that the sexual charge is only
one of the expressions of sexual energy. There is the rutting compulsive energy
related to the monthly ovulation cycle, that is designed for reproduction. There
is also the pleasure of the sensual-erotic in which all of the senses can be stroked,
and the thrill of the aesthetic with perfect form or grace. Furthermore, there is
the peak experience of the transpersonal in which one surrenders to the cosmos in sexual bliss. And all of these forms, including the sexual charge, can be
romanticized into gross sentimentality, losing altogether any final particle of
the self that may remain. Sexuality is no small matter!

Returning to the pornographic, remember that the whole process is objectifying
in nature, involving sex objects, but *no persons*. Because it is a means of stimulating such sexual excitement, it can be a most effective form of control. Both
the controller and the recipient tend to become *obsessive* and then compulsive
around their behaviours. Sometimes, what began as a casual flirtation can grow
into an obsession involving threats, stalking, terrorizing, and sometimes even
physical assault. The more the fixation grows, the more the sense of the person
is lost; this is a flirtation with the death of the Self. No wonder that the charge
is so great—the stakes (real or imagined) are so high!

In relationship, these capture themes can be acted out in sexual games. If there
were no limits, no respect for boundaries, the risk of personal annihilation would
translate into fear, with a loss of the sexual charge. After establishing limits,
couples can discuss, share and role play without devastation. With close relationships—or at the least, trusting ones—there exists a sufficient level of perceived safety to allow the taking of risks, to explore the limits of the danger of
losing the Self. Without that safety, and without permission being granted, the
same acts that can be so exciting for intimate relationships would be acts of
violence. It is the permission and level of safety that make it otherwise.

An interesting aspect that may emerge is a desire to *humiliate* or to be humili-
ated. This is related to a need for revenge rising out of perceived humiliating
experiences as a child or youth. This can include such desires as to spank or be
spanked, to be tied down, or to be ejaculated upon one's body rather than within

the body. *Anonymous sexuality* such as telephone sex may prove to be highly charged, especially when the parties are able to control one another's sexual excitement; the element of anonymity highlights the depersonalization involved.

For some pairings, taking time out from routine sexual intercourse can make room for novel and exciting sexual games. Many couples enjoy being able to masturbate one another, sometimes whispering sexual fantasies into one another's ears. Even more risky—and hence potentially more exciting, might be to masturbate oneself in front of one's partner. For many people, this means confronting their vulnerable shame and guilt over voyeuristic and exhibitionistic desires. What has been most prohibited could well prove to be most exciting!

There are a number of commonly held pornographic fantasies in any society. These classic themes include the travelling salesman and the farmer's daughter, the soldier on a final date before leaving for battle, a minister and a member of his flock in church, a student and a teacher, a patient and her doctor, an encounter with a rapist or a hostage-taker, an anonymous phone caller talking dirty, a peeper with someone undressing or taking a shower. The more forbidden the fantasies, the more charged they will be. Add to those the array of individually created fantasies, and there will be endless situations that couples can explore in the privacy of their own homes. Permission and safety must always be stressed; it is also important for couples to agree upon some password that would signal that one of the members really does wish to stop the fantasy—a signal that would immediately be respected. Once they embark upon this exploration, the possibility exists that as one level of fantasies is recalled, shared, or acted out, deeper layers of repression will become available for the future. Thus, in that process, each person's history can be revealed and expressed and understood.

Intimacy and Objectification

Couples seeking intimacy, who want to connect through loving, need to identify and acknowledge any impulse toward objectification. In intelligent, highly complex individuals, the sexual object choices can be very variable and exotic. Knowing one another's source of objectifying excitement can enhance the intimacy. At this point, to deepen intimacy, it is important that both agree to share their inner fantasies of excitement, *even if the object of that charge is someone (past or present) other than the partner!* By so doing, what was impersonal and political in nature becomes personal. As with all personal information, such sharing is accompanied by considerable vulnerability and may result in much pain and anger, which also must be shared to further the intimacy even more.

During these kinds of sharings, it is important that the parties remain non-judgmental, uncritical (both of the self and other), and curious. As people come to know more and more about their partner's past experiences and sexual orientations, they catch glimpses of that person's inner power desires and feelings of inadequacy. Frequently, during those times, the sexual charge for one another may become strong, and they can bring it into sex play between them. As they become more familiar, they may begin to realize that they have previously really known very little about one another—and what they thought they knew might be revealed to have been only projections upon one another!

With the information revealed about those innermost objectifying secrets, the partners can be co-creative. One day, Cindy revealed to her partner that often when they were having sex, she had become excited by a fantasy of being seduced in her own home by a travelling salesman. Without telling her what he planned to do, Sam dressed up one day as a salesman and rang the doorbell; when Cindy answered the door, he proceeded to seduce her into the bedroom where they enjoyed some of their most exciting sexual encounters! The exploration of these fantasies with one another is another way to turn the impersonal into something personal and revelatory.

In time, people involved with such an exploration of their sexual charges will begin to notice how the intensity of their charge over the issues they have revealed will diminish in intensity. This is a natural process of growth as intimacy increases. At this time, the idea of going exploring outside of the relationship may arise; generally, this is not the best solution for the average couple. Frequently, people in Apathy can confuse their listlessness with the calming that comes with Integration, and are prone to have affairs; for these apathetic people especially, moving outside of the primary relationship for sexual excitement is very risky. For the rare couple who can successfully operate within these parameters, the partners must reiterate their commitment to holding their relationship as being primary, and be stringent about always revealing such inclinations, activities and feelings to each other.

Submission versus Surrender

In *submission*, one person gives over to the other. In this power situation, there tends to be a loss of oneself. With submission one is placed in a subordinate relationship to another, in an objectified victim position. People often submit to one another to play roles in relationships; this can be exciting, and can serve to provide security. Such submission commonly arises in the stages of Romance and Power Struggle.

In *surrender*, one lets go into an experience of intense ecstasy; investments are relinquished, and the life force flows unabated—this is often identified as a spiritual experience. People do not surrender to anyone else; they let go and fill with themselves. In surrender, there is an acceptance of both self and other, with no attempt to change anything. Thus, surrender can create profound intimacy with the self, with an openness and acceptance that permits intimacy with another.

Ecstasy, as reported by saints such as St. Theresa, involves a profound surrender, in which one feels full of the cosmic life force; some theologians believe this to be a joining with one's God, a union with the universe.[13] When this occurs in sexuality, people fully let go of their boundaries; in this way a transpersonal dimension is possible in orgasmic release. Too often, people get caught in the ambition for cosmic liberation and then become attached to the goal of surrender; holding such a romance often prevents authentic surrender and ecstasy to occur.

Sexual Charge and Passion

The sexual charge with its objectifications, fantasies, obsessions and compulsions produces a sense of electrical excitement, accompanied by various levels of self-doubt and self-hatred, because of its denial of the personal. The accompanying desire to dominate and capture the other makes a victim of both of the parties involved. According to Sartre, such sexual desire is doomed to failure.[14] Unless people address their inclinations to objectify, they can never reach a point of knowing either themselves or others; hence, most people do not fully come into being.

On the other hand, people who discover themselves as persons located in the scheme of the universal order might find that what was previously sexual excitement becomes replaced with a sense of *passion* for life. They relate to the universal life force in a more direct way, beyond the roles, idealizations, and objectifications of one another. Life might become less exciting but much more *fulfilling*, a whole person should be capable of both.

Performance Anxiety

People are responsible for creating their own feelings—including all of their sexual excitement. Thus, one person does not "turn on" the other or "excite" the other. Indeed, people's passions and sexual interests are generated within themselves, based on their life experience, imagery, and personal tastes. Thus everyone can learn a great deal about themselves when they are turned on or off. But, they should not blame themselves or their partners when they are not turned on. They can investigate why they are not turning on, and can learn about their own limitations.

This relieves each partner of performance demands. Instead of the common (and doomed) approach of trying to excite each other, we recommend dialogue between sexual partners to discover what each other finds exciting. People cannot turn their partners on; however, they certainly can increasingly learn about what partners use to turn themselves on, so that they can willingly and lovingly participate in enhancing their excitement and pleasure. They can learn and learn, and can mine ever deeper veins of excitement, pleasure and self-discovery.

Varieties of Orgasms

Although simultaneous orgasm is possible, and sometimes occurs, too much has been made of this phenomenon. The idea that people should orgasm together is often based on a romantic idea that they will then be joined in a cosmic way. Indeed, there is deep sharing possible in being present for the partner's orgasm, quite independent of one's own satisfaction. And there can be great joy, sharing, and excitement in participating in bringing a partner to climax after having had one's own.

Vaginal, clitoral, and anal orgasms all tend to be different in quality; but one is not better than the other. They are a matter of personal preference, and informed by each situation. If people are free to experiment, they can experience a great variety of orgasms. Indeed, there are orgasms possible without even being touched! And contrary to the myth that men are only able to orgasm once, many men can come twice, and some can let go several times in an hour. The orgasms are often different each time. Sometimes, they are more like what their female partners describe—whole-body shudders of pleasure, rather than an ejaculatory release. Sometimes women can ejaculate like a man. When it comes to orgasms, men and women both are capable of much more than people commonly realize!

One notion that interferes with people having sequential orgasms is the idea that the only valid orgasm involves a penis in a vagina. Indeed, often the most exciting orgasms are from manual or oral or anal stimulation, or from masturbating oneself in the presence of one's partner. When people become creative about sexuality, they can openly masturbate themselves; and their partner can have pleasure and excitement in being a witness to this. This relieves great pressure from relationships where one partner has a higher sexual drive than the other; not every sexual feeling needs to result in intercourse or recriminatory pouting. If he is excited, and she is not interested in intercourse, she can be present with him, and share in his pleasuring himself, and vice versa. In this way, one can share sexuality without demanding anything in return. Then partners are freed of the necessity to become aroused every time the other is sexually interested; indeed, with this freedom, people often find that they become aroused by their partner's sharing.

Open communication is the key. Keep talking about how you feel, what you want, and don't want, at any given time.

The Isomorphism of Sexuality With Life

"Isomorphic" means "having the same pattern" (see "Spirituality and Relationships," p. 203). The expression of one's sexuality is a reflection of one's entire life. People who are interested in domination/submission in sexuality are likely to have these issues elsewhere in their lives. It is not necessary to act out all the forms of one's sexual interest; the very investigation to discover where attractions, charges, or disgusts reside can provide a key to the basic patterns of one's existence. Thus, sexuality can be an investigation ground for self-discovery. Whatever passions people have in their sexuality can be discovered in other areas of their life. For years, we have made the statement:

As you are in your sexuality, so are you in your life.

Transcendence and Transformation

In many religious approaches, there is a denial of the body and its sensations; people are expected to rise above carnal experience. This is the philosophy of *transcendence*, and is generally linked to a moral position where the body is somehow deemed to be bad, dirty, inferior, or undesirable (see "Spirituality and Relationships," p. 203). The spirit is seen as separate from the body.

Looking back over the history of the church, it is apparent that earlier leaders were fully aware of the importance of the sensual-erotic impulse in seeking and expressing the spiritual. Intense, uplifting feelings permeated the music commissioned by the church to be played during services, to fulfil the spiritual appetites of the masses. In the same vein, cathedrals were filled with art, sculptures, richly woven tapestries, elegant candelabras, and wondrously coloured stained glass. The rituals were full of the sounds of choir and organ, the scents of incense and candle wax, and the sights of rich vestments and moving symbols. Where else have the senses been so stimulated in such an erotic fashion? What an effective way to call forth the senses to rise above the humdrum existence of the bodily self to *surrender* one's self to God! Unfortunately, such experiences also left the worshippers vulnerable to control, so that what could have been an exercise in surrender was used by the church to demand *submission* to its moral authority; it converted what could have been spiritual into the *religious* experience. In spite of that, spiritual transcendental experiences can still be gleaned from the masses of the great composers, in the lofty cathedrals that still stand as silent sentinels throughout the western world, and in the priceless treasures of the Vatican!

In the *transformative* approach to spirituality, all of human experience is an expression of the universe. There is no need to rise above daily life in transcendence. God is not located somewhere outside of the self—the self is an holographic expression of God. Hence, in this approach people are encouraged to fully experience their sensations, feelings and passions because they *are* of God. The transformative approach accepts all feelings—be they angry, ugly, altruistic, dark, light, or sexually exciting! The spirit *is* the body, *and* the mind, *and* the emotions.

> The glory of God is man fully alive. —Saint Irenaeus[15]

Notes

1. David Heller, *Growing Up Isn't Hard to Do If You Start Out As a Kid* (New York: Random House, 1991).

2. B.R. Wong & J. McKeen, *A Manual for Life* (Gabriola Island, BC: PD Publishing, 1992), p. 111.

3. David Heller, *Growing Up Isn't Hard to Do If You Start Out As a Kid* (New York: Random House, 1991).

4. B.R. Wong & J. McKeen, *A Manual for Life* (Gabriola Island, BC: PD Publishing, 1992), p. 113.

5. N. Webster, *Webster's Collegiate Dictionary* (Springfield, MA: G. & C. Merriam Co., 1947), p. 742.

6. Robert Johnson, *He* (New York: Harper & Row, 1986), p. 31.

7. Robert Johnson, *She* (New York: Harper & Row, 1986), p. 42.

8. C.J. Jung, *The Portable Jung* (Joseph Campbell, ed.) (New York: Viking Press, 1971), pp. 148–162.

9. J.M. Russell, "Sartre's Theory of Sexuality," *Journal of Humanistic Psychology, 19*(2), Spring 1979, pp. 35–45.

10. Philip Wylie, *Generation of Vipers* (New York: Rinehart & Company, Inc., 1942), pp. 68–69.

11. Noah Webster, *The Living Webster Encyclopedic Dictionary* (Chicago: The English Language Institute of America, 1975), p. 741.

12. R.J. Stoller, *Perversion* (New York: Pantheon Books, 1975), pp. 64–65.

13. Jock McKeen, "The Ecstasy of Saint Theresa," in *As It Is In Heaven* (Gabriola Island, BC: PD Publishing, 1993), pp. 183–84.

14. J.M. Russell, "Sartre's Theory of Sexuality," *Journal of Humanistic Psychology, 19*(2), Spring 1979, p. 41.

15. St. Irenaeus, quoted in E.A. Johnson, *She Who Is, The Mystery of God in Feminist Theological Discourse* (New York: Crossroad Publishing Company, 1992), p. 14.

Developmental Stages of Loving

The Meaning of Love

Introduction

"Love" is one of the most frequently used words in the English language. People long for love, fight for love, and even die for love. They tell one another that they love each other. Most people assume that love exists between family members. Yet, there is very little agreement about what is really meant by "love." When the word is spoken, each person assumes that the meaning heard is the one intended. Frequently, that is not the case. Yet, on such misconceptions are built many relationships that are doomed to fail, with all the resulting emotional pain and complications that we know so well! We have written at some length in other places about the development of loving.[1,2] However, over the years, these ideas have ripened, and we wish to put them forward again in a more extensive manner, and to amplify the discussion about the various phases and aspects of loving.

No Such Thing as "Love"

Loving is not a thing, not an object, nor is it even a noun. It is an *action*, expressing emotion, a *verb*. There is no such thing as love; there is only *loving*. Loving is a process; there is no end point where one finds something called "love." There is only a *journey*, a developmental *project* in life, wherein one can *discover* oneself and others to be in loving relationships. It is a quality of interaction, something that is felt within, that could be shown on the outside by appearance (the "look" of love) and by deed (loving behaviour). Too often, love is treated as though it were a commodity, some thing that can be exchanged or bartered, or withheld and used for ransom or control. When it is seen as something limited in quantity, it must be carefully guarded, and slowly measured out in amounts that do not deplete a person. Such a view of love as object is mechanistic in nature. In this view people have only so much love to give, and so they must become shrewd investors in order to ensure a healthy return when they dedicate any to another. Children are viewed as empty vessels that

175

must be filled with love so they will have some to give in the future. Parents and children become fixated in the pattern of exchanging love as if it were an object, a commodity to be used for control of one another.

> Love is the chain whereby to bind a child to his parents.
> —Abraham Lincoln[3]

Energetic View of Loving

Another view of loving is an energetic one in which loving is seen to be the energy of *union* flowing between people, nurturing their growth and providing their pleasure. With such a view, there is a corresponding need to *be loved*: loving without reciprocation drains people of their energy. It is apparent that this view of love is still mechanistic in nature.

In contrast, we believe that energy is not transferred or exchanged. Instead, energy within one resonates with the energy within another—all in the context of the universal harmony. What others see as a "love bond" we see as a *meaningful relational resonance* (see "Resonance," p. 11). Thus, there is no need to be loved; people need to discover and activate the energy of their own loving resonance (see "Love, Obsession and Addiction," p. 136).

Empathetic View of Loving

When people are finely tuned to one another, a resonant vibration occurs between them. Such loving people are sensitive and vulnerable, willing and able to be in harmony with others. Energy is not lost or passed between them, as the mechanistic views of energy would have. In this state of being, people can allow the energy of the universe to flow within them in an unimpeded way, creating the possibility of being in *empathetic* vibration, responding with others. In this proces, people become *recognized* to themselves and to each other. Loving does not join; what is *revealed* is the joining that already exists, because people are not really separate.

Loving is Relational

Loving is relational. We disagree with the simplistic dictum that is bandied about, "You can't love someone else until you learn to love yourself." Indeed, this notion has led to much self-involved indulgent behaviour, where people waste their time waiting for love to arrive, and fail to develop into their potential fullness and depth. People don't have to be loved first; as they learn to take an interest in others, they can discover their own feelings and responses. As they learn to experience empathy with another, they will be activating their own loving potential. Rather than having to first be loved, they need to exercise their initiative and courage, to take the risk to enter into a loving relationship.

Loving provides people with a way of seeing beyond their defences, masks and roles. They make visible what hitherto has been invisible. Loving is not the glue that holds together their personality, as the mechanistic view would have it. Rather, it is a way of *illuminating*, *revealing* and *locating* the Authentic Self in the overall scheme of things.

Development of Loving

As people grow and mature, the meaning of love changes. This change is not sequential in nature; it is cumulative. Infants have a need to be loved in a way that is nurturing and protective. As they grow, that need grows less important, but never entirely disappears. Other meanings of loving unfold, taking on various degrees of importance at different times. The more a person matures, the more encompassing and complex becomes the meaning of loving.

Loving is not a constant entity—rather it is a *process* that is different in different situations and at different times. An infant in its mother's arms experiences different loving from the mother who is the co-participant. And that same mother means something different when she says to her husband, "I love you." And the same woman means something different again when, as an adult, she says "I love you" to her own aging parent.

Loving develops as the individual grows and gains experience. The quality of loving changes at different ages; furthermore, loving is different at the same age in various relationships. So, you can love pizza, your dog, Mozart, your child, your husband, yourself, or God. Each "loving" is different, even though in the vernacular, the same word "love" is used to describe them all. Much as the Eskimo people have dozens of words to describe various qualities of snow, there probably should be dozens of words to describe the variations in loving.

Stages of Loving

In *A Manual for Life*, we noted the Stages of Loving that occur in developing a mature relationship with others, with oneself, and with life.[4] The following list is a refinement, with some changes and additions from the original.

Stages of Loving
Loving is Supportive
Loving is Enstrengthening
Loving is Enlightening
Loving is Valuing The Person
Loving is Pleasuring
Loving is Recognition
Loving is Being Vulnerable and Intimate
Loving is Accepting
Loving is Sharing
Loving is Co-Creating
Loving is Eternal

Note that these stages of development are additive and cumulative. Although they tend to proceed in order from the top to the bottom, these *aspects* of loving are more like elements in a rich tapestry of experience, rather than sequential phenomena.

At any point in time, depending upon the level of maturation, people may have the capability of loving in a great variety of ways. They choose the way their loving will be expressed, depending upon their personality and circumstances.

Loving Is Supportive

Dependency

At birth, the infant is helpless. Anxious, frightened and needy, the baby is dependent upon parents (or parental substitutes) for survival, for comfort, and for reassurance. When these basic physical and emotional needs are met by parents, the child experiences being loved. Parents express this loving by caretaking; infants experience this loving as the recipient of the care.

It is this basic kind of interaction—this "taking care of" and "being taken care of"—that is most universally interpreted as love. For infants, it is an essential transaction, as they live with a vague but very real fear that not to be loved would be to perish; if they were not loved, they might be abandoned, which would make survival impossible. Whatever natural bonding exists between a mother and her child is reinforced by this *mutuality of dependency feelings.* Such strong bonding is indeed a matter of life and death to the child in all aspects—

physically, emotionally, and spiritually. The physical is of less importance to the parent; however, the emotional and spiritual needs can be even stronger in the parent than in the child.

This kind of "love"—this *seeming* need to be protected and needed, remains with each person throughout life. With maturity, people come to recognize their ability to take care of themselves; indeed, each person has an increasing need to be independent, to separate and make individual choices. No matter how mature people become, they will always carry this infantile feeling of dependency, which can never be erased. As people grow, they can learn to more freely *choose* when, how and with whom that feeling is expressed.

Unmet Needs

The idea of *needs* is a thorny one. Although it appears that children "need" to be loved, they probably just need protection and stimulation. Further, what they really need is to discover their own capability for loving. Without finding this, people persist in the infantile desire for attention.

When the craving to be loved is not adequately met, a child will respond first with anxiety, then fear, then anger and rage, then depression, and finally despair. When a person loses a "loved" partner, the process is often exactly the same. There is likely to be a similar process of feeling anxiety, fear, rage, depression, and despair. However, there is a major difference between children who feel abandoned and adults who feel the same; the children are in real danger of dying, whereas abandoned adults only feel as if they might perish. Many obviously competent adults readily respond to their infantile fear of abandonment.

The Myth of Loving as Supportive

This view of love as involving need and dependence has been mythologized in the romances that people see as role models, such as the story of Romeo and Juliet. Underlying this great love story is a theme of two people not being able to survive without one another; they sacrifice themselves in the name of their "love." The majority of the populace seems to yearn to participate in some version of this romantic (and tragic) tale.

Security and Control

In the immaturity of such dependent "love," people attempt to control the loved person to maintain a base of security. Such control is established between "loving" persons in a great variety of ways. Placating, manipulating, threatening, being pleasing, or becoming indispensable to the other—these are some of the more socially acceptable ways of gaining control, and hence, feeling secure.

In both children and adults, such a dependent "love" is usually accompanied by feelings of possessiveness and entitlement; people think they "own" their loved ones. Jealousy occurs when that ownership is threatened. Too often, in their fear of being abandoned, people use their jealousy as a means of control of the loved person.

Obviously, this is *love objectified*, not loving. In such fixation upon dependency and ownership, people do not come to recognize each other; hence genuine loving cannot flower.

Pleasing the Other

Children learn to please their parents because of their insecurity and fear of abandonment; this sets the basic motif for all relationships that follow. As they grow, youngsters continue to look outside for support and attention, and try to be pleasing to keep this security intact. As they enter school and establish relationships with peers, pleasing continues as a theme. People carry this motif on in trying to please teachers; this continues later on with employers, and in their spousal and partnering relationships. Oddly, parents are often confined by their intense need to please their own children. All of this pleasing and desire to be protected relates to an ongoing infantile fear of abandonment; this theme lurks under the surface of most adult relationships.

Accepting Neediness

Most everyone has these unresolved infantile dependencies. They only become a problem if they become the central motif in relationships, because the relationship will be limited by them. Indeed, in a developing relationship, this theme of loving as support is an important building block. Not only is this a necessary early stage of relational development, but this stage also involves feelings relating to personal vulnerability. When people make each other important, they are afraid to lose that person, in the same way infants are afraid to lose their parents. People can share much vulnerability with each other in working through this dependency to more autonomy. As long as one partner does not try to control the other with this felt need, there can be nutritive times of mutual pleasure and satisfaction when such feelings are shared with vulnerability.

Love comforteth, like sunshine after rain. —Shakespeare[5]

Loving Is Enstrengthening

Enstrengthenment, not Empowerment

In earlier writing, we titled this next phase "Love is Empowering." Now we recognize much confusion exists for people in distinguishing between power and strength. We ourselves confine the use of the word "power" to situations of domination, submission, and control. People have power over one another. Strength, on the other hand, originates from within, asserting the person's genuine autonomous self; it involves self-awareness and responsible choices and actions that are not "over" anyone else. We have written at length elsewhere on making the distinction between power and strength.[6]

Recognizing that the use of the term "empowerment" seems to perpetuate much confusion, we do not use this term any longer. For us, more distinct meaning can be associated with the term "enstrengthening."

When people become *empowered* (accumulating power), they remain tied to the very thing that they are gaining power over. *Enstrengthenment* (growing strength) comes with an embodied sense of self, where people have their own viewpoints, perspectives, values, thoughts and feelings. In expressing strength, there is no need to oppose, or to move away from anyone or anything.

Self-Reliance

As a child grows, a natural development of skills is required for self-sufficiency (first grasping, then crawling, then walking and talking). The mastery of these skills affords the child a sense of confidence and a feeling of self-worth (which others call "personal power"). The better these skills are developed, the less the child will have to rely upon others for survival. Anxiety and fear are reduced as the child becomes increasingly self-reliant. During this process, the child anxiously checks out the reactions of the parent upon whom survival depends.

As youngsters experiment, they constantly check back with parents, looking for reactions of approval or disapproval for newly found independence. If parents have a need to be needed, then their children will get the message that it is not OK to go out and explore; these children will remain emotionally tied to their parents, and will develop guilt feelings to keep them from pursuing their natural desires to explore and learn. In this overprotective environment, the parents are using the children as a means to not face their own insecurities. In their limited logic, they have made their significance to their children so important that they find it unthinkable that their children can grow and develop on their own.

This is often expressed as overprotectiveness when the children are young. When the children are older, the parents frequently give rules and admonitions "for their own good" that serve to keep the children tied to the parental view of the world, rather than encouraging the young people to develop their own views. This excessive control also occurs when little children bring a school project to the parent; parents often make suggestions as to what their child should draw, or write about, thus inhibiting the development of the youngster's own creativity. If parents were able to say, "What do *you* want to do?" rather than "Here's an idea for you," children could become stronger with their own viewpoints and initiatives. The "good enough" parent[7] will encourage the children's ever-increasing steps toward autonomy and independence.

Parents Who Won't Let Go

Some parents themselves have not developed beyond the belief that to love is to take care of another. When these parents are possessive or controlling, they are usually expressing their loving as they know how, through offering support and protection and control; because this tends to foster dependence, it can be very limiting for both parents and children. At some unconscious level, these parents experience a fear of losing their dependent children. Aware of this fear in the parents, children can react in a variety of ways. They can believe that it must be dangerous to become independent, and so can lose interest in acquiring the tools of self-sufficiency. On the other hand, when children want to be independent and do not feel supported toward that goal, they can feel resentment, anger and defiance.

In adult relationships, people are often attracted to one another in a desire to support and be supported. When either becomes interested in growing as a separate person, the security of the dependent relationship is threatened. The other person will likely feel anxious, hurt, angry, and blaming, and might try to regain control over the other in some way. To feel loving and supportive of another's growth as a separate individual seems beyond that person's comprehension. When people persist in such control, they can become alienated from each other and feel neglected. These relationship dynamics often began in the nuclear family with overprotective parents.

Roles

Roles are based on expectations of performance that demand adherence to rules and conventions, rather than valuing the growing independence and autonomy of both parties. Seeking security, needy persons often want their partners to fulfil roles rather than explore their own interests. For example, the husband might expect the wife to stay at home as a homemaker, even though she might prefer to be out in the work force; conversely, the wife might expect the husband to go out and work, even though he is more interested in being the homemaker. Mature, loving individuals take pleasure in witnessing their loved ones becoming more of themselves as persons, full of their own strength, and less needy of the approval of others.

Autonomy

When loving is enstrengthening, both partners are recognized as separate individuals; in their mutual solitariness, they can embrace each other without leaning. Thus, both persons become strong in their own individuation.

> *Love consists in this, that two solitudes protect and touch and greet each other.* —R.M. Rilke[8]

Loving Is Enlightening

Order Out of Chaos

To the infant, both the inner and outer worlds of experience seem senseless and anxiety-producing. Through developing personal abilities and skills, a child acquires particular viewpoints, with individual likes, dislikes and aspirations. Loving that child involves an offering of stimulating experiences that will sustain that learning, to cast a light into the shadow of ignorance. The child feels the loving of those *enlightening* situations that help to bring order into this chaos. As the child continually grows and learns, the enlightenment becomes more extensive. Such a child shines with the increasing awareness of self and others.

Children have a natural tropism to learn and to discover the world; they become illuminated as life is revealed. One aspect of loving is related to this illumination: as parents witness the light in a child's eyes as the little one learns something new, they light up, too, with loving. Curiosity is a natural function, which can be lost or underdeveloped when parents do not appreciate their children's native ability to learn.

Learning Throughout Life

People have the ongoing capacity to further develop and strengthen their curiosity, through investigation of the world and themselves. Life provides the possibility to learn unceasingly. People can have a strong sense of fulfilment from learning, acquiring mastery of their innate potentials. Strength accumulates, as people become more of themselves. Learning is not an accumulation of facts; rather, it is a process of relating to the world, incorporating and responding dynamically in a way that brings the whole self to bear upon circumstances. Through learning, one is fulfilled in relationship to self and others.

When people come to enjoy learning, they can have enlightening relationships later in life, with spouses and children, partners and friends. Such people take pleasure in seeing their partners learn, grow, and become fulfilled; they themselves continue to expand their vision by learning to see the world through the eyes of others.

Indoctrination vs. Discovery

Not all knowledge is freeing. Too frequently, information is taught in a way that is controlling and enslaving. In schools, children often must agree and conform to what is taught. Such indoctrinated knowledge—albeit useful and perhaps even essential to that person's successful adjustment in society—is not enlightening. It is convenient to create and maintain roles, but it does not help people to discover themselves. In accommodating to this inculcation, people's essential nature becomes stifled.

In mid-life, an urgency often develops for self-expression. This frequently occurs after a person already has established a relationship based on a mode of mutual dependency. The thrust toward self-awareness and creativity becomes a disruptive force to the set patterns of such a relationship; yet, such a disruption can be revitalizing to both parties. If they can learn to enjoy each other's creativity and learning, couples can enter the new territory of loving as enlightening.

Mirroring

We have previously discussed the various types of mirroring previously (see "The Family Garden," p. 145). Providing direct mirroring facilitates the growth of autonomous persons; distorted mirrors often occur in power-based or romantic encounters.

Every person's growth as an individual (*individuation*) involves an ever-increasing awareness and knowledge of the self. A loving person provides information, experiences, encouragement, and feedback in a caring way. Parents who are loving in this way recognize that their children are individual entities, capable of their own growth and independence—like plants in a garden to be tended, watered, and allowed to grow—stimulated by such practices as *direct mirroring* by the parents other people. Too often, feedback is not provided lovingly; it can be critical, disapproving, and controlling, fostering compliance and impairing the person's self-esteem.

Many times, parents are more concerned that their children become what the parents want. Often, the adults are more concerned for social position and what others think of the children (and by association, the family), and are less concerned for the welfare and learning of the youngsters. Some parents see their children as their chance for immortality; when parents believe that they have failed in life, they can heap unrealistic expectations upon their children to fulfil what they have not. In this atmosphere, the children are seen as tools to fulfil the parents' ambitions, rather than as individuals who have their own interests and can learn about the world from their own vantage points.

When parents offer *distorted mirroring*, they reflect back images where the children experience themselves as smaller than life (*concave mirroring*) or larger than life (*convex mirroring*); both of these faulty mirrorings fail to provide an opportunity for the child to learn a realistic sense of self and a harmonious perspective on the world. When parents praise excessively, or criticize harshly, the children do not learn accurate self-assessment.

If children are given *direct mirroring*, with honest, uninflated feedback of thoughts and feelings from guardian figures, they will be able to learn about themselves and the world around them without a distorted viewpoint. This direct mirroring provides a nutrient atmosphere for realistic learning and enlightenment.

In a relationship that values learning and enlightenment, people encourage their partner to have greater self-awareness, and, toward this end, they provide loving, honest feedback. In most relationships, feedback is not given lovingly, or with any concern for the feelings of the other. It is usually delivered and received with resentment, for the purpose of control.

> *The value of the personal relationship to all things is that it creates intimacy ... and intimacy creates understanding ... understanding creates love ... love conquers loneliness.* —Anaïs Nin[9]

Loving Is Valuing the Person

Ways to Value Children

Parents have children for a great variety of reasons—to fulfil their own need to find meaning, to avoid their own loneliness, to provide a mutual project for relationship, to find pleasure in taking care of someone, to solve an inner need for immortality, and numerous others. For each of these reasons, the parent values the child in a different way, each way transmitting a particular emotional message to the child; most of these messages are called "love."

A baby peering into a parent's eyes is looking to see how the parent values the infant. If children are valued as possessions, their behaviour will be developed accordingly, and they will tend to become placators in life. When children experience being valued as persons, they can learn to value themselves in the same way. When children feel cherished, they are helped to believe that they count, that their existence is of consequence and that their being is of some importance in this world!

Possessive Love

Some parents value their children as possessions; they "own" their children, who must behave in ways necessary to please the parents. Little regard is given to who the children are as individuals, or what they themselves might desire. They are seen as "good" children to the extent that they conform and achieve. The child's self-esteem is dependent upon how much the parent is pleased, and ultimately, how pleasing the child can be to all parental authority figures. As the child develops, self-esteem continues to be directly related to being able to please others, rather than stemming from internal assessment by the self.

> *You love me so much, you want to put me in your pocket. And I shall die there smothered.* —D.H. Lawrence[10]

Such possessive "love" often is of great value. Much of our socio-cultural achievement is related to it. A lot of people's desire to be in relationship, to raise a family and to work hard to provide for them stems from this urge to own, to caretake, and to improve others; this helps to establish a base of security. When people are "loved" in this way, they feel worthwhile; unfortunately, in this circumstance their self-esteem is dependent upon the valuation of others, rather than their own. Many children are unable to meet the expectations of their parents and teachers who love in this way. They spend their lives feeling inadequate, inferior, unacceptable, unworthy, insecure, and at the mercy of the approval of others.

Roles and Ideal Self

Usually, children are raised as *objects*, to play *roles* ("good" daughters, successful students, loving fathers), and generally do not have much experience in being valued for the persons they are. Youngsters are expected to manufacture an Ideal Self, rather than be appreciated for their beingness (the Authentic Self).[11] People raised with rewards for these roles will tend to objectify themselves, and will be inclined to lose touch with their deeper nature. Thus, they are prone to self-hatred, and lack the self-awareness and self-acceptance that would bring them back to their essential being.

Self-Esteem

In the adult years, the issue of self-esteem is central. In relationships, many people can only feel worthwhile to the extent that they have the approval of others. These *field-dependent* people seek the company of others who will hold them in high regard, and are happy to be pleasing in return. This stance works well until the expectations of one another are not met. Then resentment, anger, and rejection become real possibilities, usually followed by depression.

People of high self-esteem are able to value themselves as persons. This process is supported by experiences with parents and friends who value them in this way. When rejected, such persons will not crumble into helplessness, or react with defensiveness, violence or punishment. They will be able to clearly see the important issues at stake for what they are—nothing more, nothing less. They tend to remain vulnerable, and do not shy away from feeling emotional pain. They remain responsible for their own feelings and do not tend to blame others.

Valuing the Person

At this stage, loving involves valuing people beyond their roles and accomplishments. Each party in a relationship is seen as an autonomous being, separate and whole. Because partners are appreciated as persons, not objects, there is no ownership between them; instead, they grow together in their separateness.

Loving Is Pleasuring

A loving person takes enjoyment in seeing pleasure in another. Parents are in touch with a spark of life that is noticeable in the eyes of their children. When this spark is present, they know that it is a sign of connection with life and with them that is pleasurable, comfortable, and desirable. Much of a parent's child care is unconsciously determined by such signs. In return, much of the child's reactions are aimed to see or feel a similar sign of delight in the parent. When this spark is present on both sides, they participate in a *loving state*, which has been created by both of them.

A word of caution: it is important to note that *the other person is not the source of pleasure*. In the loving state, both parties are responsible for their own pleasure, which is stimulated by being in the presence of another loving person. Too many people become fixated in the belief that their pleasure is dependent upon someone else—that they can only be happy when they are loved by that other person or persons. They lose touch with their ability to feel their own pleasure, making others responsible for it. By being so field dependent, they are prone to be pleasing and placating in order to control others, and to prevent themselves from being rejected. The end result is often a loss of strength and autonomy. That is not loving! In loving, each person grows and is greater for it; whenever the self is reduced, then loving has been lost.

In adult loving relationships, *the pleasure is in the loving itself.* Loving people have pleasure when their partner has pleasure. People's loving does not cause the pleasure in their partners; because each is a distinct person, capable of growth and autonomous development, everyone's pleasure is self-generated. As most people carry within them the childhood desire to be loved, there is indeed a comfort and pleasure in being loved. However, the more profound pleasure for each person is in *being able to love*, to feel the expansiveness and exhilaration of loving itself.

> The pleasure of love is in the loving. We are happier in the passion
> we feel than in what we arouse. —La Rochefoucauld[12]

Loving Is Recognition

When defences are relinquished, people are exposed to themselves and to each other. When the walls are down, both parties are able to see and witness each other. In this process, each is *revealed* to the other. As people come to know one another in this way, they become increasingly able to be close, in harmonious contact with themselves and each other.

One is *recognized* in being revealed; so too, one is revealed in recognizing another. The word recognize comes from the Latin *recognoscere* (literally, to know again).[13] When people recognize their partners, they also recognize themselves, as they can only know in another what they know in themselves. As people *know* their partners to be an expression of life, they too can feel their own profound sense of *participation* in life. In recognizing each other, partners can see their place in the harmony of things, and come home to the union of themselves with each other and with the universe. Life shines forth, and events are seen with deeper meaning—a spiritual dimension opens. In the theological concept of revelation, the life force (God) is manifested. When people recognize each other, they literally shine with the emanation of the life force!

> *Every relationship, from the intense closeness of parent and child or partners in marriage to the more distant connections with coworkers and business acquaintances or even the driver of the bus we take daily to work, is an entanglement of souls. The gift of this entanglement is not only intimacy between persons, but also a revelation of soul itself, along with the invitation to enter more deeply into its mysteries.* —Thomas Moore[14]

Loving Is Being Vulnerable and Intimate

Learning Defences

During the developmental years, most of children's training is to prepare them for security and survival. Education and parenting promote defences—through the teaching of roles, achieving, and compliance to authority. Children learn social niceties and acceptable moralities at home, school, and church. People learn to contain their emotions, to overcome their impulsiveness, and to control themselves and others. Thus, a pattern of relationships is established, wherein manipulating others and controlling the self are encouraged and rewarded.

Defences and Roles

People tend to defend themselves, to assure the integrity of their own organism and being. This is a phenomenon that is necessary for survival. Psychological and emotional survival is just as important as the physical variety—to lose any of these seems like losing all. Each person may use a variety of defences to this end. The particular array of defences creates much of that individual's personality and uniqueness; in this way, such a system of defences is not only necessary, it is desirable.

Unfortunately, those very defences that ensure survival also work to inhibit the full expression of the self. People who are fully themselves risk censure, rejection, and abandonment. To the child—or the child within each of us—such rejections are seen as a threat to existence. So people learn to function in roles that are effective for survival but involve a closing down, a contraction of the energy body. The self is "put into cold storage with a secret hope of rebirth,"[15] safe from the judgments and possible rejections of others. Then such people find difficulty in being exposed either to others, or to themselves. These individuals tend to be invulnerable in relating to others.

Letting Go into Vulnerability

For personal growth—to discover an essential meaning in life—each person must ultimately *let go*, to experience spontaneity, to feel the outer limits of existence and the fullness of one's own inner space. That can only happen when the personal defences are set aside, or made transparent, or abandoned altogether—when the person is *vulnerable*.

Children are vulnerable at the beginning; in face of the threats and vagaries of life, they soon learn to develop necessary defences and roles. If they were to fail in this, they would be seen as handicapped and ineffective in life, and often judged as "stupid."

Like young children, *innocents* are vulnerable. Innocents remain like children; by somehow retaining a trust in others and in life, they neither become defended nor seemingly "stupid." They remain open, yet still they effectively survive. Frequently, their lives become exemplary and inspirational to others.

Loving is Offering Vulnerability

To be loving is to offer this vulnerability, to reveal the self openly, innocently, without guile and without control. In so loving, the person is able to experience the self in its most authentic form, without the usual amount of restricting defences. It is a fresh, open, and exhilarating emotional state. The self is expansive, and able to experience the outer reaches of its own boundaries. In this way, a rare opportunity occurs—to become reacquainted with the self, to become fully *present*, past all the defences.

> Where love rules, there is no will to power; and where power pre-
> dominates, there love is lacking. The one is the shadow of the other.
> —C. G. Jung[16]

Being Vulnerable

When people are intimate, they desires to *share* themselves with others, to become *recognized*. However, to be recognized, people must shed their habituated defences and roles. By the time people reach adulthood, these defences are so ingrained that this becomes a difficult (nearly impossible!) task.

When people present themselves in a vulnerable, defenceless way, they are revealed—becoming available for intimate contact, without guile, deception or manipulation. Hence, their relationships can be authentic; their loving involves an extreme vulnerability. In this situation, people might feel anxious and uncertain; however, they are also *present*, *revealed*, and *available* for genuine contact.

Without vulnerability, relationships involve roles and habituated behaviours, while the persons remain unknown to each other. So many marriages and long-term partnerships are between two roles; the two individuals might not ever be vulnerable and revealed to each other. Personal growth becomes possible through vulnerability; such loving offers recognition and the opportunity for *intimacy*.

This loving occurs in relationships in the Integration stage and beyond. In Romance and Power Struggle, there is limited vulnerability. When vulnerability arises, along with the curiosity about the self and the other, the state of Integration opens more fully.

Loving Is Accepting

Accepting

In relationships where roles and obligations are paramount, people do not come to kow each other sufficiently to experience loving as accepting. When partners become more curious and *less defended*, opening to each other in the Integration stage, they become aware of themselves and each other beyond the limited images of roles and objectifications. As they *reveal* this to each other, they can embrace and accept previously unacknowledged aspects of themselves and each other. As this process of *curiosity, awareness* and *acknowledgement* becomes established as a consistent theme in a relationship, partners can grow to know and accept both themselves and each other. As we have discussed (see "Developmental Stages of Relationships," p. 50), this process of accepting self and other progressively deepens, and is continually translated into new actions of growth, awareness, and acceptance. As the relationship matures, each partner becomes more *personal* and more *individuated.*

Beyond the Power Struggle

In the Power Struggle, both persons remain hidden within defences and roles, and cannot be known; hence, there is little opportunity for accepting themselves or each other. Instead of being curious, people become fixated in blame, guilt, and contempt. When loving is accepting, people move beyond the limitations of right or wrong to accept their thoughts, feelings, and attitudes; more and more, they are willing to acknowledge these in interchanges of revelation. In this process, people can overcome the limitations that accompany blame and can move to a deeper loving acceptance of their partner; at the same time, this process of acceptance operates to overcome self-hatred, and their own self worth grows.

In a dialogue of mutual acceptance, couples can accept their current situation, rather than complaining or wishing for something different. They have literally "rolled up their sleeves" and are fully engaged in the relationship project, interested in whatever comes to light. This curiosity and willingness to face any turn of events is a characteristic of the Integration stage. As the relationship deepens, both individuals become fuller in their loving acceptance of each other, and in their self-acceptance (self-loving).

Loving Is Sharing

> *A good marriage is that in which each appoints the other guardian of his solitude.* —R.M. Rilke[17]

In the early phases of relationships, people are defended in their objectifications of each other. Both are hidden behind their defences and walls, and unavailable for genuine dialogue. When partners reach the stage of Integration, they are more curious than defended, more available than hidden. In the atmosphere of exploration and curiosity, they become *revealed* to each other, vulnerable yet strong. Each becomes more individuated and autonomous, and yet capable of much deeper closeness because they can accept their separateness. When partners will be open and vulnerable with each other, free of expectations, blame, guilt or defence, they can *share* their feelings in a loving way.

Taking Care of Another, or Caring About Another

Sharing is not loving when it has an expectation in return. Frequently, parents do things for their children in order to control them, to have them do their bidding. That is not wrong; it is understandable, probably even desirable. It is a way of training a child for the future, a means of behavioural control. It is an element of *taking care of* the child. But, as the child grows, the parent should be able to do less of that, and become more able to *care about* the person who is the child. In this way, parents could then can become less "parents" and more persons with their children.

By not remaining fixated in the caretaking role, people can become more free within themselves, and more able to share themselves with others; this is especially important in primary intimate relationships. Taking care of one another reduces people to dependent objects, encouraging arrestation of personal growth and producing a relationship that is static and inhibiting. Caring about others respects their individuality. When parents love their children in this way, they can take delight in the persons, the individuating selves that are emerging. When partners in a primary relationship can share without fostering dependence, they can experience a true *communion.*

Individuation

When persons share in this way, they express more of themselves, and become more *individuated*; each is separate, yet sensitive to the other. They do not have to become distant in order to be individuals; they can be close in their interaction, through establishing of an *interdependence* (a collaborative co-mingling of separate autonomous people). When sharing is impaired (as it is in most families), the children need to rebel to become *independent* and *individualized.* Sharing helps to establish *boundaries* and *autonomy;* caretaking and obligations establish *dependency* and *walls.*

Anything that is shared can enhance intimacy. For example, anger can be shared in a responsible manner, not blaming the other for the anger, and keeping the expression of the emotion boundaried so that there is no threat of violence or control. In the same way, jealousy, possessiveness, guilt, blame, expectations and resentments can all be shared with a partner to bring further closeness (see "Feelings and Closeness," p. 34).

Learning to Share

The task in learning to share is to move beyond the limitations of one's own perspective. People can learn to recognize that their partners have valid (and often very different) points of view. In sharing, people can learn to really listen, and hear what their partners hear; in the same way, they can learn a new seeing, to witness what their partners' viewpoints offer. In this way, people grow beyond the narcissistic self-bound attitudes of childhood into a more mature empathetic responses, sensitive to the feelings and perspective of each other.

> Nothing we do, however virtuous, can be accomplished alone; therefore, we are saved by love. —Reinhold Neibuhr[18]

Loving Is Co-creating

> The most visible creators I know of are those artists whose medium is life itself ... the ones who express the inexpressible—without brush, hammer, clay or guitar. They neither paint nor sculpt—their medium is being. Whatever their presence touches has increased life. They see and don't have to draw. They are the artists of being alive.
>
> —J. Stone[19]

Co-Creativity

When people become *co-creative*, they share their acceptance and awareness in joint engagement with life. In such loving, people's lives become a creative process in dynamic interaction with others around. This results not only in fine art works, but also in inventive expression in all aspects of life (a "flourish" in home decorating, or a tasty flair in cooking). Evidence of this co-creativity manifests in people's work, family life, and leisure activities. A remarkable quality of life is revealed that comes forth in the activities and interactions of the persons involved—newness, freshness, and vibrancy are evident, even in small things. In the mutuality of their relationship, such people approach all aspects of their life as creative endeavours.

The Spirit Child of the Relationship

When loving is shared, something new is created. Some people call it a "bond"; some refer to it as a "spirit child." Any name is an attempt to describe something ineffable. In this vulnerable state of mutual sharing, caring, and revelation, each person becomes more fully present to the other, offering the fullness of the self innocently and without guile. Each experiences the expansiveness and authenticity of the self, fresh and without defences. Each is in tune with the other; some report that they feel as if there is a "joining of the souls." It is as though boundaries have been erased, and a union of two separatenesses has been accomplished.

Let there be spaces in your togetherness. —Kahlil Gibran[20]

Bonded and Separate

In actuality, the surrendering to loving does not extinguish the boundaries between people. Rather, those boundaries become more clearly defined. One often has the sharp pain of recognition that fusion is not possible. Each person will continue to be separate. However, both will know themselves more distinctly, and will know one another more intimately. It is a state of *recognition*. Because partners know each other's experience so well, separating boundaries seem absent. Union does seem possible. This is a characteristic of the *loving state* that is created between people sharing their loving.

The Inspirational Quality of Co-creation

What Co-creative people do, and how they are together, influences their environment and the products of their joint labour. Not only do others recognize such loving, but more, they are profoundly affected by it. They are *inspired* to enter into their own loving project of individuating and sharing!

All mankind love a lover. —Ralph Waldo Emerson[21]

Loving Is Eternal

Loved Ones are Never Lost

Possessions are soon forgotten; people never are. *Things that are held* closely to the self remain passively uninvolved, even though they might appear to be highly valued. *People who are loved* become part of a dynamic relationship in which both parties are transformed. The parts of one another that have been possessed more than loved will fade and disappear. But the *essence* of what has been involved in loving is forever.

Such loving does not involve the imposition of one personality on another. Rather, it is like two musical instruments that are capable of many harmonies; when the presence of the other is imminent, previously unrevealed harmonies come into flower. People are not so much *changed* by loving interactions as *called forth* into the fullness of their own nature. When this has occurred, it is never again undone—the harmonies themselves are timeless and eternal.

Loving Beyond Death

Thus, when one person dies, the loving does not stop. Indeed, often the intensity of the loving increases when the physical presence is gone. A friend lost her son to a sudden automobile accident; when we saw her, we asked her, "Do you feel closer to him now that he is not in the body?" She was at first shocked by this question; however, a few days later she reported that this perspective came to be very sustaining to her, to realize that her connection to her son is not dependent upon the bodily presence or the anticipation of his return. She realized that her loving for him is eternal.

The Harmony of Loving

The basic life vibration is not related to time and space. When people are more authentic, they are joined to the universal vibration, and hence are connected and related to all of life (see "Resonance," p. 11). In this way, the essence of people is *eternal* (not related to time) and *infinite* (not related to space); at the same time, we are distinct and individual and finite. This is the deep spiritual nature of people: each individual participates in eternity and infinity.

Universal Loving

In the diagram "The Self and Connections" (see "Resonance," p. 11), the universal wave energy of the universe could be called "God" (other words are Tao, universal energy, or universal loving). The individual person springs up as a distinct being, emanating from the rhizome of the universal energy. Each person appears separate and distinct in time and space; yet the mortal being is an expression of an eternal process. When people touch their authentic nature (by self-compassion, by breathing, and in dialogue with others), they resonate in harmony with the loving state of the universe, where they are eternally related one to another. "Loving is eternal" acknowledges the oneness of all.

This is the *transpersonal* dimension to loving. As partners discover more of themselves and each other, they are *transformed*—in their appreciation of both their uniqueness and the wholeness of which they are both expressions. This is *not transcendence,* where one rises above the body, and disidentifies with worldly existence; the very raw stuff of each individual has been transformed through the crucible of the dialogue in a loving relationship. This state of loving involves *reunion* with cosmic energy; the partners experience profound closeness, not just with themselves and each other, but also with all of life. They reunite in harmony with the all, through touching each other.

Joined Beyond Time and Space

When people open more fully to themselves and their partners, they begin to glimpse a deeper dimension, in which they are indeed joined, and not bound by time or place. In this way, loving is eternal and infinite. The experience of eternal loving involves the *revelation* of our connection with the wholeness of the universe. When people vibrate with life, they move beyond social roles, which separate them by colour, race, creed, and social class; in this *reunion,* they find themselves at one with themselves and life itself, rejoined with the harmony of the cosmic vibration (God).

> If we can find the whole world in a grain of sand, we can also find
> the soul itself at the small point in life where destinies cross and
> hearts intermingle. —Thomas Moore[22]

Persons Fully Alive in Loving Relationship

In the mature relationship, people will experience many of the dimensions of loving mentioned in this chapter. In the dialogue and appreciation of themselves and each other, the project goes on without cease. The following poem illustrates.

Thanks To A Friend

> You loved me first in a way strange to me
> As the air is strange to the fledgling bird,
> Giving support but demanding the use of wings.
> And as I trusted you,
> As I was compelled in my whole being to trust you,
> You accepted my trust in trust.
> You received my love and my dependence
> In trust for what you trust.

> You taught me to look beyond you, see what you see,
> Hear and proclaim the voice you hear and proclaim,
> Which is your voice, and mine.
> I fly in the air of the spirit of perfect love
> And whistle the dewfall song of the truth of love
> And eat forever the fruit of the Tree of Life
> Because you did not love me to possess me,
> Because you did not labour to convince me,
> Because you belong to the life that I belong to
> And you, knowing it, made me know it too.
> And now, what thanks have I
> That I might offer in a golden bowl
> To you?
> This only: that what you gave, and give,
> I give and will give and forever.
> As it is with you, so shall it be with me,
> That all may know—and may come to rejoice in knowing,
> The worth of a true friend.
>
> —Theodore Black[23]

Notes

1. B.R. Wong & J. McKeen, "To Be ...Loving...To Be," *Journal of Child and Youth Care*, 6(4), pp. 73–83.

2. B.R. Wong & J. McKeen, *A Manual for Life* (Gabriola Island, BC: PD Publishing, 1992), pp. 106–110.

3. Abraham Lincoln, quoted in E.M. Beck (ed.), *Bartlett's Familiar Quotations* (Boston, MA: Little, Brown and Co., 1980), p. 524.

4. B.R. Wong & J. McKeen, *A Manual for Life* (Gabriola Island, BC: PD Publishing, 1992), pp. 106–110.

5. W. Shakespeare, "Venus and Adonis" (line 799), in W.J. Craig (ed.), *The Complete Works of William Shakespeare* (London: Oxford University Press, 1957), p. 1082.

6. B.R. Wong & J. McKeen, *A Manual for Life* (Gabriola Island, BC: PD Publishing, 1992), pp. 56–64.

7. D.W. Winnicott, quoted in H. Guntrip, *Schizoid Phenomena, Object Relations and the Self* (New York: International Universities Press, 1969), p. 224.

8. R.M. Rilke, *Letters to a Young Poet*, quoted in *Bartlett's Familiar Quotations*, 15th ed. (Boston: Little, Brown and Company, 1980), p. 756.

9. Attributed to Anaïs Nin, source unknown.

10. D.H. Lawrence, *Sons and Lovers* (Middlesex: Penguin Books Ltd., 1948), p. 506.

11. B.R. Wong & J. McKeen, *A Manual for Life* (Gabriola Island, BC: PD Publishing, 1992), pp. 15–19.

12. François, Duc de La Rochefoucauld, *Reflections*, quoted in *Bartlett's Familiar Quotations*, 15th ed. (Boston: Little, Brown and Company, 1980), p. 293.

13. J. Traupman, *The New College Latin and English Dictionary* (New York: Bantam Books, 1966), p. 261.

14. Thomas Moore, *SoulMates* (New York: HarperCollins Publishers, 1994), p. 259.

15. H. Guntrip, *Psychoanalytic Theory, Therapy, and The Self* (New York: Basic Books, 1973), p. 152.

16. C.G. Jung, *The Psychology of the Unconscious*, vol. 7 (1943), quoted in *Bartlett's Familiar Quotations*, 15th ed. (Boston: Little, Brown and Company, 1980), p. 755.

17. Attributed to R.M. Rilke, source unknown.

18. R. Neibuhr, *The Irony of American History* (1952), quoted in *Bartlett's Familiar Quotations*, 15th ed. (Boston: Little, Brown and Company, 1980), p. 823.

19. J. Stone, "Creators," source unknown.

20. K. Gibran, *The Prophet* (New York: Alfred A. Knopf, 1966), p. 15.

21. R.W. Emerson, "Love," quoted in *The Macmillan Dictionary of Quotations* (New York: Macmillan Publishing Co., 1987), p. 335.

22. Thomas Moore, *SoulMates* (New York: HarperCollins Publishers, 1994), p. 259.

23. Attributed to Theodore Black, source unknown

The Harmonious Garden

A garden would be easy to develop and maintain if it contained only one kind of plant—but it would also be boring. Fortunately, gardens can be seeded with all manner of inhabitants, each with its own desires and requirements for growth. One kind of watering or fertilizing will not be appropriate for all. Some plants (like cucumbers) require much space to ramble and expand, while others (like carrots) will stay put where they are planted; some need to climb toward the sun while others like to creep under some shade. A well balanced garden will afford the ideal opportunities for each plant to have what it needs.

Like the vegetable garden, a good relationship garden provides for the varying conditions required by each of its inhabitants. One person may like time alone in privacy, while the other may be garrulous and social; one may like classical music, while the other may prefer heavy rock. It is important to recognize that none of these choices is wrong—they are merely *different*. Because people generally feel insecure and threatened by differences, they often judge those dissimilarities as being wrong, and set into motion (subtly or grossly) a series of strategies to change the other person; this underlies many power struggles in relationships. The desired outcome in such struggles is for one person to abandon what (s)he wants in order to become more like what the partner wants.

The turnip dreams longingly for an entire garden of only turnips, and feels more at home with fellow vegetables (such as carrots) that are like itself. Because of these similarities, they could sing in mellifluous harmony. The presence of other families in a garden creates a state of tension (this is so internationally as well as within the home). The greater the difference, the more dissonant the harmony.

In any relationship, there are likely to be many differences; the harmony is sometimes discordant. At first, people devote much energy toward changing one another. For the sake of peace, one or the other (or sometimes even both) abandon what (s)he wants to reach a *compromise*. In such instances, what has been abandoned sits somewhere deep within the person, generating unspoken resentment that, like pus in a carbuncle, must ultimately come bursting forth. In this manner, partnerships and nations create treaties for temporary peace, setting the stage for the next eruption. But for a while, they both sing the same song or some harmonious variation of that song.

Instead of submitting to being reduced to one another's wishes in order to hum a pleasing harmony, it is possible for both of the involved parties to continue with their individual songs, producing what initially seems discordant. Then, instead of changing the harmony, both might expand consciousness to be able to appreciate the divergent melodies and the dissonant harmonies produced by the differences. Such an appreciation must not be a *tolerance,* which still retains a belief in the wrongness of the other; the goal is for a true acceptance and liking of the different harmony. According to Richard Bernstein, "Deep attachment to culture is one of the things that prevents different people from understanding one another."[1]

> BEN: When I was younger, I recognized a strong dislike for pieces composed by Bartok; I found his music to be dissonant and unpleasing to my ear. In my mind, Beethoven and Chopin were the real composers because I liked their harmonies; Bartok was wrong! But even away back then I was aware that there was a large body of people who thought the world of Bartok's music. I wondered then about the possibility that there was nothing wrong with his music; perhaps the fault was my own inability to appreciate it! Being convinced about this fact, I set about to listen and relisten to such music, always looking into what I could like about it. The process has been a long and sometimes arduous one, but it has opened me up to appreciate a much broader band of music. Instead of narrowing my world, I have learned the possibility of increasing my consciousness and awareness to incorporate so many different kinds of experiences. And it all began with Bartok, for whose music, to this day, I still have a limited liking!

Our world has become increasingly aware of *diversity.* Unfortunately, this diversity is generally viewed through political eyes instead of personal ones. In the power arena, diversity produces hierarchies, with some differences being preferable over others. In democratic communities or families, the majority rules. However, the minorities fight back with resentment and victim politics; their positions become the causes aimed at correcting the faults suffered at the hands of those in power. Like the French Revolution, such causes begin with good intent, but through a process named *dérapage,*[2] this aim gradually slides into the opposite. In a similar way, relationships that begin with all good intent often deteriorate from something healthful and helpful into a destructive environment. This is especially so when important issues are ignored—swept under the rug and denied—rather than exposed, addressed, and ultimately appreciated.

These principles of relationship are directly applicable to the world stage. Centuries of recorded history have shown that treaties will not ensure a lasting peace. Repressed hostility just builds up over the years, waiting for an excuse to erupt into the use of force and conquest to wrestle the world into a sameness that is thought to be secure. Indeed, peace is not possible! More could be accomplished by diverting all those resources, time, and energy that are spent in the pursuit of peace to a project of expanding the consciousness of the involved parties. Then, a true appreciation of the different harmonies could lead to a world in which all of the divergent melodies would have a place.

A healthy garden would be a riot of colours, shapes, and sizes; so would a healthy relationship. With intact boundaries, each person would have a place in the sun, with a right to be different. Sameness that has been achieved through denial and repression begets future strife. It is preferable to make room in our hearts for differences that can be sustained only through an expansion of our consciousness. The harmonies of the differences can arouse our curiosity instead of our fears and judgments. Only through repeated exposure to those differences are we able to expand the range of our regard. This attitude in relationship furthers growth and strength while our horizons are being expanded. Such are the conditions of a healthy relationship garden.

Notes

1. Richard Bernstein, *Dictatorship of Virtue* (New York: Vintage Books [Random House, Inc.], 1994), p. 6.

2. Ibid., p. 3.

Spirituality and Relationships

Varieties of Spirituality

There are many ways to view the spiritual quest, each of them reflecting some basic assumptions about the nature of human life.

In some eastern philosophies, regular existence related to the body is often seen as illusory, producing suffering. The spiritual task involves seeking connections outside of the self, to recognize one's connection to the universe *beyond* the self—hence the use of the word "transpersonal." Practices like meditation and yoga are designed to help the follower to quiet the mind, and to see beyond the self in order to feel the unity of the cosmos. These are the *transcendental* (from the Latin, meaning "to climb beyond"[1]) approaches to spirituality; when people take a transpersonal approach to relationships, the partners are seeking to experience the deeper connection between them. From this viewpoint, materialism and matters of the flesh are suspect, potential seducers of the soul; to be free, people must deny these, and rise above them. Nirvana (an eastern version of heaven) awaits the successful adherent.

Western religions tend to focus more on the relationship of the body and soul in the current life. A common assumption is that humanity has experienced some "split," which is interpreted variously as being either a natural state of existence (viewing "sin" as a separation) or a result of morally "bad" behaviour (so that "sin" is a punishable wrongdoing). In the moralistic notion of "original sin," people are condemned to live in the shadow of previous wrongdoings, always committed to doing good deeds in order to be forgiven and allowed to return back to God in a final state of re-union. This conservative attitude is prevalent in many traditional Christian churches. It is the basis of *redemption-centred spirituality* that, like the eastern transcendental approaches, views the flesh with suspicion because it might lead a person away from a desirable spiritual path. Thus, many western religions demand prohibitions against sensual pleasures. This is in contrast to some eastern transcendental approaches that take a leaf from one of the legends about Prince Buddha-to-be; in that account, the prince's father is said to have given him a gift of numerous women to help him become satiated in matters of the flesh so that he could more easily give them up. In either case, the body is seen to limit spiritual development.

The separation idea of sin as a *split* with the Divine is incorporated into *creation-centred spirituality*, with the idea that God (or "higher power" or a unified and unifying presence) is ever being revealed at all levels of human experience. Unlike the redemptive approach, no wrongdoing is involved, so there is *no guilt* that must be expiated. The individual belongs in the universe and participates in it. Unity is "isomorphic"—meaning that the pattern of unification is the same within all levels of being—in the body, the mind, the emotions, and the soul. Each individual is a full expression of God.

Spirituality in Relationships

From a *transcendental* position, individuals can devote their spiritual practices toward improving their capacity for compassion and acceptance, and thus be able to relate to their partners in a more meaningful way; their commitment is to the self and not the relationship. Such relationships aim to rise above the pettiness of everyday struggles, which are seen as the illusions of the body and materialism. The more people are enlightened, the more they will see such issues as anger, jealousy, hurt, and control as being elements that need to be dismissed or disregarded, so that their focus can be on compassionate love and a sense of unity with the other. If for any reason a relationship stands in the way of personal freedom, people can consider leaving their partner.

Both the redemptive and creation-centred concepts of spirituality can be concerned with *transformation*. The redemptive idea is that a person is guilty of sin and needs to be saved by transforming the self into a good person in the eyes of God; forgiveness is the goal. In the redemptive approach to interpersonal relationships, partners are capable of wrongdoing by hurting each other's feelings or by breaking promises. When alleged wrongdoing occurs, it is followed by a series of steps—condemnations, feelings of guilt, behaviours aimed toward relieving that guilt, and the establishment of new commandments. In redemptive spirituality, God stands firm; the sinner must be transformed from sinner to saint. So it is with redemptive types of relationship, wherein one party does wrong and needs to be forgiven through acts of atonement; in this kind of power struggle, the hurt person stands firm and the guilty one must transform. In a redemptive spiritual mode, relationships tend to be seen as contracts with God; people live with a commandment to remain together forever. A goal of personal freedom or enlightenment is seen to be a sinful symptom of selfishness, and hence can be related to the work of the Devil. In this paradigm, people with problems in relationship are seen to be in need of prayers for personal redemption; praying together means staying together. If God (and Jesus Christ, the Son of God) were to be placed ahead of concerns for the Self, the relationship could survive.

In *creation-centred* spirituality, relationships are the way of the universal order. All separate beings are joined at a basic level in the unity of the universal love vibration. In this view, God is within (the universal deep structure), not an external agency. Humans are not separate from God; they *are* God in human form. Whereas moral imperatives are highly significant in many religions, creation-centred spirituality values responsiveness between life beings and does not impose morality. The spiritual dimension of relationship involves no guilt or blame; instead, the focus is on *revelation, sharing, discovery,* and *renewal*—all elements of the Relationship Garden.

The Hologram

The hologram is a multidimensional image, created by the interference pattern between beams of coherent (focused) light. The simple holograms that one sees in shops are quite primitive replicas of a wondrous phenomenon; in more complex versions, images can be created with such dimensionality that a person witnessing a hologram can actually walk right inside it! The concept of the hologram is itself a limited version of much more complex realities. David Bohm, the physicist who worked with Einstein and befriended Krishnamurti, says that the concept of the hologram is a first-order approximation of something much more elegant; indeed, the process of the universe is a "holomovement" of unfolding and folding. Everyday reality is the unfolded version of a deeper reality (God?), which is hidden by being folded up on itself. The *explicate order* is the unfolded, manifest order (in space and time); the *implicate order* is the result of the explicate order being folded up into the hidden patterns of chaos (see "Chaos and Relationships," p. 92). This hidden order (implicate order) is the code of existence; this is the patterning of the universal vibration (see "Resonance," p. 11). This arcane code is expressed in all creation, from the lowest mineral and inorganic life to the most subtle human feeling.[2]

In holographic theory, a multidimensional image is made by the interference patterns of two coherent light sources (lasers). If one considers an individual who is revealed and committed in relationship as being like a laser beam that interacts with another coherent energy (the partner), then the relationship can be seen as an *interference pattern* that can be resolved into a holographic multi-dimensional phenomenon. Indeed, the relationship is *another entity* that emerges and is expressed in the dynamism of interaction between two focused, coherent energy beings. Each person is expressing the universal life energy; one partner is *isomorphic* with the other (each is a unique expression of the same eternal, timeless energy; although they are different at one level, they are the same at another).

Holographic Relationships

As partners discover more of themselves and each other, they begin to have a more profound experience of the universal energy, their God, and themselves. Just as with direct mirroring each person can act like a laser beam to bring fuller awareness of the self and the other, so too the relationship that emerges from their interaction becomes like a focused beam that brings higher resolution to the holographic representation of the entire universe. Truly, they come to know their God, their oneness, by knowing their unique separatenesses together. They experience wholeness (the root of the word "holy" is the same as wholeness).[3]

Isomorphism

Isomorphism is a term borrowed from chemistry. The term literally means "same shape" or "same pattern." The universal deep structure[4] (the implicate order, the Archetypal dimension of Jung) is the same for all. We are all expressions of the universal whole.[5] Thus, I am expressing the deep pattern of the universe, and so are you.

> As it was for our star-watching progenitors, it is a belief in a world which is all of a piece, coherent and connected. Every event or object in this world is related to each other, reflected and affected by each other. And last, this world is in harmonious balance.
>
> —Edgar Levenson[6]

The human being *is* the explication of God. And two human beings in relationship are two manifestations of God, in dialogue with each other. In a fundamental way, each is the unfolding of God; each is each other, mirrored in their separatenesses. This is the concept of isomorphism. In relationship, people can learn about themselves (which at base is God) and about each other. Fundamentally (as deep structure), they *are* each other—they *are* God. People can discover their true nature by going deeply within themselves; they learn better about themselves in dialogue with another.

In the Creation-centred idea of spirituality, the universe is seen to be holographic, with all experiences at all levels expressing the very same pattern of existence.

> It is a world of organization and order, ... a view of the world as organization and relationship. It is, largely, a world without random accident; consequences are unpredictable only because of the complex synaptical network of connections in which they occur. We know events are related; we often do not know how or why.
>
> —Edgar Levenson[7]

Divinity in Relationship

To develop ongoing intimacy, the Creation-centred, holographic idea of spirituality is very useful. Thomas Moore describes the "Soul" as being "not a thing, but a quality or a dimension of experiencing life and ourselves. It has to do with depth, value, relatedness, heart, and personal substance."[8] One person's pattern of existence is God's pattern of existence, as is the partner's; indeed, each person is God.

Looking at relationships from this perspective, people can struggle together in their daily lives to learn about the Divine. Through nature, music, art, and literature, the Divine offers important and feelingful messages; but there is always some difficulty with the translation. That is exactly where interpersonal relationships (which when multiplied become "community") are important—to help decode those messages. People in so-called "primitive" cultures, because they remain closer to nature, are often more capable of relating to the messages that are revealed; more civilized people often have lost much of this skill.

With isomorphism, the whole is contained in all of the parts. Thus, one's relationship with God or the universe is replicated in one's relationship to other people, to nature, to ideas, or even to rocks. As Thomas Moore wrote, "Ancient psychologists taught that our own souls are inseparable from the world's soul, and that both are found in all the many things that make up nature and culture."[9]

In William Blake's words:

> To see the world in a grain of sand
> And a heaven in a wild flower,
> Hold infinity in the palm of your hand
> And eternity in an hour.[10]

Deciphering the Code

The feedback system from the universe requires much decoding—for which most of us have little talent. Difficult (sometimes even apparently impossible) as it may seem, human relationships can afford the best glimpse into the ultimate meaning of things—possibly more readily than solitary activities, such as sitting in meditation atop a mountain, or practising zazen by a country stream, or endlessly repeating prayers or chants to some invisible deity. In creation-centred spirituality, both the person and God are transformed with each act; instead of remaining steadfast (as in redemptive spirituality), God is in the process of *becoming*, along with the persons in relationship. Because the feedback system between persons affords a daily, common language, it is more easily understood than are the messages from God. According to Alan Watts:

> Love brings the real, and not just the ideal, vision of what others are because it is a glimpse of what we are bodily. For what is ordinarily called the body is an abstraction. It is the conventional fiction of an object seen apart from its relation to the universe, without which it has no reality whatsoever. But the mysterious and unsought uprising of love is the experience of complete relationship with another, transforming our vision not only of the beloved but of the whole world.[11]

Discovery in the Relationship Garden

People fixated at infantile levels of development are interested in finding partners who will fulfill earlier unmet needs so that they can feel safe and full in life. If they are successful in this endeavour, they move their centres from within themselves and locate them in others, or somewhere between themselves and others; in so doing, they abandon themselves and any opportunity to fully become their authentic selves. They merge with those they "love," primarily being concerned with controlling and possessing them, remaining dependent and relatively helpless; they fear rejection and abandonment because they fear being alone. When their own sense of worth is dependent upon how others value them, they focus on being liked and acceptable. They feel as obligated to others as they feel others should be obligated to them. They firmly believe in their "rights" as children and adults, feeling entitled to a life of happiness without care; when they are treated in any way that does not meet with their expectations, they feel victimized and thus owed some retribution. Guilt and anxiety become their way of life, which they handle by narrowing their experience of the world and their own range of feelings, which are then more easily controlled. When their strategies work , they remain numb and neurotic, immature and helpless, moral and judgmental, given to depression, physical illness, and a wide spectrum of self-defeating behaviours. On the outside they may appear to be models of success in our society, regardless of whether they are living lives of emotional isolation by themselves or in mutually dependent relationships.

Instead of opting for security, some people may choose to *grow*, to *discover* their relationship to themselves and to life, to *uncover* their *patterns* of existence. Such people find a greater range of options, and can experience more fully their range of feelings, the dark as well as the light ones. Doing so requires them to take the plunge into intimacy, through the revealing to another of all that is deep within. This is best accomplished in a relationship garden that can provide the safety, nurture, and proper ingredients for growth. Whereas security-based relationships are more like hothouses that provide external sources for growth in particular ways, the relationship garden stimulates growth from inside, to reveal the unfolding expression of unique lives. In a relationship garden, people can *transform from object to person*, to become all that they were meant to be. As Oscar Wilde writes through the mouths of his characters in *A Woman of No Importance*:

> The Book of Life begins with a man and a woman in a garden...It ends with Revelations.[12]

Notes

1. H.W. Fowler & F.G. Fowler, *The Concise Oxford Dictionary of Current English* (London: Oxford University Press, 1964), p. 1378.

2. D. Bohm, quoted in K. Wilber (ed.), *The Holographic Paradigm* (Boulder, CO: Shambhala, 1982), pp. 44–104.

3. M. Talbot, *The Holographic Universe* (New York: HarperCollins, 1991), pp. 59–81.

4. E. Levenson, *The Fallacy of Understanding* (New York: Basic Books, 1972), p. 40.

5. Ira Progoff, *Jung, Synchronicity and Human Destiny* (New York: Julian Press, 1973), p. 149.

6. E. Levenson, *The Fallacy of Understanding* (New York: Basic Books, 1972), p. 30.

7. Ibid., p. 22.

8. Thomas Moore, *Care of the Soul* (New York: HarperCollins, 1992), p. 5.

9. Ibid., p. 4.

10. William Blake, "Auguries of Innocence," in Poems from *The Pickering Manuscript*, quoted in *Bartlett's Favorite Quotations* (Boston: Little, Brown and Company, 1980), p. 406.

11. Alan Watts, *Nature, Man and Woman* (New York: Pantheon Books, 1958), p. 29.

12. Oscar Wilde, "A Woman of No Importance" (Act I), quoted in *Bartlett's Familiar Quotations* (Boston: Little, Brown and Company, 1960), p. 675.

Epilogue

The Garden Revisited

These twenty-six years have been full for us—full of learning, of experiencing, of loving. From simple beginnings when we first asked what intimacy was, through the original experimental design and its early frightening prospects, our relationship has been nurtured by our caring for one another and the gifts of love given so freely by others. Early on, we had no idea what we had planted— we only knew that there was something within each of us that wanted to gestate and burst forth with life! And burst forth it did, but not in the ways or directions that we had originally fantasized.

All we knew at the beginning was that we each had come through marriages wherein our authentic natures had been suppressed. This was neither the fault nor intention of ourselves or our previous partners; all of us were swimming in a social matrix that expected conformity, obligations, and rules. Having studied the field of psychiatry and sought marital counselling for ourselves, we discovered that we were all expected to give up many things (desires, wishes, hopes, and dreams) in order to make our relationships work. It quickly became evident that we were all expected to reduce the two members of each relationship to the lowest common denominator through sacrifice and compromise.

Having already abandoned much about ourselves for the modicum of success that we had achieved to that point, both of us recoiled at the thought of any further submission. Thus began our intimacy project. Even with all of our other obligations, we created the time for our investigations; as we prepared the ground for it, we soon imaged ourselves to be tending a garden in which each of us could grow. At that time, the words from the Broadway musical *The Fantasticks* rang in our ears: "Plant a radish, get a radish, there's never any doubt ... every plant grows according to the plot." Growing up in families and relationships full of expectations, radishes might never know their full potential. We early decided to discover what each of us could be if we dedicated our energies into the cultivation of this relationship garden.

Over the years, we have run into a wide variety of weeds of our own and others' making, which seemed common to most relationships that we knew. Attempting to stomp them out of existence or to turn our backs to them only made matters worse; we soon learned that we had to carefully assess each weed, know it intimately, pull it, and then carefully watch for its re-emergence. We also discovered that our relationship garden could not tolerate inattention; we needed to devote daily periods of time for routine tending. All of this we did with an ever-present fear of being captured somehow when we least expected it.

To our great delight, each us grew sturdy and full. All the while, we were discovering the exigencies of stormy relationship weather, the threats of flooding from the hurricanes of indulgent feelings and self-pity, the dangers of burning up from arid contempt, and the effects of the chilling frost of withdrawn feelings. Along with the ever-present possibility of neglect, we weathered all of these threats by rolling up our sleeves and ceaselessly attending to anything that came to light. To our great satisfaction, everything flourished!

To our astonishment, we were not the only ones to benefit from our garden! Our children, our friends, and our clients all appeared to thrive when they visited for awhile. Indeed, many of them were inspired to cultivate their own relationship gardens. Over a long period of time, we began to see that others could indeed learn what we had learned, to grow themselves *in relationship!*

This brings us to the end of the tour of our Relationship Garden. Our work is not over; our garden continues to require our attention. However, we notice that we can take longer periods of pause during which we can look lovingly and appreciatively at one another, content over what we have cultured and what each of us has grown and learned.

This book is one such pause. We hope that it has proven to be as interesting, pleasureful, and nutritive to you as it has been for us. We will close with one of our favourite poems:

To Edith

Through the long years
    I sought peace.
I found ecstasy, I found anguish,
    I found madness,
I found loneliness.
I found the solitary pain
    that gnaws the heart
But peace I did not find.

Now, old and near my end,
    I have found you,
And, knowing you
I have found both ecstasy and peace.
    I know rest,
After so many lonely years.
I know what life and love may be.
Now, if I sleep,
I shall sleep fulfilled.
                    —Bertrand Russell[1]

Notes

1. B. Russell, *The Autobiography of Bertrand Russell* (Boston, MA: Little, Brown and Company, 1967), dedication page.

Index

PRINTED AND BOUND
IN BOUCHERVILLE, QUEBEC, CANADA,
BY MARC VEILLEUX INC.
IN MAY, 1996